Following God

LIFE PRINCIPLES
FOR WORSHIP FROM
THE TABERNACLE

Following God

Life Principles for Worship from the Tabernacle

A Bible Study by

Wayne Barber
Eddie Rasnake
Richard Shepherd

AMG Publishers

Chattanooga, TN 37422

Following God

Life Principles for Worship from the Tabernacle

First Printing, 2024

Published by AMG Publishers.

ISBN: 978-1-61715-624-3

Cover design by Marc Whitaker, MTW Design, Dickson, TN
Editing and layout by Rick Steele
Interior Tabernacle illustrations by David Barber

Printed in the United States of America
POD

This book is dedicated to those who have taught each of us much about **true worship** and the Tabernacle:

Manley Beasley, Miss Bertha Smith, and Dr. Stephen F. Olford

"Remember those who led you, who spoke the word of God to you; and considering the results of their conduct, imitate their faith" Hebrews 13:7.

Acknowledgments

This work goes forth to those who have encouraged us in the publication of the first five books in this series: *Life Principles from the Old Testament, Life Principles from the Kings of the Old Testament, Life Principles from the Women of the Bible, Life Principles from the Prophets of the Old Testament,* and *Life Principles from the New Testament Men of Faith.* This series has been a labor of love, and through our study we have made friends with many saints of days gone by. We look forward to getting to know them even better in heaven. We are especially grateful to the body of believers at Woodland Park Baptist Church in Chattanooga, Tennessee, who have walked through many of these studies with us and have been a continual source of encouragement as the writing of new studies progresses. Thanks to the folks at AMG, especially Warren Baker and Rick Steele, Trevor Overcash and Dale Anderson, and to Phillip Rodgers. Most of all, we remain grateful to the Lord Jesus, who continues to teach us and lead us in what it means to follow Him with a whole heart.

THE AUTHORS

Wayne Barber

Wayne Barber was a renowned national and international conference ministry speaker, his primary goal of ministry was to spread the message of "the sufficiency of Christ." People around the world connected with Wayne's unique ability to makeGod's Word come alive through his honest and open "real-life" experiences. For more than twenty years he served as Senior Pastor-Teacher of Woodland Park Baptist Church. And for many of those years in Chattanooga, Wayne co-taught with noted author Kay Arthur of Precept Ministries and has studied under Dr. Spiros Zodhiates, who was one of the world's leading Greek scholars. On August 29, 2016, Wayne passed away suddenly after a short illness. He is survivedby his wife and two grown children and several grandchildren.

Wayne was one of the founding authors of the Following God© series.

Rick Shepherd

Richard L. Shepherd has served in churches in Florida, Texas, and Tennessee, and ministered over fifteen years as Team Strategist for the Prayer and Spiritual Awakening Team of the Florida Baptist Convention. He holds M.Div and Ph.D degrees from Southwestern Baptist Theological Seminary. He has been married to his wife Linda Gail since 1977. They have four children and nine grandchildren. They are always glad to encourage believers, and witness to listening hearts wherever they go. They now make thier home in Rolesville, North Carolina.

Rick is one of the founding authors of the Following God© series.

Eddie Rasnake

Eddie Rasnake graduated with honors from East Tennessee State University. He and his wife, Michele, served 7 years with Cru at UVa, James Madison, and as campus director at the University of Tennessee. Eddie left Cru to join Wayne Barber at Woodland Park Baptist Church where he still serves as Senior Associate Pastor. He has authored dozens of books and Bible studies and has published materials in Afrikaans, Albanian, German, Greek, Italian, Romanian, Russian and Telugu. Eddie and his wife Michele live in Chattanooga, Tennessee.

Eddie is one of the founding authors of the Following God© series.

Preface

What comes to your mind when you think of worshiping God? How you answer that question speaks volumes about your relationship with God. Of course worship is a part of every religion and every culture, but true worship is not something we all do our own way. Religion is man's attempt to find and worship God through his own efforts, in his own way. But Christianity is different, for the Christian recognizes that just as he cannot find God through his own efforts and in his own way, neither can he worship God however he pleases. Just as there is a right way and also wrong approaches to salvation, there is a right way and many wrong ways to worship. What is **the right way** to worship God? Our focus in this study is upon the right way to worship God.

Throughout history God has chosen to provide a way for man to worship, and for nearly five hundred years the Tabernacle was God's way for man to worship Him. Through the Tabernacle God expressed two important facts about worship. First, the Tabernacle represented the presence of God among His people, standing as it did in the center of their camp. Secondly, it pictured the divinely-appointed means by which sinful man could approach God, who was otherwise unapproachable because of His holiness and majesty. But the Tabernacle is more than simply a part of our Christian history. It was an object lesson to prepare the way for the Christ. Have you ever asked yourself, "Why did God bother with the Law and priests and sacrifices if He knew they would not work?" Was Christ simply the final work of God when all else failed? Was the levitical system an experiment that did not work? Absolutely not! God knew before the foundation of the world that Christ was the necessary provision for man's sin, for Christ is *"the lamb slain from the foundation of the world"* (Revelation 13:8 KJV). And yet the Tabernacle and the levitical system and later, the Temple all filled an important place in the plan of God. Understanding that place will move us a long way toward a right view of God and how He is to be worshiped.

The epistle to the Hebrews makes it clear that the earthly Tabernacle was only a picture of the true Tabernacle that is in heaven. The earthly Tabernacle and all that went with it (the Law, the priesthood, and the sacrificial system) are *"only a shadow of the good things to come. . . ."* (Hebrews 10:1). It stands to reason that if the Tabernacle (and later, the Temple) is modeled after the Temple in heaven, then it is not some relic from the past that is obsolete and irrelevant. It is significant that the Bible devotes fifty chapters in both the Old and New Testaments to the Tabernacle. Comparatively, only two chapters are devoted to the entire story of creation—which only accentuates the Tabernacle's importance. As Dr. M. R. DeHaan puts it, "There is no portion of Scripture richer in meaning, or more perfect in its teaching of the plan of redemption, than this divinely designed building." Our goal in this study is not to simply study the Tabernacle. Rather, we are going to use the Tabernacle as a vehicle to get us to study the right way to worship God. You will definitely be blessed!

Following Christ,

WAYNE A. BARBER

RICHARD L. SHEPHERD

EDDIE RASNAKE

Table of Contents

Following God

lesson I

Worship from Adam to Aaron

Principles from the Fall to the Priesthood

Man was created in a context of worship. He walked in perfect relationship to his Creator, and he enjoyed perfect fellowship with Him. Unfortunately, sin changed all of that, and, because of the fall, man's relationship with God needed rebuilding. This process of rebuilding was progressive. With each step God was revealing His nature and man's, and He was pointing to the One who would become the bridge between man and God—between heaven and earth. In this study we focus on a key component of that process, the Tabernacle, and what the Tabernacle teaches us of God, of Christ, and of ourselves. Before we begin looking at the Tabernacle itself, it is important to discuss its historical context. The primary focus of this week's lesson is on what worship was like from the time of Adam after the fall until the time of Aaron, the first high priest. Understanding events and styles of worship practiced before the construction of the Tabernacle will help us immensely as we study the Tabernacle itself. Even from the beginning of time, we see God taking the initiative to provide a way for man to worship Him. Before we progress any further in this study, let's establish some type of definition for the word "worship." When we use the word "worship," we are talking about a prac-

Man was created in a context of worship…but sin changed all of that. As a result of the fall man's relationship with God had to be rebuilt.

Worship from Adam to Aaron

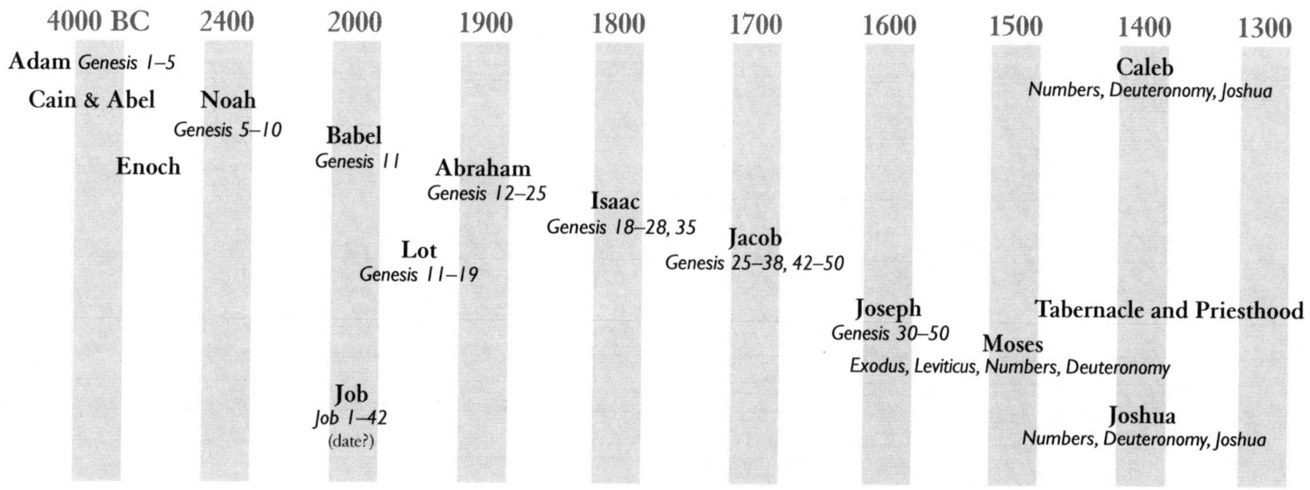

tice that goes beyond religious ritual. We are really describing man's walk and relationship with God—a relationship that respects God's holiness, majesty, and worth.

Lesson One **DAY ONE**

HOW CAN A SINFUL MAN WORSHIP GOD?

We don't travel very far into the biblical narrative before we see a serious problem arising in man's relationship with God. Three chapters into the book of Genesis we see that sin, a deliberate choice of man to go his own way independent of God, has left its stain on man's relationship with God. Can you imagine how Adam and Eve felt? For the first time in their lives, they were not walking in fellowship with God. For the first time they tasted guilt, grief, and emptiness. For the first time their hearts knew fear. Their Garden of Eden had been shattered by sin through their own choices. They had offended God instead of worshiping Him. By their rebellion they ceased to reflect that God was worthy of being their authority, and they supplanted Him with self. His image in their lives was marred and perverted, and He could no longer be clearly seen in them. No longer could they walk with Him in the garden in the cool of the day. What could they do? How could they restore their relationship with God? Could they do something to force God to take them back? At first they hid, but God found them out. Then they tried to pass the blame. Adam said, "the woman whom Thou gavest. . ." and turned the blame on Eve and God. Eve in turn passed the buck as well: "The serpent deceived me. . . ." Their worship of God had ended, for when we choose to sin, we are worshiping our own will over God. Man could not close the breach. God would have to act. For sinful man to return to worship, sin would have to be dealt with, and it would have to be dealt with God's way, not man's.

Put Yourself In Their Shoes

THE WRONG WAY TO DEAL WITH SIN

Notice the mistakes that Adam & Eve made in dealing with their sin...

- They tried to hide their nakedness from each other (Genesis 3:7).
- They tried to hide from God (Genesis 3:8).
- Adam tried to blame God & Eve (Genesis 3:12).
- Eve blamed the serpent (Genesis 3:13).

Mankind shows the same mistaken tendencies today. We try to hide our sins from each other and God, and we try to blame others for them.

Look at the story of Adam and Eve eating the forbidden fruit (Genesis 3:1–7).

What was the first thing Adam and Eve did after they sinned?

Why do you think they did this?

Did their efforts to cover their sin and hide from God succeed?

They at first tried to cover themselves, but their innocence was already gone. We see their shame in the fact that they hid from God. Sin always separates man from God and ruins worship. It is significant that their attempt to clothe themselves was not sufficient or acceptable. God knew that their sin problem still remained. Already we are beginning to see the fact that man cannot deal with his own sin. Only God can deal with our sin, for we are saved by grace, not our own works (see Ephesians 2:8–9).

🕮 Clearly, if man's relationship with God is to be restored it must begin with God, not man. Look at Genesis 3:21 and answer the questions that follow.

Who took the initiative?

____

What did God do?

____

____

God made garments for Adam and Eve. Fig leaves would not suffice. Evidently there is more at stake here than the need for clothing. Before the fall, they were both "naked and unashamed" (Genesis 2:25). One of the first consequences of the fall was a conscious sense of shame. Adam and Eve's shame was over their sin, not just their nakedness.

Adam and Eve tried to cover their nakedness with fig leaves, but God *"made garments of skin for Adam and his wife, and clothed them."* Where did the skins (the Hebrew word usually refers to animal hides) come from?

____

____

____

Obviously animals had to die for Adam and Eve to be covered. The text doesn't explicitly tell us, but it infers a sin sacrifice. The fact that Abel sacrifices an animal indicates that man had some understanding of why the animals died.

🕮 Look at Hebrews 9:22. Why do you think God killed animals to clothe Adam and Eve?

____

____

____

Hebrews 9:22 teaches us that "without shedding of blood there is no forgiveness." Animal sacrifice may seem cruel and barbaric to us, but only because we do not appreciate the seriousness of sin. The animal substitute is a reminder of our own guilt and pictures the coming substitution of Christ.

This particular Genesis account does not give much detail regarding the sacrifice of the animals for Adam and Eve's sin. However, taking the Bible as a whole, we can deduce that Adam and Eve understood that those innocent animals died in their place. The clear point from Genesis to Revelation is

Doctrine

COVER-UP

Adam and Eve's "fig-leaf fashions" could not cover their guilt, shame, and fear. Their attempt to cover their shame was the best they could do, but it was useless. Only God can cover or atone for our sins. Physically, God gave Adam and Eve garments of skin (lasting leather). These garments suggest that an animal was sacrifice, and this sacrifice symbolically spoke of atonement—the covering of sin by the blood of God's chosen sacrifice. Jesus is that sacrifice for us, the Lamb of God, who not only covers our sin but takes away our sin (John 1:29).

that sin is "serious business." Perhaps to us the whole idea of animal sacrifices seems a barbaric and outdated practice, but we need to place ourselves in the shoes of those who lived during Old Testament times. Unlike today, Old Testament believers functioned in an agricultural society. They had probably raised the innocent, sacrificial lamb since its birth. They would have grieved over the death that they deserved. God wants us to understand the reality that sin is costly. We don't know all that God told Adam and Eve, but we can assume they had some understanding of what was going on. The ultimate message from Adam and Eve is that if we are to worship God, we must deal with our sin!

Lesson One **DAY TWO**

WORSHIPING GOD'S WAY

God made clear to Adam and Eve that sin would have to be dealt with before worship could happen. It would have to be covered. The sacrifice of animals could not take their sin away, but it could cover it. In the garden we see that there is a right and wrong way to deal with sin, and a right and wrong way to worship. In the next chapter of Genesis we see through Cain and Abel that not all worship is acceptable to God.

> *". . . Abel was a keeper of the flocks, but Cain was a tiller of the ground. So it came about in the course of time that Cain brought an offering to the Lord of the fruit of the ground. And Abel, on his part also brought of the firstlings of his flock and of their fat portions. And the Lord had regard for Abel and for his offering; but for Cain and for his offering He had no regard. . . ."* (Genesis 4:2–5)

"And according to the Law, one may almost say, all things are cleansed with blood, and without shedding of blood there is no forgiveness."
Hebrews 9:22

You probably know the rest of the story, but what we want you to see is the fact that God accepted Abel's offering and did not accept the offering of Cain.

📖 Read Genesis 4:2–5 again and answer the questions that follow.

Why do you think God accepted Abel's offering but didn't accept Cain's?

____

____

____

____

____

Is there any significance to the fact that Abel's offering was an animal and Cain's was not?

____

____

____

____

____

Some theologians believe that God had already mandated animal sacrifice, and rather than give an offering from his brother's work, Cain rebelled and wanted to worship with the works of his own hands. We cannot say this with certainty, but you can see why some would believe this. What we do know is that *"the Lord had regard for Abel and for his offering; but for Cain and for his offering He had no regard."* God did not accept Cain's offering, and there can only be two reasons for this: **a)** it was the wrong offering, or **b)** it was an acceptable offering given with a wrong attitude or **c)** it was the wrong offering combined with a wrong attitude. Clearly, whether Cain's problem was a wrong heart or the wrong type of offering, or both, the message of Cain's story is that we cannot worship God however we please.

"And the LORD had regard for Abel and for his offering; but for Cain and for his offering He had no regard. So Cain became very angry and his countenance fell."

Genesis 4:4–5

Another observation that is significant is that Abel offered "the firstlings" of his flock, while Cain's sacrifice is only called "an offering." Abel prioritized his relationship with God by giving first to the Lord instead of to himself. Some have suggested that by giving of the flock Abel is giving from the blessing of God, while the fruit of the ground was the fruit of Cain's hands since now the ground had to be tilled with sweat.

📖 Look at Hebrews 11:4. What do you learn there about the basis of Abel's offering?

____

____

____

____

While Hebrews 11:4 makes it clear that Abel offered a better sacrifice than Cain, it does not state with certainty why. It does, however give a couple of important clues. First, it states that the way Abel gave a better offering was by faith. Abel was trusting the Lord in his offering. Hebrews also states that through the acceptance of his offering Abel obtained the testimony that he was righteous. In other words, God affirmed that his heart was right.

📖 Looking at Hebrews 12:24, what do you learn there about "the blood of Abel" (presumably the blood of his sacrifice rather than his own blood)?

____

____

____

____

"And without faith it is impossible to please Him, for he who comes to God must believe that He is, and that He is a rewarder of those who seek Him."

Hebrews 11:6

While Abel's sacrifice was acceptable at the time and covered sin, proclaiming righteousness, it could not do all that needed to be done. It could cover sin, but it could not take it away. A better sacrifice was coming. Hebrews 10:1–2 tells us, *"For the Law, since it has only a shadow of the good things to come and not the very form of things, can never, by the same sacrifices year by year, which they offer continually, make perfect those who draw near. Otherwise, they would have ceased to be offered. . . ."*

We see from Cain and Abel that not all worship is acceptable to God. We must worship Him in His way, not our own.

WORSHIP AND OBEDIENCE

We saw first in Day One that that worship requires dealing with sin. We cannot worship God if we have sin in our hearts that we have not repented of and confessed. In Day Two, we saw in the study of Cain and Abel that we cannot worship God in just any fashion that fancies us. We must worship in His way, or our worship is unacceptable. In today's study, we will learn through Noah and Abraham that there can be no worship without obedience. When we read the story of the Great Flood, we will see in the character of Noah someone who was accepted by God.

Word Study

"NOAH FOUND FAVOR"

Chen ("favor")—the Hebrew word is from a root word that means "to bend, stoop," and it carries the idea of condescension or favor from a superior to an inferior. It is a synonym of such words as grace, kindness, etc. This is the first time the word is used in the Old Testament.

Genesis 6:8 tells us, *"But Noah found favor in the eyes of the Lord."* Why, according to verse 9, was Noah acceptable to God?

___

___

___

Noah was "blameless" (Literally: "complete" or "perfect," or "having integrity"); but more importantly, he "walked with God." The idea of "walking" with God speaks volumes. It implies not simply a decision at a point in time, but a process—a lot of "baby steps" in the same direction.

📖 What else do you learn about Noah in 6:22 and 7:5?

___

___

___

___

___

One important thing about Noah (which God already knew would be true) is that he did all that God commanded him to do. In fact, Genesis 6:22 repeats this for emphasis. We should also emphasize the word "all" in verse 22, for partial obedience isn't really obedience at all. If I only obey God part of the time, it is probably because I obey my own desires and don't object to obeying God so long as it doesn't get in the way of what I want to do.

📖 What does 8:20–21 add to your understanding of Noah's worship?

___

___

___

___

Notice the word "clean." What does this tell you about Noah's worship?

___

___

___

Here we see Noah recognizing the seriousness of what God has done. Clearly, this idea of animal sacrifice came from somewhere. It is safe to assume that God had already communicated that this was a way to worship. With the word "clean" we see some of Noah's heart. Noah clearly had a concern for what was acceptable to God. We undoubtedly can see in Noah that there can be no worship without obedience. The concept of obedience in regards to worship is even clearer in the life of Abraham.

Look at Genesis 22:1–18.

What does God call Abraham to do?

____

____

What in verse 5 does Abraham tell his servants he plans to do on the mountain?

____

____

____

God called Abraham to sacrifice his son. This request would be a lot to ask of any father, but you must recognize that Isaac is not just any son; he is the son of promise. When Abraham laid Isaac on the altar, he intended to sacrifice all that God had promised him. Abraham laid his own dreams on the altar with his only son. It is noteworthy that, as he leaves his servants behind, he says they will "worship."

There can be no true worship without obedience, no matter how costly that obedience is. In fact, the more costly the obedience the more an act of worship it becomes.

There can be no true worship without obedience, no matter how costly that obedience is. In fact, the more costly the obedience the more an act of worship it becomes.

Read through the rest of the narrative and write down any other observations you find about worship.

____

____

____

____

Obviously Abraham didn't know how, but he believed that God would either raise Isaac from the dead or fulfill His promises another way (see Hebrews 11:17-19). With the "ram in the thicket" we see a beautiful picture of the "lamb of God who died in our place." Notice what God says in verse 12, *"I know that you fear (reverence) God."* Obedience is the measure of our reverence for God. The blessings we receive from God are related to our obedience to God (v. 17).

It is worth mentioning that Genesis 22:5 is the first verse in the Bible where the word "worship" appears. It is also noteworthy that this same location on Mount Moriah shows up much later when King David purchases the threshing floor of Ornan the Jebusite. If you recall the story, when Ornan hears what David intends to do, he offers to give David the land along with a team of oxen for the sacrifice and an ox cart for the wood. But David responds, *"I will not offer to the Lord my God that which costs me nothing"* (1 Chronicles 21:24). You see, true worship is costly. So significant is the worship of

Doctrine

ISAAC AS A TYPE OF CHRIST

Isaac may be one of the most complete Old Testament types of Christ. The "*only son*" of his father, he apparently did not resist his own sacrifice and carried the wood on which he was to be offered up the mountain. God's last minute replacement of Isaac with the sacrificial ram is a beautiful picture of Christ's substitutionary atonement—He suffered the death that was to be ours.

Abraham and David on Mt. Moriah that God later instructed Solomon that this would be the site of the first temple (see 1 Chronicles 21:18–30; 22:1–2).

Lesson One **DAY FOUR**

THE RESPONSE OF A GRATEFUL HEART

In our study of Adam and Eve, we saw that worship requires dealing with sin. We also saw through Cain and Abel that we must worship God in His way, with the right methods and the right motives. We observed a third reality in Noah and Abraham—that there can be no worship without obedience. A fourth reality of worship is that **it is a response of a grateful heart.** God has created us with the ability to reason. Not only can we comprehend what is happening in our lives, but through reasoning we can begin to understand why. Romans 12:1 tells us that to present ourselves to God is our "spiritual service of worship." Another way of translating that phrase is that presenting ourselves to God is our "reasonable expectation." Worship is a logical response when we understand all that God has done for us. One of the expressions of worship is the response of a grateful heart.

"I urge you therefore, brethren, by the mercies of God, to present your bodies a living and holy sacrifice, acceptable to God, which is your spiritual service of worship."
Romans 12:1

Look up the following passages in Genesis and observe what motivated the worship.

Genesis 12:1–8

____

____

____

Genesis 24:26, 48

____

____

____

____

Genesis 26:25

____

____

____

____

Genesis 47:31

____

____

____

____

____

In Genesis 12:1–8 we see worship flowing from God speaking to Abraham. Abraham is blessed by the encounter, and he worships God. In Genesis 24:26, 48 we again see worship as a response of gratitude. Notice in Genesis 26:25 that not only is an altar built as a place of worship because of the revelation that had been given, but also as a place to seek God. Although the text makes no mention of a sacrifice, it is implied by the normal use of an altar. When you look at other references about worship and you see the mention of an "altar," remember that an altar is a place of death. It is the Old Testament equivalent of the cross. Finally, in Genesis 47:31 we see that Israel worships in remembrance of the promise. In each instance of worship we have studied, it is clear that gratitude motivates the worship.

Look up the following passages in Exodus and observe what motivated the worship.

Exodus 3:12

Exodus 4:31

Exodus 12:27

Exodus 17:14–16

Exodus 24:3–6

In Exodus 3:12 God tells Moses he will worship at Mt. Horeb (another name for Mt. Sinai, site of the "burning bush") after God delivers Israel from Egypt. In other words, God is saying, "I promise you that you will see Me deliver Israel, and when I do, you will worship." In Exodus 4:31 Israel worships in gratitude that God has heard their groanings from Egypt. Exodus 12:27 points out that the people worshiped during God's deliverance through the Passover. In Exodus 17:14–16 Moses builds an altar to worship in gratitude as a result of God's deliverance of Israel from Amalek. Finally,

True Worship
ALTARS

The Law gave specific instructions about altars. In Exodus 20:24–25 we read, *"You shall make an altar of earth for Me, and you shall sacrifice on it your burnt offerings and your peace offerings, your sheep and your oxen; in every place where I cause My name to be remembered, I will come to you and bless you. And if you make an altar of stone for Me, you shall not build it of cut stones, for if you wield your tool on it, you will profane it."*

in Exodus 24:3–6 Moses builds an altar to worship in gratitude at the giving of the law.

It doesn't take much reflection to find reasons to be grateful to the Lord. Whenever we take the time to express our heartfelt gratitude to God for what He does, it is an act of worship.

Lesson One DAY FIVE

FOR ME TO WORSHIP GOD

You may not realize it, but you have already looked at virtually every biblical reference on worship from Adam to Aaron. It is our hope that you are beginning to see some of God's desire for how we worship. Worship is more than an emotion, more than an experience, more than a service—it is connecting with our Creator. Worship is walking in relationship with Him, enjoying His fellowship. God has progressively revealed many aspects about Himself in His Holy Scriptures. This week we have seen that God laid the all-important foundation for worship years before the Tabernacle style of worship began to function. There is much revelation in worship from Adam to Aaron that still applies to you and me today.

"Search me, O God, and know my heart; Try me and know my anxious thoughts; And see if there be any hurtful way in me, And lead me in the everlasting way." Psalm 139:23–24

One key principle we learn from the garden is that sin must be dealt with if worship is to happen. We cannot worship God without dealing with sin. Scripture identifies two main ways we sin and offend God. Ephesians 4:30 states, *"And do not grieve the Holy Spirit of God. . ."* and in 1 Thessalonians 5:19 we read, *"Do not quench the Spirit."* In these two admonitions, two types of sin are addressed. In Ephesians the context indicates that we "grieve" the Spirit when we are guilty of sins of "commission"—doing what we are not supposed to do. In Thessalonians, the indication runs in another direction. Apparently, when we "quench the Spirit," we are guilty of sins of "omission"—not doing that which we are supposed to do.

APPLY Has God quickened your heart about dealing with sin? As you seek Him, is God reminding you of sins that you need to confess? You need not necessarily be introspective, for one of the ministries of the Holy Spirit is to convict us of sin. Why not take a moment to invite Him to search your heart and reveal any sin not yet taken to the altar. Make David's prayer in Psalm 139:23–24 your own…

> *"Search me, O God, and know my heart; try me and know my anxious thoughts; and see if there be any hurtful way in me, and lead me in the everlasting way."*

Is your worship of God based on the teaching of His word or your own feelings? Has God convicted you concerning your methods or motives in worship? Don't feel like you have to have all that figured out yet, for the entire course will teach you concerning the proper manner of worship. However, if any inadequacy in your worship of God is already apparent, then write about it in the space provided.

___

___

___

Can you think of any examples from others where people worshiped God in their own way instead of His?

____

____

____

APPLY Is there a directive from the Lord toward which you have been disobedient? Are you "quenching the Spirit" by not obeying His leading in some area? Write down any acts of obedience to which you sense God is calling you.

____

____

____

____

What are some ways it has "cost" you to worship God?

____

____

____

____

For what areas should you be grateful to God? Using the areas listed below to remind you, think about all that you have for which to be grateful.

___ career	___ home	___ family	___ health
___ car	___ freedom	___ provision	___ salvation
___ love	___ friends	___ your church	___ possessions

___ other______________________________

Express to the Lord in writing some of the things for which you are grateful.

____

____

____

____

____

____

"I will not worship the Lord with that which costs me nothing."
—King David

Congratulations! You are worshiping! Worship is far more than attending a church service. Over the next eleven weeks, we will learn more about the way to worship God. Stick with the study, and you are sure to be blessed!

Notes

Where We Meet God

Walking Where God Is Truly Worshiped

Where do we meet God? Where do we worship Him? Those questions have been asked and often debated for centuries. Throughout history, every culture has had certain places set apart to worship a god or goddess of some sort, even if that "god" was some exalted man or woman. We saw in Lesson One that God took the initiative in providing a way for man to worship Him. Again, when looking at worship, we find God taking the initiative to bring man to the right place. In Genesis 2, God placed Adam in the garden to cultivate and keep it. It was the place of meeting God and the place of worship for Adam and Eve. But, you may say, there was no church building or temple. How could Adam worship? How could we worship in such a place? In this lesson, we will look at what God says about where we meet God and worship Him. Where are the places of worship?

God has always wanted the place of meeting Him to be a joyful place of worship.

The Tabernacle with Fence and Outer Court

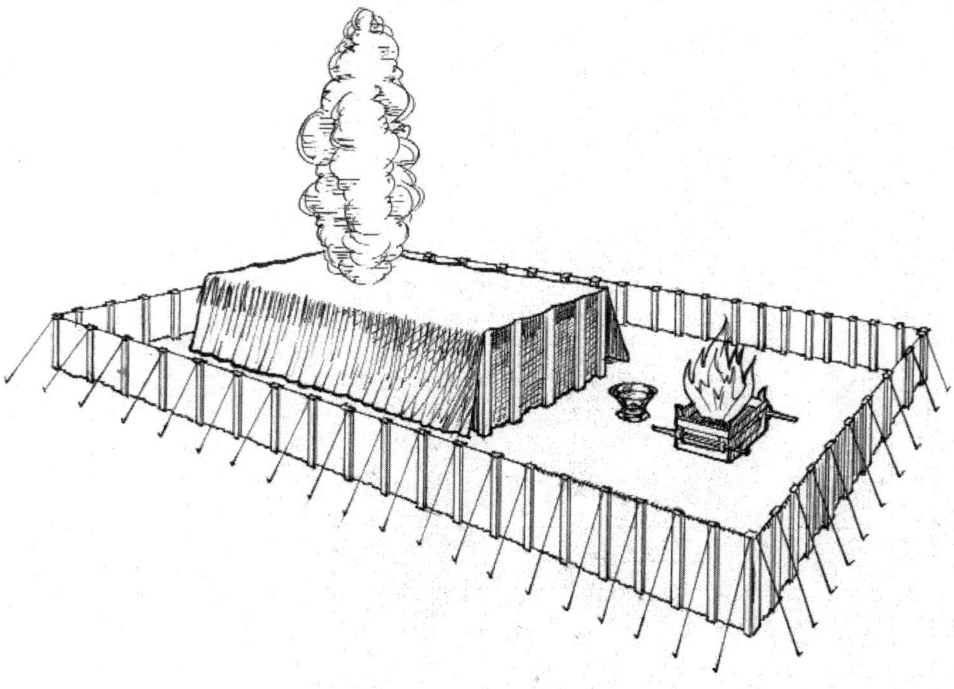

Lesson Two **DAY ONE**

God Comes to Meet with Us

In the Garden of Eden, where man was first created, his relationship with God was pure and unhindered. He recognized God as his Creator, Lord, and Provider and honored Him as such. Everything Adam and Eve did reflected a life and heart of worship because they were sensitive to God's voice—to His every wish; they were submissive to God's will, and they were ready to obey God's Word.

When Adam heard God speak, he responded in obedience. He honored God as God. For example, consider the naming of the animals in Genesis 2. Adam fully obeyed and honored God in that task. Everything Adam did was an act of worship. Everywhere Adam went was a place of worship.

Everything Adam did was an act of worship. Everywhere Adam went was a place of worship.

Then sin entered. With sin came spiritual death—separation from God, lack of sensitivity to God's voice, no submission to God's will, no heart to obey. Man was then preoccupied with his own desires, his own will, his own self-centered choices. Everything he did was touched with selfishness. Every place he went was infected with sin and its deadly results.

God came to meet Adam and Eve in the Garden. There He confronted them about their sin and promised them a Savior who would crush all evil. He also gave them a temporary covering in the skins of slain animals, a reminder of blood shed because of sin and His provision to cover their shame. God took the initiative in showing man how to return to Him and worship Him. We saw in Lesson One several examples of worship from Adam to Aaron. Let's look at some of the **places of worship** then and thereafter, **places where God and man met together.**

📖 Over one thousand years after Adam lived, God revealed Himself to Abram and called him to leave his country and resettle in Canaan. Read Genesis 12:1–7, and record your insights about what Abram did in that **meeting place**.

____

____

____

In response to God's revelation of Himself, Abram obeyed and left Haran, then built an altar at the place **where God appeared to him** in Canaan. An altar is a place of sacrifice and giving, a place where one acknowledges his relationship to God and accountability before God. The altar Abram built honored the Lord in His very presence. By His presence and His promise the Lord hallowed and set apart that land, and it became a place of worship "to the LORD who had appeared" to Abram. The place where Abram and God **met** became a place of worship.

📖 What happened at the place called Bethel as recorded in Genesis 12:8?

____

____

____

When he moved east of Bethel, Abram *"built an altar to the LORD."* At this place, Abram acknowledged His relationship to the LORD again. He recognized the land as belonging to the LORD and there *"called upon the name of the LORD."* That is at the heart of meeting with God, calling on Him out of our sense of dependence and trusting Him to act on our behalf. Calling on the Lord is the mark of those who follow God wherever He leads.

True Worship

WE CALL ON THE NAME OF THE LORD

We start our walk with the Lord by calling on His name, for He says *"whosoever shall call upon the name of the Lord shall be saved."* (Romans 10:13) As believers, we continue following the Lord *"with those who call on the Lord from a pure heart"* (2 Timothy

📖 In Genesis 14, Abram went to war to rescue Lot and his family, and God gave him victory. As Abram returned, he came to another place of worship. We find this place mentioned in Genesis 14:17–24. What happened at this place? Record your insights.

Abram met Melchizedek, king of Salem, in the valley of Shaveh. There Melchizedek, who was a priest of *"God Most High (El Elyon), Possessor of heaven and earth,"* gave Abram wine and bread and blessed him and his God. Melchizedek and Abram acknowledged that God had given Abram victory in the battles and was his provider. Because Abram knew this God as his God, he needed none of the spoils offered by the king of Sodom and rightly refused them. This valley became a place of worship for Abram, a place of acknowledging God as his provider. There Abram showed his surrender to the Lord and his trust in the Lord's care and provision.

Word Study

"EL-ELYON"

El Elyon means "God Most High" and refers to the Lord as the one who is over all, the one above all else. He is the highest, the Most High.

After the war of the kings, the Lord appeared to Abram in a vision. He revealed Himself as Abram's Shield and Reward (Protector and Provider). At that meeting place, Abram called on the Lord about the provision of a son, a promise God had made years before. At that place the Lord gave him a visual picture (the countless stars) and renewed His promise. What was Abram's response in that place? Read Genesis 15:1–21 and record your insights.

Abram believed God and His promise. When God revealed Himself as a Shield (his Protector) and as his Reward (his Provider), Abram placed his faith and trust securely in the Lord. He surrendered to Him and His will, trusting His Word. He knew that God would give him a son and many descendants and that the Lord would indeed be to him his Shield and his Reward.

In Genesis 22:5 we find the first mention of the word "worship" in the Scriptures. Read carefully the account of Abraham and Isaac in Genesis 22:1–9. What do you see about this meeting place, **the place** where they worshiped? (Note that the word "place" occurs in verses 3 and 9).

GOD'S TEST

God tested Abraham's trust, and Abraham trusted God's test. It is the same in our day-by-day walk of faith.

____

____

____

____

This was the place of a faith test. God tested Abraham's faith in this place. He was watching the man and his heart. God told him what He wanted as an offering, and Abraham obeyed, trusting the Lord. Abraham considered this call of God the call to come and worship the Lord at the meeting place God designated. In that place he would offer up a "burnt offering," a total sacrifice, fully consumed, fully offered up. In this place of God's test, Abraham truly worshiped. The Lord made three statements about what Abraham did at this meeting place: **1)** *"now I know that you fear God"* (22:12); **2)** *"you have not withheld your son, your only son, from Me"* (22:12); and **3)** *"you have obeyed My voice"* (22:18). God defined worship in this place. There Abraham walked in the fear of the Lord with prompt, full obedience to His Word, withholding nothing from Him. It was truly a place of **meeting the Lord—a place of worship!**

True Worship

WALKING WITH GOD

God wants every place we walk to be a meeting place with Him and a place of true worship. True worship means walking in the fear of the Lord with prompt, full obedience to His Word, withholding nothing from Him.

In the following years, the Lord appeared again to Abraham's son Isaac at Beersheba, assuring him of His covenant promises. At that meeting place Isaac responded by building an altar of **worship** (Genesis 26:23–25). His son Jacob did the same at Bethel and at Beersheba (Genesis 28:10–22; 35:1–7; 46:1–7).

In each meeting place, we see the LORD truly revealing Himself and His people responding with worship. Each place of worship was a place of an altar—a place to deal with sin and express surrender to the Lord. It was a place of *"calling on the name of the LORD"* and gratefully acknowledging His provision. God wants to meet with us. He comes to us, calls us, and desires for us to call on Him in faith. He wants us to walk **with** Him. He wants everyplace we walk to be a meeting place with Him and a place of true worship. We will see that in greater detail in Day Two.

Lesson Two **DAY TWO**

GOD DWELLS WITH US—MOSES AND THE TABERNACLE

We have seen that each of the places of worship has been a place with an altar, a place of sacrificial death. (No sacrificed animals had died accidentally or naturally of old age or disease.) Through these sacrificial deaths, the altars became places of worship towards God. What else can we learn about worshiping and walking with God?

📖 What marked Moses' meeting with God in Exodus 3:1–12? What did the Lord say about the **place** of their meeting?

God revealed Himself to Moses through a burning bush that was not consumed. He called the place "holy ground"—made holy (the word means "set apart") by the presence of God. There God revealed His purposes and plans for His people and, in response, Moses hid his face in fear and reverence.

Exodus 3:1 and 3:12 reveal God's purpose in sending Moses back to Egypt. The LORD wanted to meet with His people in person. That planned meeting with God occurred at Mount Horeb (also called Mount Sinai).

📖 Read Exodus 19:1–25 and 20:1–24. What marked that meeting? What do you observe about that **place** of worship?

God brought the people of Israel to Himself at Mount Sinai, a place of reverence and fear of the Lord. God wanted them to treat Him with utmost respect. He warned against any irreverent regard for the Lord or this place (19:13–25). There God revealed Himself and His Law. He wanted a people who would honor Him and His Word "in every place" where He revealed Himself (20:24). At Mount Sinai, God wanted His people to worship Him with a willing, surrendered heart.

At the "mountain of God," the Lord gave His Law. A major portion of that Law concerned the **Tabernacle** along with the regulations for the Priesthood and the offerings that were to be brought there. What did God say about this Tabernacle in Exodus 25:8–9?

The Tabernacle would be the tangible dwelling place of the Lord, a place where He could dwell in accord with His character, His holiness. There He would meet with His people, tell them what He is like, and guide them to where He wanted them to be. The Tabernacle was a "sanctuary," meaning "a set apart place." It was important for Moses and all the people to understand that God does not dwell in a place according to man's ideas and standards. Therefore, this place had to be built according to His pattern (see 25:9).

We find in Exodus 25—31 and 35—40 the details of the Tabernacle and the priesthood. The people obeyed the Lord in establishing this place of meeting and worship. In all of this, God instructed the children of Israel regarding Himself and their relationship to Him. They received training and instruction as a nation of children. Surely, they asked the following questions: "How is the Holy God to be treated?" "What is He like?" "How are

Did You Know?

THE FIRE OF GOD

God often manifested Himself in fire. He stationed the Cherubim at the entrance to the Garden of Eden holding a flaming sword. He met Moses at a bush that burned but was not consumed. He came down on Mount Sinai in fire. He manifested Himself in a pillar of fire when the children left Egypt, and He revealed Himself as a fire inside the Tabernacle at night. When God met Manoah and his wife before the birth of Samson, He consumed their sacrifice with a touch, and it went up in the flames. Upon the completion of the Temple, He consumed the sacrifice with fire from heaven. He sent fire to consume the sacrifice and altar that Elijah built in the confrontation with the prophets of Baal. God rested on each of the disciples with a tongue of fire on the Day of Pentecost. God will reveal Himself in fire at the end of the age.

we to approach Him?" "How are we to worship Him?" God set aside this special **place** we call the "Tabernacle" to reveal these things.

Construction of the Tabernacle took place "just as the LORD had commanded Moses." Its pattern, design, and order of worship were God's, and God had a definite plan and purpose in what He revealed and commanded. Worship of the living God is by revelation from Him; it is not a man-generated form, program, rite, ritual, or ceremony. Each piece of the Tabernacle signified some aspect of the nature and character of God and His relationship with His children. God wanted to show and teach the Israelites who He is and who they were in relationship to Him. It is important to note that these instructions regarding the construction of the Tabernacle were commands—not optional suggestions. In Exodus 40:18–33, there are seven divisions, each of which concludes with "as the LORD had commanded" (verses 19, 21, 23, 25, 27, 29, 32). It was all by God's design and pattern, none of it by man's suggestions or thoughts.

"And there I will meet with thee, and I will commune with thee from above the mercy seat, from between the two cherubims which are upon the ark of the testimony, of all things which I will give thee in commandment unto the children of Israel."

Exodus 25:22 (KJV)

APPLY Did you know God had a design and a plan for your life? Why not pause right now and talk to the Lord about this? He wants **the place where you are this moment** to be a place to meet with Him.

📖 What did God do in Exodus 40:34? What did Moses do (40:35)? What was significant about that place?

____

____

____

____

God revealed Himself in His glory with a visible cloud covering the tent. It was the visible sign of His presence and His favor. The children of Israel had done what He asked according to the directions He gave. The presence of the Lord left Moses awestruck. The significance of the Tabernacle is found in the manifested presence of the Lord—not in anything about the place in and of itself. Because the Lord was present, it was a place of awe, reverence, and worship. It was a place marked by the fear of the Lord, by obedience to His Word, and by unquestioning surrender to Him.

📖 Read Exodus 40:36–38. What do you see about the place of worship in these verses? What did God do? What did the people do?

____

____

____

____

____

____

The place of the cloud of glory/pillar of fire was a place of unconditional surrender. When God moved, the people moved. Where and when God stayed, the people stayed. Worship always involves submission, surrender, and service to the One you worship.

APPLY To what in our lives do we submit and surrender our time and money? Who or what do we heartily serve and follow. If our time, money, and other interests are devoted to an entity other than God Almighty, could that entity be in essence our god? How readily do we follow the true and living God?

Who or what is your God?

God with Us—The Temple and Jesus

Lesson Two **DAY THREE**

The Israelites used the Tabernacle for over 470 years. After traveling through the wilderness for almost forty years with Moses, the Israelites moved into Canaan under the leadership of Joshua. For several years, the Tabernacle stayed at Shiloh (noted for the ministries of Eli and then Samuel). It stayed there during the reigns of Saul and David and then was moved to Jerusalem. Under the leadership of Solomon, God directed Israel to replace the Tabernacle with a magnificent temple structure in Jerusalem. It took seven years to build and was completed in 959 B.C. (1 Kings 6:37–38). What was God showing His people about meeting with Him, about this new place of worship and its importance, and about walking with Him?

Look at 2 Chronicles 5:1–14 where Solomon and the priests finished getting everything in place. What happened when the Ark of the Covenant and the priests were all in place?

____

____

____

____

____

The priests had walked through the necessary ritual cleansing and sacrifices. Many offerings were made. They and the people had dealt with sin and surrendered their hearts and lives to the Lord. All were in an attitude of worship. The priests had done all that was necessary to stand before the Lord ceremonially clean and were ready to offer their sacrifices and services in the new temple as He had commanded. The priests brought the Ark of the Covenant to its place in the Holy of Holies. Then, the priests along with the levitical singers and musicians began to praise and glorify the Lord. They proclaimed *"He indeed is good for His lovingkindness is everlasting."* Then *"the house of the Lord was filled with a cloud"*—the Shekinah Glory Cloud of the Lord's presence. The priests could not stand because of the awesome presence of the Lord, just as in the days of Moses when they completed the Tabernacle (2 Chronicles 5:13–14; Exodus 40:33–35).

This was an awesome day in the life of Israel. There in Jerusalem, the place chosen by God to establish His name and to reveal Himself (6:6), He once again revealed His Presence in the cloud of glory. Solomon began to testify of the faithfulness of God to Israel, to his father David, and now to himself.

Word Study

THE SHEKINAH GLORY

The word "dwell" is a translation of the Hebrew word *shakan*, which means to dwell, to reside, to permanently stay or settle down. God did this in the cloud and the pillar of fire in the wilderness. In this visible manifestation, Israel saw the glory of the Lord. This has been called the "Shekinah (from *shakan*) Glory"—the visible dwelling of God revealing His glory through fire or a bright light, as with Jesus on the Mount of Transfiguration (Luke 9) or with Saul (Paul) on the Damascus Road (Acts 9).

In his prayer, Solomon asked a question of great importance concerning this Temple and what God would do there. Read 2 Chronicles 6:18–21 and summarize what Solomon said.

____

____

____

____

True Worship
MUSICIANS AND SINGERS

Several musicians (singers and instrumentalists) are mentioned in I Chronicles 5 that were not included in the Tabernacle. These musicians were added to the order of worship during the reign of King David (see I Chronicles 24–26).

Solomon knew that the temple was in no way adequate as a dwelling place for God, a place to contain God. Yet, he knew God's promise to meet with His people at this place—in His temple. This would be a place of prayer, a place of communion with God, of fellowship with the Lord of heaven and earth, as well as a place to find forgiveness of sins. Even for the foreigner or for the Israelite in a foreign land, this place represented communion and fellowship with the living Lord. Solomon concluded his prayer by asking the Lord to be *"attentive to the prayer offered in this place."* He also asked the people to walk together with the Lord and experience His salvation and rejoicing in His goodness (6:40–41).

What happened after Solomon's prayer of dedication according to 2 Chronicles 7:1–3? What marked that meeting place as a place of worship?

____

____

____

____

____

At the place of prayer where Solomon and the priests had offered the sacrifices for sin and showed their surrender to the Lord, the Lord revealed Himself in fire—*"fire came down from heaven and consumed the burnt offering and the sacrifices."* Then the glory cloud filled the Temple. The people of Israel, upon seeing God reveal Himself in fire and in the cloud, fell on their faces before Him and worshiped Him. *"And when all the children of Israel saw how the fire came down, and the glory of the Lord upon the house, they bowed themselves with their faces to the ground upon the pavement, and worshipped, and praised the Lord, saying, For he is good; for his mercy endureth for ever"* (2 Chronicles 7:3 KJV). This place of worship was marked by the fear of the Lord, by obedience to His Word, and by a people who surrendered themselves to Him in worship.

Did You Know?
"THIS PLACE"

The place of the Temple, also known as Mount Moriah (see Lesson One), is mentioned in accounts concerning Abraham and Isaac (Genesis 22:1–19); David and Ornan the Jebusite (I Chronicles 21:18–30; 22:1–19) and of the Temple built by Solomon (2 Chronicles 3:1–2).

Jerusalem was the place set aside by the Lord for this temple. There Solomon built the temple according to the pattern given by God, even as Moses followed the Lord and His pattern for the Tabernacle. The Tabernacle and the new Solomon's Temple were places of genuine worship. Solomon's Temple stood for over 350 years and then was destroyed in 586 B.C. because of the people's idolatry. It was rebuilt under the leadership of Zerubbabel and finished in 516 B.C. When we come to the New Testament, we find Herod's Temple, a remodeling of Zerubbabel's Temple. That remodeling began around 20 B.C. and continued for many years. When the Lord Jesus came to that temple, the renovation had been ongoing for forty-six years. There the Lord Jesus gave new revelation concerning the place of worship.

Read John 2:13–22. What did Jesus say about the Temple? What was His main point in this confrontation over this meeting place, this place of worship?

Jesus confronted the merchants selling in the Temple. They had turned the Temple, the meeting place for the worship of God, into a marketplace. Jesus had begun to reveal who He was, the very dwelling of God—the God-Man in flesh, but many did not recognize Him at that time. His body was the dwelling place of the true and living God. He had the power of life and death and declared that He would one day reveal it in His resurrection. He was (and is) God, the one worthy of worship.

The Gospels record who Jesus is and what He did. Each one reveals some unique aspects of His life. We want to look at two of them—Matthew and John. Read Matthew 1:18–25. What does Matthew say about Jesus? Then, read John 1:14 and record further insights about the person of Jesus Christ. (Note: the Greek word translated "dwelt" [*skenoó*] literally means "to pitch one's tent or tabernacle" or "to tabernacle.")

Matthew reveals that Jesus was conceived by the Holy Spirit in the virgin Mary. His name Jesus (which means "Savior" or "Salvation") matched both His person and the work He was to do—He would *"save His people from their sins."* One of His names would be Immanuel, a Hebrew word translated "God with us." John adds significance to this truth with what he reveals. The eternal Word (John 1:1–2), the Creator of the world (John 1:3), became flesh and "tabernacled" in a divinely human body. He was God dwelling with us in the divine tabernacle of His body. By His presence, the glory of God was manifested as at the Tabernacle and at the temple. He revealed the fullness of God as no one else had ever done. He "explained" the Father as John 1:18 says. Jesus Christ, "the Word made flesh," is our worthy Savior and Lord. He is worthy of our trust and obedience. He is the Lord who deserves our reverence and fear. He is our Savior who deserves our all. From Him we should withhold nothing. In Him we meet God because He is the Lord, "full of grace and truth" (John 1:14), and in worshiping Him our worship becomes all God wants it to be.

Jesus revealed much more about how we can meet with God, know God, and walk with Him, and He revealed aspects about the presence and work of His Spirit. We will study these aspects further in Day Four.

Extra Mile

"THIS PLACE" (THE TEMPLE)

Read 2 Chronicles 7:4–22. What added insights do you find about this place—the Temple? What do you discover about worship? What is God seeking to teach you about your walk with Him?

True Worship

THE CLOUD OF GLORY

The Transfiguration accounts (Matthew 17:1–8; Mark 9:2–8; Luke 9:28–36) give us another glimpse of the "glory" of God revealed in Jesus Christ. *". . . His face shone like the sun, and His garments became as white as light"* (Matt 17:2). This reminds us of the accounts of the presence and glory of God meeting with Moses and with Solomon.

Lesson Two **DAY FOUR**

God in Us—The Work of the Holy Spirit in His Temple

We have seen that the place where we meet God is always a place of an altar where we deal with sin and surrender. With the coming of Jesus, we find the Cross to be **The Altar** where God dealt with sin once and for all. The Cross is where we come to deal with our sin and surrender and begin our new life in Him. Jesus said a vital part of our walk with Him would involve His Holy Spirit, who would point us to Jesus, reveal any sin, and allow us to know His Life—that Living Water He promised. Jesus showed how the Spirit would be active in our meeting with and walking with God. In fact, He promised His disciples that the Holy Spirit would be **in** them (John 14:16–18). How would this occur? What relationship did this have to meeting God and worshiping Him? How did this connect with what had occurred in the Tabernacle and the Temple?

Acts 1 and 2 begin answering some of these questions. Read Acts 2:1–4 and carefully summarize the details. (You may want to look at Acts 1 to understand the events surrounding all that happened in Acts 2.)

____

____

____

____

____

Did You Know?

THE HOUR OF INCENSE

Incense was offered on the Golden Altar of Incense in the Temple twice each day; once at 9:00 A.M. and at 3:00 P.M.—the same hours that the lamb was offered as a burnt offering.

Acts 2 recounts the events of the Day of Pentecost, the day the Jews celebrated the Feast of Pentecost, fifty days after the Feast of Firstfruits (the day Jesus resurrected). Ten days before Pentecost, the resurrected Lord Jesus had ascended into heaven with the promise to His disciples that they were to wait in Jerusalem for what the Father had promised. He told them they would receive power from the Holy Spirit to bear witness of who Christ is and all Christ had done. At 9:00 A.M. on Sunday morning, the hour of the incense offering as well as the hour of prayer at the Temple, there came a noise like a mighty, rushing wind. That noise filled the whole place where the disciples gathered, so much so that a great crowd also heard that noise. "Tongues of fire" rested on each of the 120 disciples, and Acts 2:4 says, *"they were all filled with the Holy Spirit."*

Think back to the manifestations of God at the Tabernacle and the Temple. The fiery glory cloud rested on each of these places when all was in place, when the people had done what He had told them to do. In Acts 2, we read of a tongue of fire resting on each one of the disciples. It appears that these tongues of fire were like individual pillars of fire, representative of the presence of the Lord Himself, and they rested on and filled each disciple as **a temple** of the Holy Spirit—just as Jesus had promised. Then, the disciples spoke in several languages proclaiming the message of *"the mighty deeds of God."* Doubtless, these "deeds" refer to the deeds done in and through the Lord Jesus—His life, death, and resurrection. Like the glory cloud of old, they glorified God and revealed who He is and what He had done. His presence was being revealed in a new way, and God was at work. A crowd gathered, and Peter began to preach that most powerful message to them.

We have seen that worship always involves dealing with sin and surrender, with the need for forgiveness and submission to the Lord and His provision for salvation. In Acts 2, as Peter preached, the people cried out, "What shall we do?" Peter told them to repent of their sin, the very sin that placed Jesus on the cross, and he told them to turn to Jesus Christ for forgiveness.

What was the promise Peter made in Acts 2:38–39?

____

____

____

Peter promised the people that if they listened to the call of God, turned from their sin, and received the forgiveness offered by Jesus Christ, they would receive the Holy Spirit. This promise was for any that would repent and turn to Jesus Christ.

"Your body is the temple of the Holy Spirit who is in you, whom you have from God. . . ."
I Corinthians 6:19 (NKJV)

The Apostle Paul experienced the convicting call of Jesus Christ in his life while he was on the road from Jerusalem to Damascus. He received forgiveness of sins and the coming of the Holy Spirit into his life. The Lord even gave him a commission to carry that message to the Jews and the Gentiles (Acts 26:14–18). One group to whom he carried that message lived in Corinth.

📖 Read 1 Corinthians 6:19–20. What exactly did Paul tell these Corinthian Christians when he wrote to them about their walk with God? You may want to look at 6:1–18 to see the background for what he said to them.

____

____

____

____

____

____

Paul wanted the Corinthian Christians to know that they were to live a different life now that Jesus Christ was their Lord and Savior. They were to live as those forgiven and cleansed, as those made right with God through the death and resurrection of Jesus Christ. The Holy Spirit indwelt them. That meant their lives and their relationships with others were to be marked by holiness. In fact, Paul made a special point about the indwelling of the Spirit in verse 19: their bodies were the very temple of the Holy Spirit. There are two Greek words for "temple"—*hierón* (the entire Temple including the outer courts) and *naos* (the inner court or the Holy of Holies). This verse uses *naós*, which describes the most sacred place in the Temple, the place of highest honor, a dwelling place, just like the Tabernacle or the Temple of the Old Testament. That is what our bodies are. Each Christian is a temple, a *naós,* a dwelling place and a meeting place of the Holy Spirit. Therefore, each one is to glorify or reveal what God is like in and through one's body and in one's words and actions.

Each Christian is a temple or tabernacle —a dwelling place and a meeting place of the Holy Spirit.

APPLY Read 1 Corinthians 6:19–20 again. What applications do you see for your life knowing that **your body** is the temple of the Holy Spirit? Think of this. The Temple/Tabernacle was the place where God dwelt with His people in the Old Testament. It was a place of meeting with God, hearing from God, and even seeing God in the form of the cloud of glory and the pillar of fire. It was the visible vehicle God used to communicate His will to His people. His presence marked that place. It is to be that way with each Christian. Each is the dwelling place of God. Each one is to be a visible vehicle for communicating who God is, what He is like, what His will is.

The word "glorify" means"to form a good or correct opinion about." That is what God designed the Tabernacle and Temple to do—to give a clear, accurate, and good opinion about the living God. This is also what He has designed each of His disciples to do.A Christian's daily walk should reflect how God would act in any place or situation. A farmer should reveal what it would look like for God to farm. A lawyer should reveal what it looks like for God to practice law. A wife and mother or a husband and father should reveal what it looks like for God to be in that labor of love. That is what it means to glorify God in our bodies.

Lesson Two **DAY FIVE**

For Me to Worship God

The places where people have met God, the places of worship, have been many and varied throughout history and throughout Scripture—from the Garden of Eden to the wilderness of Sinai and from the Temple in Jerusalem to the city of Corinth. Each meeting place was marked by the fullness of the presence of God and the work of the Spirit of God. The questions we must ask today include these: "Am I marked by His presence and His fullness? Am I, as His Temple, revealing who He is?" If you are walking in the fullness of His Spirit, you are revealing Him in some way. How can we know if we are revealing God? Let's look at some Scriptures.

We have been talking about God's meeting place, the place where He is truly worshiped. First, we must make sure our meeting place is open—open to God's way.

📖 Read Isaiah 57:15 and James 4:5–6. What kind of dwelling place or meeting place does God desire? What applications do these verses have for your life? Is your life a good meeting place for the Lord?

____

____

____

____

The place where God delights to meet us is marked by an open, honest, contrite heart—no prideful show, just an honest humility that honors the Lord and looks to Him in all of life. He delights in simple meeting places, places where He can be heard and understood, followed and worshiped.
We have seen that each believer is a temple of the Holy Spirit. Each

Christian's body is designed to be a place of worship, a place of meeting with God and interacting with Him. What characteristics should mark that place? In 2 Corinthians 6:14–18, 7:1, we see some insights into the characteristics God wants to see in each Christian and in his or her relationships.

📖 Read 2 Corinthians 6:14–18, 7:1, and record your insights.

____

____

____

____

____

____

Our lives and our worship (individually and corporately) are never to be a mixture of darkness and light, never the truth of Christ mixed with the lies of Belial, never partaking or sharing in the unbelief of an unbeliever. We are new creatures in Christ. Ephesians 5 speaks of putting off the "old" and putting on the "new man." We never need go back to the old, rotten garments of unbelief. God has nothing in common with idols, and neither should we. Idols do not belong in our hearts. Our hearts are reserved for the one and only true and living God. God has promised to dwell in us and walk among us, to guide us in holy living. He wants to reveal what He is like in the way we think, choose, and live, especially in our relationships with one another.

As Christians, we never need to go back to the old, rotten garments of unbelief.

📖 Look at 2 Corinthians 6:14–18, 7:1 once again. Paul makes some clear applications in 7:1 based on the promises of God in 6:16–18. List the promises and then the specific applications.

____

____

____

____

____

____

God has promised to dwell in His children and to walk among them. He will be our God and Father and we will be His people, His children. We are His family and ought to act like it. He calls us to come out from the midst of the world and away from anything that is unclean in His sight. He wants us to be separate, set apart to Him and His purposes and designs. He wants us to become mature in holiness. Because of that, He exhorts us to deal with anything sinful, any defilement of flesh or spirit, any touch of sin. That does not mean He wants us to act differently merely for the sake of being different. It means He wants us to deal with anything that grieves or quenches His Spirit. (We grieve Him when we say "yes" to sin, when we do what we should not do. We quench Him when we say "no" to His Spirit, when we do not do what He had told us to do.) He wants us always walking in the fear of the Lord, obeying Him promptly and fully, surrendering to Him, and experiencing the fullness of His Spirit in our lives.

APPLY How are you doing? Stop and look at your "temple." Look at each area, and ask the Spirit of God to search you, especially in light of what we have observed in 1 Corinthians 6:19–20 and 2 Corinthians 6:14–18; 7:1.

Stop and take a look at your "temple."

- ❒ **Your eyes**—What do you read? Watch on TV? How do you look at others? Do you lust? Envy others? Do you covet what others have?
- ❒ **Your ears**—What do you listen to? Music or conversation that builds up or tears down? Do you listen to gossip or pointless criticism?
- ❒ **Your tongue**—Do you speak right words? Do you live according to Ephesians 4:29? Do you tell others about Jesus . . . who He is and what He came to do?
- ❒ **Your eating**—Are you grateful for the food you have? Is there any gluttony or the reverse—excessive dieting?
- ❒ **Your thoughtlife**—On what do your thoughts dwell? Do your thoughts correspond with Philippians 4:8?
- ❒ **Your moral purity**—Is your body surrendered to the Lord?
- ❒ **Your feet**—Where do you walk or drive?
- ❒ **Your hands**—Are they used for good or evil?

How are you glorifying Him in your body?

Spend some time with the Lord, asking Him to give you His wisdom and His evaluation about how you are doing.

APPLY Let's place all we have seen into one final application. What does it mean for my life to be God's Dwelling Place, **a place of meeting with God** daily, **a place of worship**? It means walking as His temple, where sin is dealt with, forgiveness is experienced, and the fulness of His Spirit is real and lasting. How can I know those things in my life? How can I walk in the fullness of the Holy Spirit, being the temple He wants me to be? Someone once shared with me three very simple truths that summarize and help us apply this on a daily basis.

How can I walk in the fullness of the Holy Spirit, being the temple He wants me to be?

1) Confess all sin to God. Agree with Him about your sin—do not argue about it (1 John 1:9).

2) Present yourself to God to be filled and controlled by His Spirit (Romans 12:1–2). To surrender means to withhold nothing.

3) Ask Him in faith to fill you with His Spirit. He commanded us to be filled (controlled) in Ephesians 5:18, so we know that is His will (1 John 5:14). He is not reluctant to fill you! (Don't depend on feelings, but depend only on Him and His Word by faith.) When you obey God's Word, you can expect the fullness of the Holy Spirit!

What would you say if someone were to come up and ask you, "Where do we **meet** God?" or "Where is the **place of worship**?"?

Spend some time with the Lord in prayer right now.

Lord, thank You that You seek those who would worship You in spirit and truth. Thank You for revealing the way to return to You, worship You, and walk with You. Thank You for speaking to me about truly walking in the fear of the Lord, of obeying You promptly and fully, and of giving all to You—withholding nothing. May I keep growing in knowing what it means to surrender to You, to Your Word, and to walking in Your ways. May I walk more consistently in the fullness of Your Spirit as Your Temple, dealing with any and every sin and yielding to You moment by moment. In Jesus' name, Amen.

Spend some additional time talking with the Lord. Make the place where you are reading this study a place of meeting God, a place of true worship. Write out your prayer of worship to Him in the space below.

The Manifestations of the Presence of the LORD— The *Shekinah* Glory Dwelling on Earth

SCRIPTURE	EVENTS	PLACE
Genesis 3:8–21	There was some manifestation of the Lord in the Garden of Eden. God came seeking Adam and Eve, and they knew He was there, and they talked with Him.	Garden of Eden
Genesis 3:24	The Cherubim and a flaming sword guarded the way to the Tree of Life.	Garden of Eden
Genesis 11:31; 12:1–4; Acts 7:2–4	The Lord of glory appeared to Abram in Mesopotamia (Ur).	Ur of the Chaldeans
Genesis 15:7–21 (verse 17)	The Lord entered into covenant with Abram and appeared in a cloud of smoke (like a smoking oven) and a flaming torch.	Hebron
Exodus 3:2–6	The Lord appeared to Moses in a burning bush that was not consumed by the supernatural fire.	Mount Horeb
Exodus 13:17–22	The Lord led the people of Israel out of Egypt with a pillar of cloud by day and a pillar of fire by night.	Egypt and in the Wilderness
Exodus 14:19–20	The pillar of the presence of The Angel of the Lord shielded the Israelites from the Egyptian army	At the Red Sea
Exodus 14:21–31	The Lord confused the army of Egypt and brought the waters of the sea upon them.	Through the Red Sea
Exodus 16:4–12	The glory of the Lord appeared in the cloud, and the Lord gave them meat in the evening and manna in the morning.	Wilderness of Sin
Exodus 19:1–25	The Lord came down on Mount Sinai in smoke and fire.	Mount Sinai
Exodus 20:1–21	The Lord spoke to the people from the smoke-covered mount.	Mount Sinai
Exodus 20:21–26; 21–23	The Lord spoke to Moses and gave him the various laws for His people.	Mount Sinai
Exodus 24:1–11	Moses went up to meet the Lord with Aaron, Nadab, and Abihu, along with seventy elders of Israel.	Mount Sinai
Exodus 24:12–18	Moses and Joshua went up to the mountain. After seven days, Moses entered the midst of the cloud on the mountain to receive the stone tablets of the law and the instructions for the Tabernacle (Exodus 25–31).	Mount Sinai
Exodus 33:7–11	Moses often met the Lord at the Tent of Meeting, and the "pillar of cloud" would descend and rest there. The Lord spoke with Moses face to face.	Outside the camp of the Israelites.
Exodus 33:12–16	Moses prayed for the presence of the Lord to go with them on the journey.	Mount Sinai
Exodus 33:17–23; 34:6–9	Moses prayed to see God's glory, and the Lord revealed His glory, *"passing by"* Moses.	Mount Sinai
Exodus 34:29–35; (2 Cor. 3:7–18)	Moses' face shone temporarily from being in the presence of the Lord.	Mount Sinai
Exodus 25:8, 22; 29:42–46; 40:34–35; Numbers 9:15	The Tabernacle fulfilled the purpose for which the Lord commanded it be constructed. It was the dwelling place of the Lord where He met with His people.	Mount Sinai
Exodus 40:36–38; Numbers 9:15–23	The cloud of glory rested on the Tabernacle by day and the pillar of fire by night. When the cloud was taken up, the people followed the Lord wherever He led them.	Wilderness journey
Leviticus 9:1–24	The cloud of glory appeared, and fire from the Lord consumed the sacrifices Aaron and his sons offered.	Mount Sinai
Numbers 12:1–15	The Lord came down in a pillar of cloud and dealt with the complaint of Miriam and Aaron against Moses.	Hazeroth in the Wilderness
Numbers 13–14	The glory of the Lord appeared when the Israelites grumbled in unbelief over entering the land of Canaan. The Lord sentenced them to die in the wilderness	Wilderness of Paran at Kadesh

SCRIPTURE	EVENTS	PLACE
Numbers 16:1–40	Korah, Dathan, and Abiram rebelled against Moses and Aaron as God's chosen leaders and declared themselves as equal leaders. The glory of the Lord appeared, and the ground swallowed the men and their families. 250 others offering incense were slain by the fire of the Lord.	The wilderness
Numbers 16:41–50	The glory of the Lord appeared, and the Lord sent a plague to judge those who complained against Moses and Aaron	The wilderness
Numbers 20:2–13	The Lord appeared when the people complained about no water at Meribah. Moses struck the rock and forfeited going into the land of Canaan.	Wilderness of Sin at Kadesh (Meribah)
Deuteronomy 4:32–33; 5:4–5, 22–33	At Moab, before the people crossed over into the land of Canaan, Moses recounted the times the Lord appeared and spoke out of the fire on the mountain, giving them the Law.	At Moab, telling of Mount Sinai
Joshua 4:15–24; 5:1–15; 6:1–5	The priests carried the ark of the covenant into the Jordan River, and the river dried up. The people marched through and camped at Gilgal, where the Captain of the Host of the Lord appeared to Joshua, giving him the battle plan for Jericho.	Jordan River, Gilgal, Jericho
Judges 6:11–24	The Angel of the Lord appeared to Gideon and caused fire to consume the offering he made.	Ophrah
Judges 13:1–24	The Angel of the Lord appeared to Manoah and his wife, promising them a son and then ascended in the flame of the altar where they were offering a burnt offering.	Zorah
1 Samuel 3:21	The Lord appeared at the Tabernacle at Shiloh, where Samuel ministered as a prophet.	Shiloh
1 Samuel 4:11–22; 5–6	The Philistines captured the ark of the covenant from Israel, and God brought great turmoil and sickness to them. God cannot be captured.	Ebenezer, Ashdod, Ekron, Beth Shemesh
Psalm 26:8	David prayed, *"O Lord, I love the habitation of Thy house, and the place where Thy glory dwells"* [literally, "the place of the tabernacle of Thy glory"].	Israel
Psalm 73:21–28	Asaph spoke of being in the presence of the Lord, of being received *"to glory,"* and declared, *"the nearness of God is my good."*	Israel
1 Kings 8:1–11; 2 Chronicles 5:2–14; 6:1–2	In the reign of Solomon, the priests brought the ark of the covenant into the newly-built Temple, and the cloud and glory of the Lord filled the Temple.	Jerusalem
2 Chronicles 6:12–42; 7:1–3	When Solomon finished praying at the dedication of the Temple, the fire of God came down and consumed the burnt offering, and the glory of the Lord filled the Temple.	Jerusalem
Ezekiel 10:1–4, 18–19; 11:22–24	Ezekiel saw the glory of the Lord depart from the Temple to the East Gate to the Mount of Olives.	Jerusalem (Temple and Mount of Olives)
Ezekiel 43:1–12	Ezekiel saw a vision of the glory of the Lord returning to a reconstructed temple.	Jerusalem
Isaiah 6:1–13; John 12:41	In the year King Uzziah died, Isaiah saw a vision of the Lord in heaven.	Heaven
Isaiah 40:5; 60:1–2; 66; Habakkuk 2:14; Zechariah 2:5	Several prophets spoke of the coming kingdom in which the presence of the Lord would be manifested in His glory being seen.	Israel and the earth
Haggai 2:6–9	Haggai prophesied about the glory of the Lord appearing in a future Temple.	Jerusalem
Daniel 7:9–10	Daniel saw a vision of the Ancient of Days in His glory.	Heaven
Daniel 7:13–14	Daniel saw a vision of the Son of Man coming in the clouds of heaven.	Heaven and earth
Luke 2:8–20	The glory of the Lord appeared to the shepherds in the fields outside Bethlehem at the birth of the Messiah Jesus.	Shepherds' fields near Bethlehem
Matthew 2:1–12	The magi followed His star to find the Christ Child in Bethlehem. That star went before them and stood over the house where the Child was. Many believe that supernatural "star" which appeared and led these men was the *Shekinah* fire of God.	Bethlehem
Matthew 16:27	Jesus promised His disciples that one day He would come in the glory of His Father with His angels.	Earth

SCRIPTURE	EVENTS	PLACE
Luke 9:28–36; Matthew 17:1–8; Mark 9:2–8; 2 Peter 1:16–18; James 2:1; John 1:14	On the mount of Transfiguration, Jesus' face and clothing changed, Moses and Elijah appeared in glory, and the Father overshadowed them in a cloud. Peter, James, and John saw this.	The Mount of Transfiguration (possibly Mount Hermon)
Daniel 7:13–14 Matthew 24:30, 26:64; Mark 13:26; 14:62; Luke 21:27	First to His disciples and then later to the Jewish leaders at His trial before His crucifixion, Jesus promised that He would come as the reigning Son of Man in the clouds of heaven (a manifestation of His glory).	Heaven and Earth
Acts 1:9–11	Jesus ascended in a cloud of glory forty days after His resurrection. The angel promised that Jesus would one day return in the same way.	Mount of Olives in Jerusalem
Acts 2:1–4 1 Corinthians 6:19; 2 Corinthians 6:16	Tongues of fire rested on each of the believers gathered on the morning of Pentecost. These appear to be individualized pillars of fire resting on the new temples of the Holy Spirit. Paul speaks of believers being the temple (Greek, *naos,* "inner sanctuary") of the Holy Spirit.	Jerusalem
Acts 6:15; 7:54–60	Stephen's face appeared as the face of an angel. When the authorities were seeking to execute him, he saw the glory of God and Jesus standing at the right hand of God.	Jerusalem and Heaven
Acts 9:1–9; 22:3–16; 26:9–18	A very bright light from heaven, brighter than the sun, flashed all around Saul as he was on the road to Damascus, and then the Lord Jesus spoke to him.	Damascus Road
2 Corinthians 3:8–9	The ministry of the Spirit is marked by the glory of God	Wherever
2 Corinthians 3:18	Believers in Christ are being transformed into the image of Christ "from glory to glory."	Wherever
2 Corinthians 4:3–6	God *"has shone in our hearts to give the light of the knowledge of the glory of God in the face of Christ."*	Wherever
2 Corinthians 4:16-18	An eternal weight of glory is being worked in us as God renews the inward man day by day in the midst of the light affliction we face.	Wherever
Romans 8:18-21	We and the creation await the glory of the revealing of the sons of God	The creation
1 Thessalonians 4:17	Believers in Jesus will be caught up in clouds [of glory] to meet the Lord in the air.	Earth and Earth's Atmosphere
Hebrews 1:3	Jesus is the radiance, or the outshining, of the glory of God	Throughout heaven and earth
Hebrews 2:10	Jesus is bringing many sons to glory, to a life full of the Shekinah glory.	Heaven
Revelation 1:9–20	The apostle John saw the Lord Jesus in His resurrected glory and received the Revelation of things to come.	Island of Patmos
Revelation 15:5–8	John saw the Temple in Heaven filled with smoke from the glory of God. This was in addition to the many manifestations of the Lord throughout the Revelation.	Temple in Heaven
Revelation 21:1–27; 22:1–5	The Tabernacle of God (the New Jerusalem) appears, and the Lord and His people live eternally in the glorious presence of the Lord.	New Heaven and New Earth

Notes

Notes

Enter His Gates

Principles from the Fence, the Gate, and the Outer Court

How can sinful man approach God? Only in God's way! Throughout history God has chosen to provide a way for man to worship Him, and for nearly five hundred years the Tabernacle was that way. Through the Tabernacle, God expressed two important facts about worship. First, the Tabernacle represented the presence of God among His people, standing as it did in the center of their camp. Secondly, it pictured the divinely appointed means by which sinful man could approach God, who was otherwise unapproachable because of His holiness and majesty. But the Tabernacle is more than simply a part of our Christian history. It was an object lesson to prepare the way for Christ. Have you ever asked yourself, "Why did God bother with the law and priests and sacrifices if He knew they wouldn't work?" Was Christ simply the final work of God when all else failed? Was the Levitical system an experiment that didn't work? Absolutely not! God knew before the foundation of the world that Christ was the necessary provision for man's sin, for He is *"the lamb slain from the foundation of the world"* (Revelation 13:8 KJV). And yet the Tabernacle and the Levitical system and, later, the Temple all filled an important purpose in the plan of God. Understanding that purpose will move us a long way toward a right view of God and how He is to be worshiped.

"Enter His gates with thanksgiving, and His courts with praise."
Psalm 100:4

The Tabernacle with Fence and Outer Court

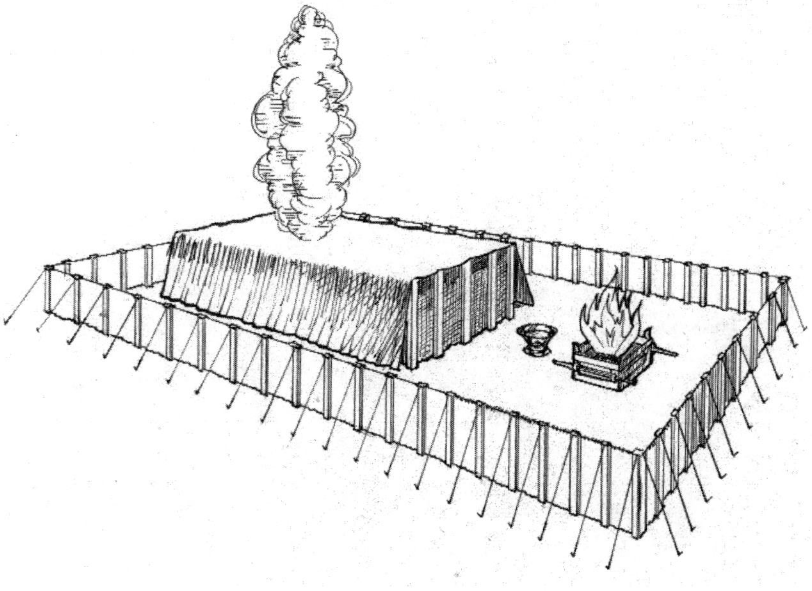

Lesson Three **DAY ONE**

According to Pattern

Hopefully by now you are no longer asking the question, "What does the Old Testament Tabernacle of more than three thousand years ago have to do with me?" What we have seen so far makes it clear that the Tabernacle is far more than simply part of our religious history. It is an object lesson to teach us how to relate with God. In studying the path the priest took as he moved toward the presence of God, we learn so much about how God desires to be approached. For the next three lessons we will study this pathway of the priest. This week we will look at the fence around the tabernacle, the gate of entrance, and the outer court. In the following weeks we will study the inner court and its contents as well as the "Holy of Holies" where the presence of God dwelt. It is worth noting that when God called Israel to build a "tent of meeting" so that He might teach them how to worship, the result was one of the most expensive houses of worship ever. Moreover, it was amazingly simple to dismantle and reassemble and was completely portable.

True Worship

A PATTERN FOR WORSHIP

The Scriptures clearly show that the Tabernacle was to be constructed according to a specific pattern. This same pattern was followed with each of the temples as well. Each of these places where man met with God was modeled after the true Tabernacle in heaven.

The Tabernacle
Built under Moses' leadership about 1430 B.C., replaced by Solomon's Temple 960 B.C.

Solomon's Temple
Built under Solomon's leadership about 960 B.C., repaired by Jehoshaphat (ca. 870 B.C.), renovated under Jehoash (ca. 780 B.C.), destroyed by the Chaldeans about 586 B.C.

Zerubbabel's Temple
Built under Zerubbabel's leadership about 516 B.C., plundered and defiled by Antiochus Ephiphanes (162 B.C.), taken by Pompey in 62 B.C.

Herod's Temple
Zerubbabel's Temple was renovated under the leadership of Herod the Great about 20 B.C., and destroyed by the Romans in A.D. 70.

The Lord's Tabernacle in Heaven
"From everlasting even unto everlasting" (Eternal [1 Chr. 16:36ff.]).

What did this place of worship look like? In answering this question, we must recognize one essential truth: its design was very specific.

Look at Exodus 25:8–9. What point does God make here?

Notice how many times the idea of "pattern" is repeated (see also Exodus 25:40). The key point is that God's design for the Tabernacle is very specific, for there is meaning in every aspect of it. God didn't leave it to man to design this house of worship. He Himself planned it in great detail. An implicit application from this detail is that there is a right way to worship God. Just as the Israelites could not build the Tabernacle according to their own whims and fancies, we cannot worship God in our own way, but God's way.

When God spoke through the author of Hebrews (8:1–5) to explain the meaning behind the Tabernacle, what was His explanation of the "pattern" idea of Exodus 25:8–9?

Verse 2 makes it clear that the "true tabernacle" is the one in heaven made by God, not man. Verse 5 clarifies even further that the plans God gave to Moses for the earthly Tabernacle (and later the Temple) were to create a copy of the true Tabernacle in heaven. The end of verse 5 clearly shows that this is the meaning of Exodus 25:40. Scripture is the best interpreter of Scripture, and here we see that the New Testament gives us needed commentary on how to understand what is stated in Exodus.

📖 Look up these other verses and identify what the Bible teaches us about the meaning and purpose of the Tabernacle.

Hebrews 9:23

____

____

Hebrews 9:24

____

____

Hebrews 10:1

____

____

In Hebrews 9:23 and again in 9:24, we see that the earthly Tabernacle is a copy of the heavenly one. In Hebrews 10:1 a different word is used, "shadow," implying how much greater the heavenly Tabernacle is than the one on earth. When you read the writings of Moses (Genesis, Exodus, Leviticus, Numbers, Deuteronomy), at first glance these historical records do not appear to have much to say to the New Testament believer. But clearly that is not the case. In fact, one could legitimately say that Christ is the central figure in each of these books.

📖 Write what you learn from the verses below about Christ being pictured in the Old Testament.

Luke 24:26–27

____

____

John 5:39

____

____

John 5:46

____

____

"You search the Scriptures, because you think that in them you have eternal life; and it is these that bear witness of Me"
—Jesus Christ
John 5:39

Luke, writing in his gospel in Luke 24:26–27, quotes the words of Jesus as He states that both Moses and the prophets wrote *"the things concerning Himself* [Jesus]." Likewise, in John 5:39 Jesus teaches that the Scriptures bear witness of Him. The Scriptures Jesus speaks of here are the Old Testament writings. In other words, He is the main figure of the Old Testament. Again, in John 5:46 Jesus says, "Moses wrote of Me." These verses make it abundantly clear that Christ is not only pictured in the Old Testament, but is also the prominent figure.

THE FENCE OF THE TABERNACLE

We have clearly seen that the Tabernacle is far more than an obscure relic from Israel's past. We have seen that even before the Tabernacle, God instructed His people about worship. And we have seen that the whole purpose of the Tabernacle is a continuance of that instruction. What we will see in the weeks ahead is that every item in the Tabernacle has something to say about Christ, about the Christian, and about worshiping God. It will take several weeks to look at every component in the place of worship, but it will be well worth the time. In order to approach our study systematically, we are going to start from the outside and move inward in the same manner that the priest would make his approach to God. Here in Lesson Three, we will focus on the fence, the gate, and the outer court with the bronze altar and bronze laver. Next, in Lesson Four, we will focus on the Holy Place with the golden lampstand, the table of showbread, and the altar of incense. In Lesson Five, we will move into the Holy of Holies through the veil and will look at the ark of the covenant with the golden jar of manna, Aaron's rod that budded, the tablets of the covenant, the mercy seat, and ultimately, the cloud of glory. Below is a diagram that should help you identify the layout of the tabernacle.

The Tabernacle

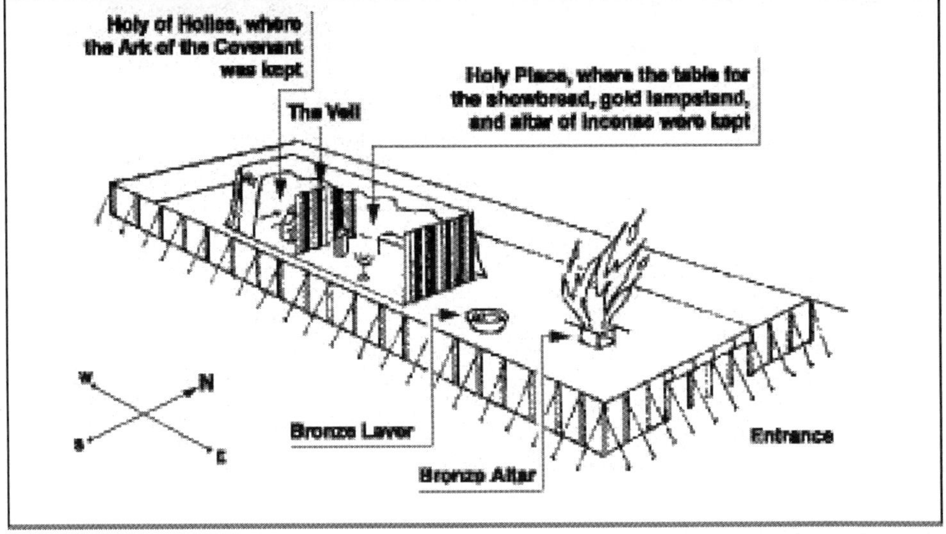

📖 Today we want to begin our look at the components of the Tabernacle by focusing on the fence. Read Exodus 27:9–19 and write down what you see about the fence.

This fence around the Tabernacle is called "the court of the tabernacle." It was rectangular and made of *"fine twisted linen."* It had only one entrance on the east side, and was about seven-and-a-half feet tall (five cubits), which means it was tall enough to prevent anyone from looking inside.

Before we look at the specifics about the fence, we need to ask the question, "Why a fence?" If God desires that all humanity worship Him, why would He close off the place to meet with Him?

📖 Look at Isaiah 59:2 and identify the truth you find there.

____

____

____

____

Isaiah 59:2 states that our sins have separated us from God. It would seem that the fence pictures the fact that man is separate from God, who is holy and pure. The fence of the Tabernacle served four purposes: **a)** it was a barrier that prevented unlawful approach; **b)** it was a protection, keeping out all wild beasts; **c)** it was a clear line of demarcation between the world and the holy presence of God; and **d)** with its single gate, it was a way of approach to God. It spoke of separation to those on the outside and security to those on the inside. It is possible to overdo the apparent symbolism of the Tabernacle by attaching a symbolic meaning to everything relating to God's ancient house of worship. However, we must recognize one distinct truth regarding the Tabernacle. We must recognize that, whether literal or symbolic, there is both meaning and mystery in every aspect of the Tabernacle. We will glean some of the meaning by looking at the rest of Scripture, but we will never understand all the majesty and mystery of God's design this side of heaven. As we seek to understand the fence, let's look at what it is made of. Exodus 27 teaches us that the fence is made of fine twisted linen.

📖 Look up the following verses and see if you can identify any significance to the material of the fence.

Revelation 3:3–4

____

____

____

Revelation 19:8

____

____

____

Revelation 19:11–14

____

____

____

Did You Know?

A CUBIT

In the days of antiquity and long before the advent of the ruler, yardstick, and tape measure, construction was usually done with two primary measurements: the span and the cubit, These were tools that a worker carried with him everywhere he went. The "span" was a measurement from the bend of his wrist to the tip of his middle finger (approximately 5–6 inches). The "cubit" was the distance from the elbow to the tip of his middle finger (about 18 inches).

What can we conclude from this about the spiritual meaning of the fine white linen?

____

____

____

Did You Know?

"FINE TWISTED LINEN"

Linen was derived from the flax plant. Twisted linen was a thicker cloth made by two, three, or more threads being twisted together. Through beating the flax plant with clubs, boiling the thread in water and then wringing it out carefully, a finer version was made that was both whiter in appearance and better suited for twisting and weaving. This time-consuming process meant that it was a very expensive and valued type of cloth.

There is a consistent message in Scripture that values and affirms garments of white. In Revelation 3:3–4, we see that white points to being "worthy." By implication, this color speaks of holiness, for Jesus intones that there were those in the church at Sardis whose worthiness stemmed from the fact that they had not *"soiled their garments."* In the Mediterranean culture with its dry, dusty roads, it was difficult to keep garments clean and white. In Revelation 19:8 we see fine linen in connection with *"the righteous acts of the saints."* Obviously, the color white is a picture of righteousness and holiness. Again in Revelation 19:11–14 we see fine linen (clarified as *"white and clean"*) as that which clothes the saints. It is worth noting that these are the saints after they are glorified. The fact that the fence is built of white linen speaks to the holiness and righteousness of God and to the requirement of holiness and righteousness on the part of those who would worship Him.

Lesson Three **DAY THREE**

THE GATE OF THE TABERNACLE

The word "Tabernacle" means to dwell. It speaks of God's desire to dwell with His people, yet a fence is erected around the dwelling place. We saw yesterday that the fence speaks of the holiness of God as separate from man's sinfulness. We saw that it speaks of the holiness and righteousness that God requires of those who would worship Him. Although the fence separates man from the worship of God (and this is significant), it is also important to see that there was a provided entrance to the Tabernacle that was invitingly wide. While guarding His holiness, God has always desired to make Himself accessible to man. Man cannot approach God in any way he wants, but he can approach God through the provided way.

Word Study

TABERNACLE

Mishkan ("tabernacle")— the word was a masculine noun derived from the Hebrew word "*Shakhan*," meaning "to reside permanently, to inhabit, abide, settle down, to dwell." It has the basic meaning of a residence. The Tabernacle was a physical and symbolic representation of God's presence among His people.

Exodus 27:16 begins giving us a description of the gate to the Tabernacle. Look at this verse and write what you see.

____

____

____

The verse tells us that it was to be 20 cubits wide. If a cubit is about eighteen inches, how wide would the gate be in feet?

____

____

We see in Exodus 27:16 that the gate was a beautiful object with blue, scarlet, and purple material on a backdrop of fine (white) linen. If the gate is twenty cubits and a cubit is eighteen inches, then the gate was about 30 feet wide.

The width of the gate speaks of a great spiritual truth found elsewhere in Scripture. Look up these verses and write what you see.

John 3:16

____

____

2 Peter 3:9

____

____

Revelation 22:17

____

____

In John 3:16, perhaps the most familiar verse in the New Testament (and rightly so), we see that the invitation to come to God is "whosoever will." Salvation is open to all, but only to those who come in the prescribed way. In 2 Peter 3:9 we see that God desires all to come to repentance. Revelation 22:17 speaks of the openness of the invitation to worship God. It would seem that the wide gate speaks of the open opportunity to all.

Not only is there meaning in the width of the gate, but in its very existence. Look up the following verses and see what Jesus taught about the gate.

John 10:9

____

____

____

John 14:6

____

____

In John 10:9, Jesus calls Himself "the door," the way of salvation. In John 14:6, Jesus teaches that He is "the way." As with John 10:9, the Greek definite article is used, indicating exclusivity ("the one and only"). There is no other way to God. Another picture of this is found in that there was only one door to the ark, God's means of deliverance for Noah. When we speak of the gate, we see that the way to God is wide, open to all, but that the only way to God is through Jesus. Just as there was only one entrance to the tabernacle, there is only one way to God.

The final aspect of the gate is its location. Remember that the Tabernacle was a portable building that was moved many times during its 470-year-history. Every time the Tabernacle was reassembled, the gate was to be placed to the east. This meant that the way to approach God was to enter at the east and go west. We don't know all of God's purposes for placing the gate where He did, but we see that, throughout Scripture, heading east is a picture of moving away from God, and going west is a picture of pursuing God. Again, God was very specific in His demands for the way He was to be worshiped.

Doctrine

JESUS AS "THE DOOR"

In John 10, Jesus called Himself the "Good Shepherd." In the shepherd culture of the Middle East, it was customary at night for sheep to be placed in a pen with the shepherd sleeping in the space of entrance. He functioned as a "door," allowing entrance and then keeping the sheep inside. In the parable of the Good Shepherd, Jesus identified Himself as the **only** entrance into the fold.

THE BRONZE ALTAR AND THE BRONZE LAVER

Did You Know?

GO WEST, YOUNG MAN!

With the gate to the Tabernacle being on the east side, to go east would be to move away from God and to go west would be to move toward Him. The entrance to the Garden of Eden was on the east side (Genesis 3:24). When Adam and Eve headed away from Eden and the presence of God, they apparently traveled east. When Cain separated from the people of God he settled to the east (Genesis 4:16). Ishmael settled east in relation to Isaac, the son of promise and father of Israel (Genesis 16:12). When Solomon's heart turned away from God, he went to the east to erect a place to worship other gods (1 Kings 11:7). In Isaiah 2:6, we see that the "influences from the east" were the antithesis of God. Virtually every time Scripture speaks of the east it is in a negative sense. The "east wind" was an ill wind of bad tidings. It would seem clear that "east" is a type of evil.

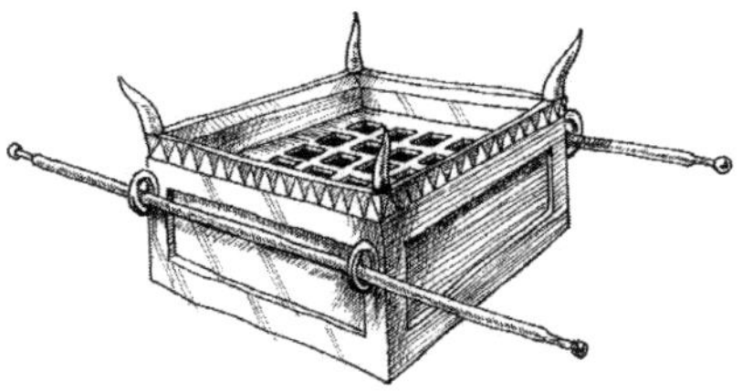

The Bronze Altar

The Bronze Altar

Once those who would worship God had entered into a relationship with Him by the divinely-appointed way, the gate, the first item they would encounter was the bronze altar. As with every area of the Tabernacle, God was very specific in His instructions for building the altar. In Exodus 27:8 God reminds Moses, *"as it was shown to you in the mountain, so they shall make it."*

Looking at the drawing below, read Exodus 27:1–8 and jot down the dimensions of the altar. You may also write down anything else that stands out to you in the passage

___

___

___

The bronze altar, called *"the altar of burnt offering"* in Leviticus 4:7, 10, 18, was the most frequently used piece of furniture in the Tabernacle. It was made from acacia wood and was square with horns and rings on each corner. It was then overlaid with bronze, accompanied with bronze utensils, and was carried by bronze-plated poles. The High Priest went into the Holy of Holies (the innermost room) once a year on the "Day of Atonement" to sprinkle blood on the mercy seat. The ministering priests went into the Holy Place (the outer room) twice a day (morning and evening), but the bronze altar was used all day long as people came to offer their sacrifices. In fact, the Hebrew word for altar (*mizbeach*) literally means "slaughter place." The bronze altar had a two-fold ministry: **expiation** and **consecration,** as seen in the types of offerings given there. Let's look at the ministry of the altar.

EXPIATION

Expiation means "to atone for, to make amends for." The ministry of expiation is expressed in two of the five offerings found in the first five chapters of Leviticus: the sin offering and the guilt offering. These blood-sacrificial offerings made atonement or reconciliation for those on whose behalf they were presented. This idea of a blood sacrifice probably seems gruesome and morbid to us today, partly because it is our fleshly nature to desire a religion that requires no sacrifice. However, sacrifice is essential to relating with God.

Look up the verses below and write what they say about the necessity of a sacrifice.

Leviticus 17:11

___

___

Hebrews 9:22

___

___

1 Corinthians 2:2

____

____

Leviticus 17:11 teaches us that it is the blood (the fountain or wellspring of life) which makes atonement. Hebrews 9:22 goes so far as to say that almost all things are cleansed with blood, and without shedding of blood there is no forgiveness. In 1 Corinthians 2:2 we see that the essence of Paul's message was the sacrificial death of Christ which makes atonement for our sins. It is worth noting that, without an understanding of the Old Testament sacrificial system, we can never adequately appreciate all that Christ's death means to us.

CONSECRATION

The second ministry of the altar was consecration or dedication. Hebrews 5:1 teaches that the ministry of the priest was to offer both gifts and sacrifices. The gifts are the dedicatory offerings. This included the meal or grain offerings, the peace offerings, and the burnt offerings. Similar to the expiation-based sin and trespass offerings, the burnt offering dealt with sin, but its main purpose was to indicate a life devoted or dedicated to God.

📖 Look up Romans 12:1–2 and write how this practice of consecration applies to us today.

____

____

____

____

As Christians, we are called to present ourselves as a living sacrifice. The altar pictures our "dying to self" with its desires and demands. In the Old Testament sacrificial system, as the fire would burn down, sometimes the sacrifice would shift away from the center of the altar. Just as the priest used the flesh hooks to keep moving the sacrifice back to the center of the altar, as Christians we are called to continually maintain and readjust our yieldedness to the Lord.

The Laver

The last component of the outer court we will observe is the **laver.** The word "laver" is a name for a large basin designed for ancient ceremonial washing. We are probably more familiar with its Modern English equivalent word, "lavatory." We know nothing of the size or shape of the laver, but we do know of its building material.

The Bronze Laver

📖 Read Exodus 30:17–21 and identify what materials were used to make the laver, along with anything else that stands out to you.

____

____

____

____

____

The laver was made of bronze and mounted on a base. Its purpose was for washing and for ceremonial cleansing. Positioned between the altar and the tent of meeting, the laver remained filled with water. It was necessary for the priests to cleanse themselves in this basin before meeting with God lest they die.

Where did the materials for it come from? (Exodus 38:8)

____

____

____

____

The laver was made from the "mirrors of the serving women." Highly polished copper mirrors were much used by the ancient Egyptians, and the women of Israel must have brought out with them great quantities of these looking glasses.

📖 The idea of a spiritual emphasis to water is implied in several places in the New Testament. Look up these passages and write what you see.

John 7:37–39

____

____

Ephesians 5:25–26

____

____

John 17:17

____

____

Psalm 119:9

____

____

"How can a young man keep his way pure? By keeping it according to Thy word."

Psalm 119:9

In John 7:37–39 we see the Holy Spirit referred to as water. Ephesians 5:25–26 adds another dimension as we see that the Word of God performs a washing function in our lives. In John 17:17 we also see this idea as we see that truth is the vehicle of our sanctification. Therefore, since sanctification is the ongoing process of our being cleansed from the stains of sin, the imagery of truth (the Word) is obviously suggested by the water of the laver. In Psalm 119:9 we are told that a young man can keep his way pure by keeping it according to the Word.

While the altar teaches us about the ministry of reconciliation, the laver speaks of the ministry of separation or sanctification. Through the priesthood's use of the laver, we see two aspects of this sanctifying ministry: the **initial** cleansing and the **continual** cleansing. When the priests were ordained into their office, they were bathed all over at the laver (Exodus 29:4). The only other time a priest was bathed all over was when the high priest cleansed himself on the Day of Atonement (Leviticus 16:4), which represented a new beginning each year for the whole nation.

📖 Look at these New Testament references to understand the significance of this:

Titus 3:5

____

____

____

John 13:10

____

____

____

Titus 3:5 teaches that we are saved by the *"washing of regeneration"* by the Holy Spirit. In John 13:10 we see that once a person has bathed (is saved), he or she only needs to maintain cleanliness. It would seem that Jesus has the initial bathing of the priests in view when He speaks of His disciples already being clean. Later in John 15:3, Jesus says that the disciples are clean *"because of the Word"* He had spoken to them.

📖 The continual cleansing of the priests is explained in Exodus 30:20–21. Read it and write what you see.

____

____

____

____

____

While we deal with forgiveness once for all at salvation, we must still keep short accounts with God about our sins as a Christian.

📖 Now, one final task. Look at John 13:3–10 and write how the basin applies to the New Testament believer (who is a priest [1 Peter 2:9]).

____

____

____

____

____

According to Exodus, priests bathed their whole bodies only once, but were to maintain cleanliness every time they approached God. When Jesus washed the disciples' feet, He had more in view than just being a servant. Clearly, He painted a picture of the normal Christian life. The Old Testament concept of cleansing and the New Testament account of Jesus washing the disciples' feet are excellent pictures of the fact that, while we deal with forgiveness once for all at salvation, we must still keep short accounts with God about our sins as a Christian.

FOR ME TO WORSHIP GOD

God has provided a way for man to draw near to Him. He desires our fellowship. Yet His holiness demands that man cannot approach Him in whatever way he desires. There was a fence to the Tabernacle, but there was also a gate. When we look at the physical components of this way of worship that functioned in Israel for nearly five hundred years, we must be able to see beyond to grasp the spiritual truth behind them. God has provided a gate for us to enter, and that gate is Christ. Once we enter through that gate, we can draw near on a regular basis. Every day, all day long, offerings and sacrifices were on the bronze altar. Throughout the day, the priests would maintain their cleanliness at the bronze laver, preparing themselves for the presence of God. We approach God in much the same fashion today. The priesthood and the Tabernacle are our tutors for worship.

As we look to application today for this week's lesson, we want to understand all that God says to us through these components we have studied. In Day One, we saw that there was a definite and prescribed pattern to God's design for the earthly Tabernacle. It was to be a model of the true Tabernacle in heaven. Every component holds a spiritual significance. In the same way that Moses could not build a tabernacle according to his own desires and hope that God could be worshiped there, we cannot erect our own approach to God and demand that He accept it.

Did You Know?

THE HOLINESS OF GOD

The holiness of God is guarded by a whole class of angels called *"seraphim,"* who are continually in His presence (for example, Isaiah 6:1–4).

THE FENCE

The fence speaks of guarding God's holiness. As you reflect on your own worship, and what you observe in others, what are some ways that we try to approach God without respect for His holiness?

____

____

____

____

____

What can we do to respect God's holiness more as we approach Him?

____

____

____

____

____

THE GATE

The Gate of the Tabernacle was the only way to enter. It was wide and inviting; nevertheless, it was the only entrance. In the same way, our entrance into relationship with God is always and only through Jesus Christ. Have you begun a relationship with God through faith in Christ?

If not, there are three main issues (the "ABC's," if you will) which you must address. You must . . .

Admit that you are a sinner (not just that you have sinned, but that you have a sinful nature). Only a sinner needs a savior. (Galatians 2:21 – *"I do not nullify the grace of God; for if righteousness comes through the Law, then Christ died needlessly."*)

Believe in your heart that Jesus died for your sins and rose again. His death paid the penalty, and His resurrection proved God's acceptance of that payment.

Confess Him with your mouth. You must make a choice, a decision of the will.

Romans 10:9–10 states, *". . . if you confess with your mouth Jesus as Lord, and believe in your heart that God raised Him from the dead, you shall be saved; for with the heart man believes, resulting in righteousness, and with the mouth he confesses, resulting in salvation."*

The Bronze Altar

The bronze altar had a two-fold ministry: **expiation** and **consecration,** as seen in the types of offerings given there. Each of those has application to us in our walk with the Lord.

Expiation speaks of atonement. The offerings of expiation were the sin offering and the guilt offering. Even those granted entrance into the Tabernacle had to make atonement for their sins against God and their trespasses against their fellow man.

APPLY As you look at your own heart, ask God to bring to mind any offenses against Him that are unresolved. Have you offended Him through disobedient acts (directly or indirectly)? If so, write down what comes to mind.

Consecration speaks of dedication. The offerings of consecration were the meal or grain offering, the peace offerings, and the burnt offerings. Though the burnt offerings dealt with sin as did the expiatory sin and guilt offerings, their main purpose was one of indicating a life devoted or dedicated to God.

As you evaluate your worship of God, in a tangible sense, the most important thing to place on the altar is ourselves. Have you dedicated yourself to the Lord?

The Bronze Laver

While the altar teaches us about the ministry of reconciliation, the laver speaks of the ministry of separation—or sanctification. Through the priesthood's use of the laver, we see two aspects of this sanctifying ministry: the **initial** cleansing and the **continual** cleansing.

True Worship

THE OUTER COURT

The outer court of the Tabernacle was a place of cleansing and atonement in preparation for meeting with God. One could not enter the Holy Place without coming by way of the gate, the bronze altar, and the bronze laver.

As you look at your own walk with God, you must invite Him to shine the searchlight of His Holy Spirit in your heart to reveal any "maintenance" cleansing that needs to take place. In Psalm 139:23–24, King David models how we should approach God—not with introspection, but with invitation for Him to show us anything that needs to be dealt with. It reads, *"Search me, O God, and know my heart; Try me and know my anxious thoughts; And see if there be any hurtful way in me, And lead me in the everlasting way."*

Why not make David's prayer your own? Use it to express your heart to God, and then listen to Him. Use the space below to write a prayer of response to Him.

Notes

Notes

lesson 4

The Holy Place

Principles from the Lampstand, the Table, and the Altar of Incense

In the previous lesson, we followed the path of the priest past the fence and through the gate, by way of the bronze altar to the bronze laver. We saw the beautiful pictures that the various Tabernacle components paint of our relationship with God. However, our journey into the Tabernacle is only beginning. As we walk the way of the priest, we must remind ourselves that we, too, are priests. First Peter 2:9 teaches us that we are *"a royal priesthood."* Each of us as New Testament believers can walk the way of the Old Testament priest. In fact, as we will see in more detail next week, through the blood of Jesus and the veil of His flesh, we are able to enter the Holy Place and the Holy of Holies with confidence. We can enter the very presence of God. That is what worship is all about. As we study the way to worship God, our tutor is the Tabernacle. This week we want to focus on the tent and the Holy Place with the golden lampstand, the table of showbread and the altar of incense. As we begin to enter this holy place, we must prepare our hearts just as the priest prepared himself. Remember, if it took the illumining work of the Spirit of God for men to write Scripture, then it will take His illumination for us to understand it. Yet we will not experience His illumining work unless our hearts are in right relationship with Him. Take some time to write a prayer of preparation, reflecting what you have learned so far about the way to worship God.

As Christians, we are "a royal priesthood . . . a people for God's own possession" (I Peter 2:9).

The Holy Place: The Tent of God

Lesson Four **DAY ONE**

THE TENT OF GOD

Today we move past the outer court and approach the "tabernacle proper." Although sometimes the term "tabernacle" refers to the tent and the outer court and fence, it is generally used only of the tent in the middle of the court. The word "tabernacle" literally means "to dwell." The promise of God is *"I will be your God, you will be My people, and I will dwell (tabernacle) in your midst."* This statement is repeated in various forms throughout the Old and New Testaments (see Exodus 6:7; Jeremiah 7:23; Zechariah 2:10, 11ff). The Old Testament Tabernacle was the beginning of God's renewing His intent to dwell with man that had been interrupted in the garden of Eden by Adam's sin. It gave way to the incarnation when *"the Word became flesh and dwelt* ["tabernacled"] *among us"* (First Advent of Christ [John 1:14]). The incarnation will give way to the Second Advent of Christ when *"the tabernacle of God is among men, and He shall dwell among them, and they shall be His people, and God Himself shall be among them"* (Revelation 21:3). The Lord, who dwelt among His people Israel with a pillar of fire and a cloud of glory, will one day come in all His glory to dwell among His saints forever. That is our hope. But we don't have to wait for the culmination of the ages to begin to experience dwelling with God, for He inhabits the praises of His people.

Today we want to look at the tent itself and all of its various building materials. The roof of the Tabernacle (detailed in Exodus 26:1–14 and 36:8–19) consisted of two inner curtains and two outer curtains, each very different from the other. Let's look at them.

THE INNER CURTAINS

The inner curtains covered the two parts of the place of meeting. This place of meeting was known technically as "the tabernacle" (Exodus 26:6) and "the tent" (Exodus 26:11).

THE LINEN CURTAIN

The linen covering was made from four colors of cloth: white, blue, purple, and scarlet. As you think through Scripture and biblical culture, what do these colors bring to mind?

White

Blue

Purple

Scarlet

Word Study

NAMES OF THE TABERNACLE

The Tabernacle was referred to in several different ways, each one giving added emphasis to its purpose…

"The Tabernacle of the Testimony"

- mentioned in Scripture eight times
- speaks literally of the tablets of testimony in the ark
- points figuratively to the Word of God

"The Tabernacle of the Tent of Meeting"

- mentioned five times in Scripture
- a place for man to meet with God and God with man

"The Tabernacle of the Lord"

- mentioned seventeen times in various forms
- called: "My Tabernacle," "The Lord's Tabernacle," and "His Tabernacle"

As we have seen before, the color white speaks of holiness and purity. This is suggested both by its appearance and by its usage in Scripture. We do see that most of the tabernacle furniture was to be covered in blue cloth. Scripturally, we can see no identifiable significance to the color blue. What its meaning is no one can say for certain. Some have suggested that blue, being the color of the sky, speaks of heaven. They base their suggestion on Psalm 19:1, which states that *"the heavens are telling of the glory of God."* Perhaps this verse is an indication as to why blue is so prevalent in the Tabernacle. Purple was a color associated with royalty in the culture of the day. It was rare and costly and would remind the people of the majesty of God. Scarlet speaks of blood, a reminder of the necessity of blood to cover sin. It should be noted that embroidered into the covering were cherubim, the angels associated with the presence of God.

The Goat's Hair Curtain

The covering made from goat's hair obviously speaks of the sacrificial offerings.

🕮 Look up the verses below and identify how goats were used in the offerings.

Leviticus 9:3

____

____

Matthew 25:32

____

____

"The Word became flesh and dwelt [tabernacled] among us. . . ."
John 1:14

In Leviticus 9:3 we see the goat used in connection with the sin offering. Goat's hair was a course but sturdy type of material, one that would last for some time. In Matthew 25:32 we see that God will separate the sheep from the goats. Sheep picture the saved, and goats picture the unregenerate. However, we may be reading too much into it to see a spiritual point in the goat hair curtain as it relates to other components in the Tabernacle.

The Outer Coverings:

The Ram's Skins—The ram's skins were to be dyed red, probably as a reminder of the blood which covers sin, pointing ultimately to the blood of Jesus which covers us.

🕮 Look up the passage below to see what the ram's skin suggests.

Leviticus 8:22, 29

____

____

Exodus 29:35, 44

____

____

In Leviticus 8:22 and 29 we see the ram referred to as *"the ram of consecration."* The same idea is put forward in Exodus 29:35 and 44, where we see the ram used in consecrating Aaron and his sons to the ministry of the priesthood. It is important to realize that a purpose existed for every component of the Tabernacle, and there is some type of message being spoken by each of these components.

The Porpoise Skins—The porpoise skins were the outermost covering and as such were extremely durable. It is noteworthy that there is no indication they ever had to be replaced in their 470 years of use. Although we cannot say for certain what their purpose served, the passages below are viewed by some as an explanation.

📖 Look at each of the passages listed below, and write your observations.

Isaiah 53:2–3

____

____

John 1:10–11

____

____

The prophet Isaiah teaches more on the subject of the Messiah than any other Old Testament book. In Isaiah 53:2–3 we observe that Christ was devoid of outer attractiveness. We see the same idea in John 1:10–11, where those who looked at the outside failed to recognize Christ, suggesting the need to look deeper for His truth and beauty.

The Door

The last thing we want to look at today is the door to the tent. With what we have seen so far, the meaning and purpose of the door should be fairly clear as you read the passage below.

📖 Look at Exodus 26:36–37, and write what you observe.

____

____

____

Here in Exodus 26:36–37 we see the same colors used as with the inner curtain: blue, purple, scarlet, and white. Again, the message for these colors is significant.

Lesson Four **DAY TWO**

THE GOLDEN LAMPSTAND

Inside the tent of meeting, the Holy Place held three significant pieces of furniture, each with a message about our relationship with God and worship of Him. Today we will begin our examination of the furniture of the Holy Place by looking at the golden lampstand. It was, in effect, seven oil lamps connected together.

Read Exodus 25:31–40 and write down what stands out to you.

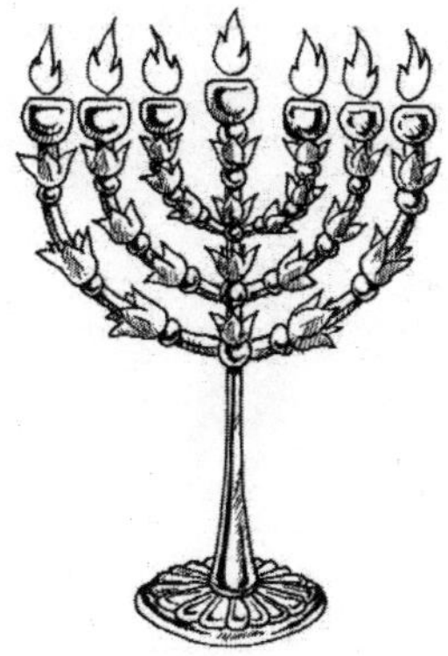

The Lampstand

The lampstand was made from one "talent" of pure gold (see sidebar explanation of "talent). Gold was the most precious metal of the day. Its smelting process speaks of purity. The lampstand had seven lamps—one central branch and three branches on each side. The golden lampstand was to be made according to the pattern shown to Moses (of the heavenly Tabernacle).

The golden lampstand would be the first item to catch the eye of the worshiper as he entered into the Holy Place. It provided the only light inside the tent, and with its ornate metalwork of almond blossoms, pomegranates, and lilies, it was by far the most beautiful object in the room. It was a continual reminder that where God dwells, there is light. We must go to the New Testament to understand fully the spiritual significance of the lampstand.

📖 Look up the verses below and write what you see.

John 8:12

John 9:5

Ephesians 5:8

Philippians 2:15

John 8:12 tells us that Jesus is the *"light of the world."* This verse intonates that Jesus' light gives direction and draws men to the Father and eternal life.

Did You Know?

WHAT IS A "TALENT"?

Exodus 25:31 says that the lampstand was to be made of *"a talent of pure gold."* A "talent" was an Old Testament unit of weight measurement equivalent to approximately 125 pounds. The market value today of this much gold would be well over half-a-million dollars.

Did You Know?

THE GOLDEN LAMPSTAND

Some translations of the Bible refer to the golden lampstand as the "golden candlestick," but such an identification is somewhat inaccurate, for candles were not invented until Roman times. The lampstand, consisted of seven oil lamps connected together on one stand.

In John 9:5, we see again that Jesus is the "light of the world," drawing men to the Father. Paul teaches us in Ephesians 5:8 that not only does this light speak of "goodness, righteousness and truth," but it also teaches that we, the body of Christ, are light. He continues in Philippians 2:15 to teach us that we are lights in the world, pointing the way to the Father.

Read Leviticus 24:1–4 and respond to the questions below.

What duty of the priests is mentioned in this Scripture?

____

____

What application does this hold for us as we seek to worship God?

____

____

Leviticus 24:1–4 teaches that it was the duty of the priests to keep the wicks trimmed and maintained so that the light of the lamps would never dim. The obvious application here is to the need for each of us to attend to our light that we might always be a witness.

Lesson Four **DAY THREE**

THE TABLE OF SHOWBREAD

Today we continue our look at the furniture by focusing on the table of showbread. You may want to refer to the diagram from the beginning of the lesson to remind yourself of where the table was in relation to the furniture of the holy place. It is also called "The Table of the Bread of the Presence" and speaks of God as the sustenance and satisfaction of His people.

Read Exodus 25:23–30 and write down what stands out to you.

____

____

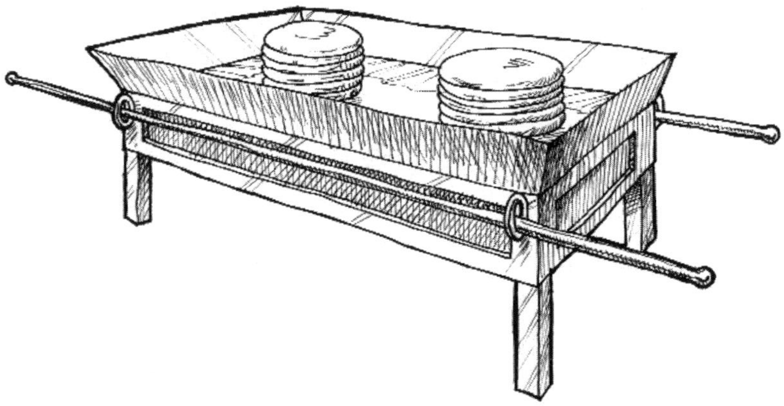

The Table of Showbread

The table of showbread was made of wood overlaid with gold. It was made in the shape of a rectangle and had four rings so that the poles could be inserted for carrying it. The table had accompanying utensils of gold, and it was to be continually set with bread.

What is suggested by a table set with food in the context of worship?

Food speaks of fellowship both in the culture of Israel and today. The table reminds us that God is continually waiting for fellowship with us. In Revelation 3:20, Jesus taught that when we open the "door" of our hearts and invite Him in, He will "dine" with us.

Specific instructions were given in Leviticus 24:5–9 that the bread of the table was to be made from fine flour, and twelve cakes were to be baked (presumably to represent the twelve tribes of Israel). This bread was placed regularly before the Lord, but the priests actually consumed it, a picture of God's provision.

Look at the New Testament passages on what Jesus taught about bread and write down anything you observe to be especially noteworthy.

John 6:35

Matthew 4:4

Word Study

BREAD OF LIFE

It is noteworthy that Jesus, the "Bread of Life," was born in the city of Bethlehem (which literally means "House of Bread") and was lain in a manger (a feeding trough).

In John 6:35 Jesus identified Himself as the "Bread of Life." This truth speaks of Jesus, who is our life. Matthew 4:4 states that not only is Jesus our bread, but His Word is to be our daily sustenance and satisfaction. This speaks of the truth that fellowship with God and one another should center on His Word, or it is not true fellowship.

It is important to remember that this sweet fellowship with God is only possible to those who have first experienced forgiveness and consecration at the altar, being cleansed at the symbolical laver. There is no other way to enter the presence of God and enjoy Him. Once we have entered the Holy Place in the proper way, we can partake of this Bread of Life. Remember that bread (food) is satisfying, but it is also sustaining. Physically, when it comes to living healthy lives, food consumption is not an option. Likewise, we spiritually stand in daily need of the Bread of God, lest we die in our ability to worship.

THE ALTAR OF INCENSE

Once we have been illumined by the light of the world which draws us to God, and as we walk in fellowship with Him through the Bread of His Word and presence, we are ready to approach the altar of incense.

📖 Read Exodus 30:1–10 and write down what you learn regarding both the construction and operation of the altar of incense.

____

____

____

The Altar of Incense

The altar of incense was to be fashioned in a square. It was made of wood overlaid with gold, with rings and poles to make it portable. The incense altar sat in front of the veil into the holy of holies. The altar was to be used twice daily.

The altar, sitting as it did just outside the Holy of Holies, was as close as one could get to God without literally being in His presence. We don't want to float our own ideas on the significance and purpose of this altar and its incense, so let's go to the teaching of Scripture for enlightenment.

📖 Look up the verses below and write what you learn about the burning of incense.

Psalm 141:1–2

____

____

____

Luke 1:10

____

____

____

It is difficult to have a low assessment of prayer when we understand the significant role prayers play in heaven.

Revelation 5:8

____

____

____

Revelation 8:3–4

____

____

____

In Psalm 141:1–2 we see that incense, rising as it does with smoke, is a picture of the prayers of the saints rising to heaven. Luke 1:10 teaches us that it was the custom for believers to gather outside the tabernacle for prayer at the time of the incense offering, indicating a link between the two. In Revelation 5:8 we see the prayers of the saints being symbolized by incense brought before the Lamb in heaven. Again, in Revelation 8:3–4 we see that the incense on the golden altar in heaven actually is the prayers of the saints. It is difficult to have a low assessment of prayer when we understand the significant role prayers play in heaven.

So we see that the incense on the altar is a picture of prayer. What a beautiful picture it is, too. It bears noting, however, that not all prayer qualifies as fragrant incense to the Lord. The instructions were very specific on the procedure for burning incense. Leviticus 16:12 indicates that the fire for the incense is to come from the bronze altar in the outer court. The picture this paints is that before one can pray in a way acceptable to God, he must first go by way of the outer court altar where a sacrifice for sin was offered. We have seen over and over again that to approach God, we must deal with sin.

Read Psalm 66:18 and record your observations.

____

____

____

____

____

____

The clear point is that the Lord does not hear prayer offered from an unclean heart, a heart filled with unconfessed sin. The prayer of the upright is His delight, but He takes no delight in listening to the pious words of those who will not order their heart aright (see Psalms 50:23; Proverbs 15:8).

"If I regard wickedness in my heart, The Lord will not hear. . . ."
Psalms 66:18

📖 Look at Leviticus 10:1–3 and write your observations.

____

____

____

____

____

____

Nadab and Abihu, the sons of Aaron, offered "strange fire" before the Lord, and they were consequently struck dead by the Lord. Scripture doesn't tell us exactly what they did wrong, but the implication is that they failed to follow the instructions laid out for the offerings. The application to us is significant, for we cannot pray as we should without a clean heart.

FOR ME TO WORSHIP GOD

Think of all we have studied so far! As we have walked the way of the priest, we have seen the holy presence of God guarded by the fence of fine linen. Yet this fence doesn't keep us from God if we are willing to enter through His provided way—the wide gate which is Christ. As we move through the gate, we approach God by way of the brazen altar. Even though our sin nature has been dealt with through Christ, we must still deal with the sins that stain our fellowship. We do this through the brazen altar and bronze laver. With our heart prepared, we enter into the holy place. We are illumined by the lampstand, satisfied with fellowship at the table, and send our prayers heavenward at the altar of incense. What truths we see in this place of worship! Hopefully, as we have studied, you have begun to view the Tabernacle as much more than an ancient relic. It is rife with applications for our walk and worship.

APPLY It is impossible to walk soundly in a dark world without light. The golden lampstand speaks of our walking in the light. Consider the different light-shedding tools listed below, and identify all the ones you are currently using to draw the light of God's Word into your life.

___ Sunday School	___ church sermons	___ Christian radio
___ small-group Bible study	___ quiet time with God	___ television
	___ message tapes	___ Christian books

___ Other ____

Is there anything you need to be doing differently to make sure you are walking in the light of God's Word? If so, write it down.

____

____

____

As Christians, we have a relationship with Christ, but that does not necessarily mean we are enjoying fellowship with Him and with the family of God.

The table of showbread speaks of enjoyed fellowship with God and His people. It is important to recognize the difference between a relationship with God and fellowship with Him. Think of a human relationship. A son can dishonor his parents and through rebellion and sin be kicked out of the home. He can break all communication and fellowship with his family, but nothing can ever change the biological fact of his parentage. He will always be their son. It is a permanent relationship. In our walk with God, if we are Christians, we have a relationship with God, but that does not mean we are enjoying fellowship with Him and with the family of God.

📖 Read Hebrews 10:24–25, and write what you notice concerning the mandate for fellowship and the reasons for this mandate.

____

____

____

____

____

In Hebrews 10:25 we are admonished to "not forsake" assembling together with fellow believers. Apparently, some Christians thought that they could walk with God as "lone rangers," but clearly, we need to come together. In fact, the closer we get to the Lord's return, the more we need to fellowship with His people. In verse 24 we see that it is in the fellowship of other believers that we will be stimulated toward love and good deeds.

APPLY How often on average do you fellowship with other believers in church each month?

How often do you fellowship with other believers outside of church each month?

Is there anything you need to do differently because of what you have seen in this study?

The altar of incense is a reminder of the role prayer plays in the Christian life. If our hearts are clean, then every time you or I lift our voices heavenward to speak to the Lord, our prayers are a fragrant aroma rising to the Father. Yet for many Christians this is a neglected privilege. Look at the questions that follow to evaluate your own prayer life.

APPLY How would you identify the regularity of your praying?

❒ throughout the day ❒ daily ❒ weekly ❒ not often

How would you rate the quality of your praying?

❒ intimate and personal ❒ dry and impersonal ❒ mere ritual

How can you improve your praying?

As we close this week's lesson, why not get some practice in your praying by writing a prayer dealing with each of the components we have studied.

Notes

Notes

lesson 5

Enter His Presence

Principles from the Veil, the Ark, and the Mercy Seat

We have followed the path of the priest past the fence and through the gate, past the altar of burnt offerings to the bronze laver. We have seen the beautiful pictures these paint of our relationship with God. But these areas are merely the entrance of our journey into the Tabernacle. Last week, as we continued following the path of the priest, we entered into the Holy Place. We saw the golden lampstand, the table of showbread, and the altar of incense. We learned that we too are priests (1 Peter 2:9) and as such, we must prepare our hearts just as the priest prepared himself. But we still have only "scratched the surface" on what it means to worship God. As we will see in more detail this week, through the blood of Jesus and the veil of His flesh, we are able to enter the Holy Place and the Holy of Holies with confidence. We can enter the very presence of God, where true worship takes place. As we study the way to worship God, our tutor is the Tabernacle. This week we want to focus on the Holy of Holies with the veil, the ark of the covenant, and the mercy seat. As we begin to enter this holy place, we must prepare our hearts just as the priest prepared himself. Remember, if it took the illuminating work of the Spirit of God for men to write Scripture, then it will take His illumination for us to understand it. We will not experience His illuminating work unless our hearts are in right relationship with Him.

A ROYAL PRIESTHOOD

"But you are a chosen race, a royal priesthood, a holy nation, a people for God's own possession, that you may proclaim the excellencies of Him who has called you out of darkness into His marvelous light." (1 Peter 2:9)

The Holy Place and the Holy of Holies

THE VEIL

Today we want to begin our study by focusing on the veil at the entrance of the Holy of Holies. The veil was the heavy curtain that closed off this most holy place. The historian Josephus wrote that it was as thick as a hand's breadth (four inches), and that a team of horses pulling in each direction could not tear it.

📖 Read Exodus 26:31–33 and 36:35–37 several times. Write down your observations on the veil.

____

____

____

____

The veil was four-colored: blue, purple, scarlet and white (fine-twisted linen). It was embroidered with cherubim, and it was erected on four gold-plated pillars. The purpose for the veil was to serve as a partition between the Holy Place and the Holy of Holies, where the ark of the covenant was kept. The veil was the work of a weaver (literally a "variegator," a weaver in colors).

What is the significance of the colors of the veil?

____

____

____

Did You Know?

COLORS AND CULTURE

When we reflect on the colors found in the Tabernacle, we must remind ourselves of the role color played (or did not play) in everyday-life in Palestine. Most all clothing was in natural hues of brown and beige. Color was reserved for the wealthy and important. Houses were in the same earth tones, as they were made from clay bricks and wood. To the agricultural and transient society of Moses' day, the Tabernacle must have been quite a sight to see.

As we have already seen, the color blue to some is symbolic of heaven, though the scriptural support for this is lacking. Purple was the color of royalty in that culture. Scarlet was the color of blood. Scarlet dye was made from the crushed bodies of a particular type of worm larvae. The color scarlet is symbolic of death and sacrifice. The color white, of course, speaks of holiness and purity.

We are told that cherubim were embroidered into the veil by skilled workmen. Scripturally, other than their association with the tabernacle and later the temple, cherubim appear in three places. First, Genesis 3:24 tells us that cherubim guard the entrance to the Garden of Eden. In 2 Kings 19:15 (along with many other Scripture passages), we see that God is enthroned *"above the cherubim."* In Ezekiel 10 we see Ezekiel's account of the glory of the Lord departing from the temple, being ushered by cherubim. Reflect on these references, and write your thoughts about the significance of cherubim.

____

____

____

____

Obviously, Eden speaks of the presence of God. Genesis 3:24 states specifically that the cherubim guard *"the way to the tree of life."* The phrase that says God is *"enthroned above the cherubim"* implies that the cherubim are attendants in His presence. This idea is underscored by the cherubim ushering His presence out of the temple. Therefore, it would seem that cherubim speak of the presence of God and the life that is associated with it.

The veil is spoken of in the New Testament in two primary methods. First, in three of the Gospels we read that at the crucifixion, at the moment Jesus breathed His last breath, the veil was torn in two from top to bottom (Matthew 27:51, Mark 15:38, Luke 23:45). Reflect on this truth and write your observations.

Obviously, the veil was a sturdy object to have lasted so many years. The veil of Christ's time was not the original veil from the Tabernacle, but a new one built for the Temple according to the same specifications. Josephus says that a team of horses pulling in each direction was not strong enough to pull it apart. Yet here we see it torn in two. Each Gospel account mentions the fact that the veil was torn *"from top to bottom,"* indicating a work of God—not a work of man. Imagine the impact this would have had on the priests. The event pictures the presence of God opened to all by the blood of Jesus.

The second way the veil is mentioned in the New Testament is in Hebrews 10:19–20. Read it and write your observations.

New Testament believers can enter the very presence of God ("through the veil") by the blood of Jesus. The veil is called "His flesh." What a contrast to the Old Testament, where only the high priest could enter, and this only once a year at the Day of Atonement.

One final note on the veil. Numbers 4:5 tells us that when the Tabernacle was moved, the veil was used to cover the ark of the covenant.

True Worship

THE VEIL OF HIS FLESH

The veil, we are told, is a picture of Jesus' body sacrificed for us. When the veil was torn in two, it painted a visual reminder of the idea of covenant. When establishing a covenant, a sacrifice was cut in half and the two halves separated. The pathway between the two parts was called "the way of death." When we walk this path, we are dying to our old way of living. When the veil of His flesh was separated, we were invited to pass through this "way of death" into the very presence of God.

The Ark of the Covenant

Lesson Five **DAY TWO**

Today, we want to move through the veil into the Holy of Holies and begin our study of the ark of the covenant. We can wax eloquent on the subject of the Tabernacle and still not do justice to the topic. Although we have taken the path of the priest and begun our study from the outside and moved inward, it is important to note that when God gave the instructions for building the Tabernacle, He started with the centerpiece, the ark of the covenant. Man builds a house, and then he thinks of the furniture. Not so with God. The Bible makes mention of the ark 180 times, thereby emphasizing its significance. It is called *"the ark of the testimony"* (Exodus 26:33); *"the ark of the covenant of the Lord of all the earth"* (Joshua 3:11); *"the holy ark"* (2 Chronicles 35:3); and *"the ark of Thy might"* (2 Chronicles 6:41). The ark of the covenant is none other than the throne of God.

📖 Read through Exodus 25:10–22 and write down what you see there about the ark and its components.

____

____

____

The ark of the covenant is none other than the throne of God.

The Ark of the Covenant with Mercy Seat

The ark (or chest) was a rectangular box of gold-plated wood. It had rings and poles to make it portable (it is the only piece where the poles were always left in). It was covered by the "mercy seat" and two cherubim made of pure gold. Inside would be placed "the testimony" as yet ungiven.

Although we think of the ark as one item, Scripture deals with it by its components: the ark itself, the mercy seat, and the items inside. Today we are going to focus on the ark itself. It was the holiest of all the furniture.

📖 Read 2 Samuel 6:1–19. What does this story reveal about the ark?

____

____

____

____

Primarily this story points to the holiness of the ark and the necessity of doing things God's way. The ark was not to be carried on a cart, nor was it to be carried by just anyone. It was to be carried by the priests. Uzzah thought lightly of the ark and did not treat it as holy and pure. Therefore, the Lord instantly struck Him dead. God does not do such things because He is vengeful, but incidents like this one and the deaths of Nadab and Abihu (Leviticus 10) are manifestations of the perfection of God's holiness and purity.

One final story will suffice in our study for today. Read 1 Samuel 4:1—7:1. Yes, it is a lot of reading, but it will be a blessing to you. After you have read, take a few minutes to reflect on the narrative and write down what comes to mind. Don't worry so much about the details; just make sure you get the overall picture.

This story clearly illustrates that God will not be manipulated. It also demonstrates the power of the presence of God associated with the ark. Even the pagans recognized the hand of God with the ark.

THE CONTENTS OF THE ARK

Lesson Five **DAY THREE**

As we saw in Day Two, the ark was essentially a large chest. We read in Exodus 25:21 that God intended something be placed in the ark (*"the testimony which I will give you"*). But that was not to be the end of it. Eventually, there would be four items in the chest. Today we want to identify those items and their significance. The first item placed in the ark was this "testimony" God discussed with Moses.

Read Deuteronomy 31:24–30; 32:44–47. Identify what this "testimony" was and why it was placed in the ark.

This "testimony" Exodus mentions is the long version of the Law. Some theologians believe that it is certain sections of Exodus such as we have in our Old Testament today. It included such laws as those related to murder, property, divorce, slaves, injuries, etc. The reason it was placed in the ark was twofold: as a reminder that these words were their life (32:47), and as a witness against them when they were disobedient to the words (31:26). We see in this a reflection of the two-fold purpose of cherubim: to guard the way to life and to guard the holiness of God.

Not only was this "testimony" (known as the civil law) placed in the ark, but three other items were placed in the ark as well. Read Hebrews 9:4 and list the items in the ark revealed there.

Doctrine

THE LOST ARK

In the 1980's a popular movie entitled "Raiders of the Lost Ark" put forth the fictional idea of Hitler trying to discover the missing ark to seek its powers in his war for global control. In the movie's end, the ark was shown to be too powerful to be controlled or used for selfish purposes. As we see from 1 Samuel 4:1—7:1, the Philistines in fact played out the movie's premise. They discovered that the God of Israel was not a magic genie with this ark as His bottle. They could not conjure Him up and make Him do their bidding.

Inside the ark was *"a golden jar holding the manna"* (a reminder of God's faithful provision in the wilderness), Aaron's rod which budded (a reminder of God's affirmation of the priesthood) and "the tables of the covenant" (a reminder of Israel's accountability to God's laws as part of its covenant with God).

Let's look at these items in order. First, we want to examine the golden jar of manna. Read Exodus 16:1–35, and write what you learn about manna.

____

____

____

____

____

____

Manna was the food God provided for Israel day by day in the wilderness. It was like "coriander seed" (a white seed about half the size of a pea) and was sweet to the taste. It had to be gathered and completely consumed each day (for unused portions spoiled [vv. 19–20]), except on the day before the Sabbath, when two days portion was gathered (vv. 22–24). Moses told Aaron to save a jar of it *"to be kept before the Lord."* The name "manna" means "what is it?" in Hebrew (v. 15). From this passage we can learn three important truths about manna: **1)** it was **sufficient** (*"he who had gathered little had no lack; every man gathered as much as he should eat"* [v. 18]); **2)** it was **satisfying** (*"its taste was like wafers with honey"* [v. 31]); and **3)** it was **sustaining** (*"the sons of Israel ate the manna forty years, until they came to an inhabited land. . ."* [v. 35]).

Jesus taught of this manna in John 6:31–35. Read this passage and write your observations.

____

____

____

____

____

____

The manna of the wilderness is a picture of Christ, the "Bread of Life." No wonder God wanted it saved in the ark of the covenant as a reminder that Christ is our lifegiver.

Jesus makes it clear that manna "gives life," and more importantly, that manna was a picture of Him, the "bread of life." No wonder God wanted it saved in the ark as a reminder that He is our life. Like manna, He is **sufficient, satisfying,** and **sustaining.**

The next item in the ark was Aaron's rod that budded. The story of the rod is found in Numbers 16 and 17 if you want to read it. There had been a rebellion against the leadership of Moses and Aaron, and the rod was God's way of proving His selection of them. A rod was taken from each of the twelve tribes (including one from Aaron representing the Levites) and laid before the Lord in the Tabernacle.

Read Numbers 17:1–10. Note what happened in this passage, and why this rod was placed in the ark.

____

____

____

____

By sprouting buds, blossoms, and almonds from the dead stick of Aaron, not only did God affirm His calling and choosing of Aaron, but He also spoke a valuable truth about Himself. He is the God who is able to bring life out of death. Aaron's rod stands as a continual reminder to Israel of God's delegated authority through the Levites, but it also speaks of the resurrection of Christ on which our future resurrection and our whole faith depends (1 Corinthians 15:12–19).

The last item in the ark is "the tables of the covenant." This of course is the Ten Commandments written on two tablets of stone. While the writings of Moses spoke of the civil law, the Ten Commandments were the moral law.

Read Matthew 5:17 and Galatians 3:24 and write what these verses teach us about the Christian and the Law.

____

____

____

____

Matthew 5:17 clearly states that Christ is the fulfillment of the law. In Galatians we learn that the purpose of the law serves as a tutor to lead us to Christ. It is significant that the Ten Commandments (which neither you nor I could ever keep) are kept beneath the mercy seat—a picture of the only one who kept the whole law.

Did You Know?

TWO TABLETS OF STONE

The two tablets of stone placed in the ark were written by the finger of God. These were not the original Ten Commandments, but a second copy. When Moses came down from Mt. Sinai with the first copy of the commands, he found the Israelites worshiping in a pagan frenzy before a golden calf they had made. Moses threw the stone tablets to the ground, fracturing them into pieces (Exodus 31:18, 32:15–20). His act pictured vividly the fact that already God's people had broken His commands. Moses had to return to the mountain to receive a second copy (Exodus 34:1–4, 27–29).

The Mercy Seat

Lesson Five **DAY FOUR**

What a tremendous study we have experienced so far as we look into the Holy of Holies! We have seen the beauty of the veil, which is Christ. We have seen the power of the ark, the throne of God. We have seen the precious reminders of the law, the manna, and the rod. Yet we still haven't covered the most exciting aspects of the Tabernacle! The most blessing-filled piece in the Tabernacle is the mercy seat. The Hebrew word *kapporeth,* translated "mercy seat," literally means "a place of covering." The word speaks of propitiation or provision being made for our sin. The mercy seat was a slab of pure gold, which served as a lid to the ark. The lid to the ark held the seat as well as two cherubim hammered from gold that covered the seat with their wings. Their faces were bent downward gazing at the mercy seat.

📖 Read 1 John 2:1–2, and identify what the mercy seat points to.

The Ark of the Covenant with Mercy Seat

Our "advocate" with the Father is Jesus Christ the righteous. Our standing with God is not based on our righteousness, but on His, for *"He Himself is the propitiation for our sins."* It is at the mercy seat we find mercy, for the sprinkled blood of sacrifice becomes our Passover, and judgment passes us by. Once a year the high priest would enter the Holy of Holies on the Day of Atonement. He would sprinkle the blood of the sacrifice as a covering for the sins of Israel. What the high priest had to do once a year, Jesus did once for all. The epistle to the Hebrews teaches us that when Christ's blood was sprinkled on the mercy seat in heaven, the work of atonement was finished. What would have been a throne of judgment to us now has become a throne of grace, for Jesus, our High Priest, has *"cleansed our conscience from dead works to serve the living God"* (Hebrews 9:14).

"Since therefore, brethren, we have confidence to enter the holy place by the blood of Jesus, by a new and living way . . . through the veil, that is, His flesh . . . let us draw near with a sincere heart in full assurance of faith. . . ."
Hebrews 10:19–22

As we saw in Exodus 25, the cherubim on the ark are perpetually gazing at the mercy seat. This points to a tremendous truth revealed in the New Testament.

📖 Read 1 Peter 1:3–12 and write your observations on the meaning of the "gazing angels."

After expounding on the wonders of our salvation and redemption, Peter reminds us that the wondrous works of Christ are *"things into which angels long to look."* I'm sure if we could look closely at the faces of those cherubim on the ark, we would see expressions of amazement. They, who understand so much more than we do about God's righteousness and holiness, must look in awe at the mercy seat. It is as if God caught a glimpse of the awe on the faces of angels as Christ sprinkled His own blood on the mercy seat in heaven, and then captured that expression on the golden images of the earthly ark.

FOR ME TO WORSHIP GOD

You have followed the path of the priest. You have gone from outside the gate, past the brazen altar and the laver, into the Holy Place with the lampstand and table of showbread. You have passed the altar of incense and have gone through the veil into the very presence of God. You have gazed at His throne and experienced the wonder of the angels at His mercy. You have worshipped. As we finish this week's study, lets take some time to reflect on all the wonderful truths we have learned.

In Day One, we observed that the veil speaks of God's holiness, His separation. As you see His purity, has He quickened your heart about dealing with sin? As you seek Him, is He reminding you of anything that needs to be dealt with? You don't need to be introspective. One of the ministries of the Holy Spirit is to convict us of sin.

APPLY Why don't you take a moment to invite Him to search your heart and reveal any sin that has not been taken to the altar. Write down what comes to mind.

____

____

____

____

____

____

____

Take a minute to look at your notes for Day Two. In your worship of God, have you seen His power at work—or is your faith mere religious ritual? Has God convicted you concerning the fact that He is holy and pure and must be treated as such? Have you come to the realization that God will not be manipulated? Don't feel like you have to have that all figured out yet, for the entire course will teach you of the proper way to worship, but if anything has already come to mind, then write it down.

____

____

____

____

____

____

____

"Remember His wonderful deeds which He has done, His marvels and the judgments from His mouth."
I Chronicles 16:12

In Day Three, we studied the contents of the ark of the covenant. God had them place inside the ark remembrances of milestones from their relationship with Him. Repeatedly, we see modeled in the Scriptures a reminder of God's past faithfulness.

Is there something God is calling you to remember about your relationship with Him? Look to your own spiritual past and try to come up with as many milestones as you can that remind you of God's faithfulness to you in the past. Write down some things of which He reminds you.

"For the Mighty One has done great things for me; and holy is His name. And His mercy is upon generation after generation toward those who fear Him."
Luke 1:49–50

In Day Four, we studied the "mercy seat." Have you come to the place in your walk with Christ where you recognize your need for mercy?

Take some time to express to the Lord in writing a prayer of gratitude as you reflect on His mercy.

Do you realize that you have just now worshiped the Lord? Worship is far more than attending a church service or having an emotional experience. We are almost half-way through our study of the Tabernacle. We hope that you are already seeing the fruit of this study in your own walk with God. Stay with us, for it only gets richer from here!

Notes

Notes

Ministers to the Lord

Principles from the Priesthood

So far we have studied the Tabernacle from the standpoint of why it was needed; we have studied its construction, its furniture and coverings, and we have looked at the many pictures of the Lord Jesus in this beautiful building. However, we cannot fully appreciate each of these components without studying the priesthood that ministered there. It is significant to realize that out of all Israel, one entire tribe was set apart to the service of God. Setting one tribe apart from the others was God's idea and God's desire. Even though God desires every member of His family to walk with Him, worship Him, and serve Him, He wants some to devote their full-time labor to Him. Tabernacle work was full-time work. The tribe of Levi was set apart for the work of the priesthood. Members of this tribe were completely supported by the other eleven tribes. Though eleven out of twelve family groups were involved in secular labor, one was to be supported by the other eleven in the service of God. As we study the priesthood this week, keep in mind all that it says about the importance of "laborers in the harvest" (Matthew 9:36–38).

A Royal Priesthood

"But you are a chosen race, a royal priesthood, a holy nation, a people for God's own possession, that you may proclaim the excellencies of Him who has called you out of darkness into His marvelous light." (1 Peter 2:9)

The High Priest and His Priestly Garments

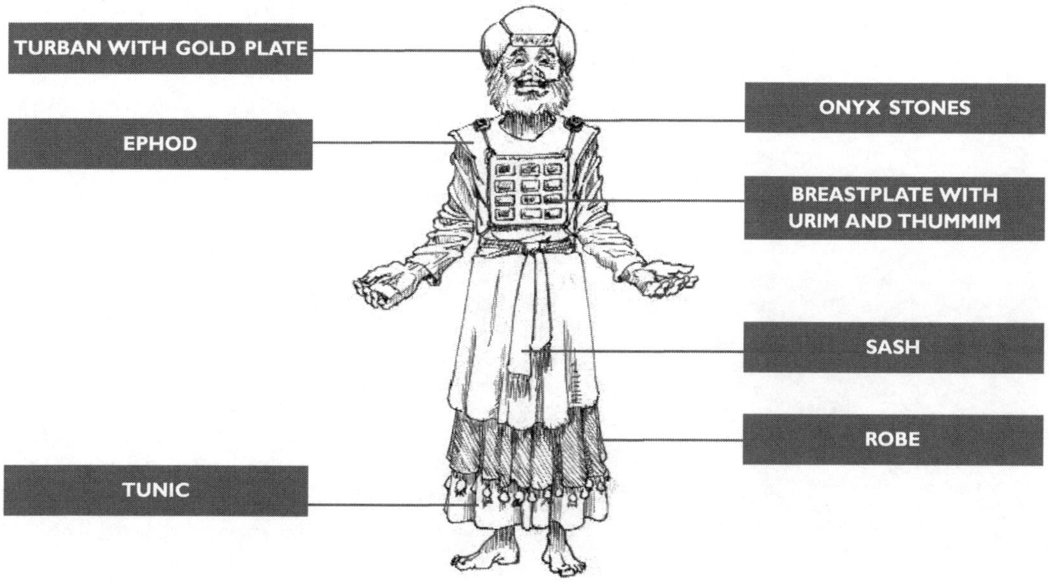

Lesson Six **DAY ONE**

The Priestly Appointment

> ***When Aaron, as high priest, is considered alone, he serves as a picture of our Lord Jesus Christ, "high priest of the good things to come" (Hebrews 9:11).***

The priesthood is divided in Scripture into three components: Aaron, his sons (Nadab, Abihu, Eleazar, and Ithamar), and his tribe (the Levites). When Aaron, as high priest, is considered alone, he serves as a picture of our Lord Jesus Christ, *"high priest of the good things to come"* (Hebrews 9:11). Aaron and his sons typify the priestly ministry of the Church, emphasizing the corporate body of believers, while Aaron and his tribe picture the priestly ministry of the children of God, emphasizing the individual believer. As we study the priesthood and the high priest, keep these distinctions in mind.

📖 Read Exodus 28:1 closely. To whom were the priests to minister?

____

____

____

____

____

Exodus 28:1 clearly shows that the priests were called to minister to the Lord, not the people. The distinction is significant. This does not mean that the priests would have no ministry to the people, but their focus always was to please the Lord. Sadly today, many ministers and pastors are enslaved to the expectations of their congregations.

We looked briefly last week at Aaron's rod, which was placed in the ark. To fully appreciate the story of Aaron's rod and why it was significant enough to be kept for posterity, we must look at the background. In Numbers 16 we have the record of Korah's rebellion. Korah was a Levite and led a revolt against the leadership of Moses and Aaron. The central point of Korah's argument was that he believed that the entire congregation of Israel was holy. This statement was true, for in Exodus 19:6 we read that all of Israel was *"a kingdom of priests and a holy nation."* However, this is a one-sided truth, for even in this, God had His divinely appointed ministers just as He has today. By rebelling against God's appointed leaders, Korah and his companions were *"gathered together against the Lord"* (Numbers 16:11; Acts 4:26). Consequently, the Lord judged them, and the earth swallowed them alive.

📖 Re-read Numbers 17:1–10 and write what you learn there about how God affirmed His selection of Aaron.

____

____

____

____

____

By calling all twelve tribes to submit a rod to be placed before Him, the Lord is involving everyone in affirming His calling of Aaron and the tribe of Levites. As these rods were placed before the Lord inside the Tabernacle,

God miraculously affirmed His choosing of Aaron and the Levites by causing his rod to bud and bloom and to bear fruit. This rod was set aside in the ark as a continual reminder against grumbling (v. 10).

📖 Now look at Hebrews 5:1–4 and write what you see there about the appointment of the priests.

____

____

____

____

____

They were *"appointed on behalf of men"*; they were to *"deal gently with the ignorant and misguided"*; and, most importantly, verse 4 makes it clear that no one could take this honor on himself, for it required a calling from God. Likewise, today, men should not decide to become ministers; they must be called of God. True ministry that is of God is "received," not "achieved."

Once the issue of calling was settled, the priests were ordained as recorded in Exodus 29:1–46. The consecration of Aaron and his sons in an act of ordination served to underscore the seriousness of the mission they had been given in the whole act of the worship of God. Aaron and his sons were installed as high priest and ministering priests respectively. The ordination procedure for the high priest was more involved than that of the ministering priests, but both involved **purification** and **consecration.**

RECEIVED MINISTRY

True ministry is received, not achieved. Paul told Archippus in Colossians 4:17, *"Take heed to the ministry which you have received in the Lord, that you may fulfill it."* Paul said of himself in Acts 20:24, *"But I do not consider my life of any account as dear to myself, in order that I may finish my course, and the ministry which I received from the Lord Jesus."*

📖 As we consider the purification of the priests, notice in Exodus 29:4 how this was to take place. What was to be done to the priests, and where would you find water at the doorway of the tent of meeting?

____

____

____

____

____

The priests were to be bathed with water. Of course, this cleansing was to take place at the laver that sat at the doorway of the tent of meeting. This ceremonial bathing was practiced only once a year, but the hands and feet were washed regularly.

📖 As you consider Jesus, our High Priest, read Matthew 3:13–15 and identify how His ordination was fulfilled in His life.

____

____

____

____

Jesus was bathed by being baptized in the Jordan by John the Baptist. Jesus did not need to repent of anything (which John recognized), but He made it clear that this baptism fulfilled God's purposes.

Now back to the Tabernacle for a few minutes. Not only were the priests purified by washing and then clothed with dignity and honor, but the high priest was to be consecrated to God.

Read Exodus 29:7 and 29:20. Identify how consecration was accomplished.

Did You Know?

ORDINATION SERVICES

Today, ministers are often consecrated to God at the beginning of their ministries in what is called an ordination service, much as the priest was in the Old Testament. While most churches do not anoint with oil and blood, they observe another Old Testament practice, the laying on of hands. This originated in the priestly practice of laying hands on the forehead of a sacrifice as a means of identifying with it. When a church ordains a minister, they are identifying with his future ministry.

Aaron was anointed with the holy anointing oil poured on his head. In Scripture, oil is a symbol of the Holy Spirit. Then sacrificial blood was applied to the right ear (symbolizing a consecrated hearing of God), the right thumb (symbolizing consecrated service), and the right big toe (symbolizing a consecrated walk).

According to Matthew 3:16–17, how was the Lord Jesus anointed?

After His baptism, the Holy Spirit descended upon Jesus in a true (not symbolic) anointing, which is affirmed by the statement of verse 17—*"This is My beloved Son, in whom I am well pleased."*

Lesson Six **DAY TWO**

THE PRIESTLY APPAREL

The garments of the priests were of great importance to the Lord. In Exodus 28:2 we are told that Aaron's garments were to serve the purpose of giving him *"dignity and honor"* (NIV). This same phrase is used in verse 40 of the garments of the other priests. In fact, in many denominations the ministers wear robes today for the same reason. God is always concerned that His people have a proper respect for leadership. Everything about the priestly apparel is designed so that they might be set apart. There is also much spiritual truth wrapped up in the symbolism of the garments.

To begin our study on the priestly apparel, take some time to read through Exodus 28:1–43 and write down the high points.

Obviously, much can be said concerning this lengthy passage, but let's stick with the "big picture." This is just a "first pass" overview, so don't get bogged down in the details. Two things that stand out about the priestly apparel are that the garments are **specific** and **special.** The garments are very specific indicating that, like the rest of the Tabernacle, there is meaning in each part. They are also special, emphasizing that the priests are to be set apart.

Now let's get more specific. Re-read Exodus 28:4 and identify the six components to the priestly garments.

The priestly garment was made up of the breastpiece, the ephod, the robe, the tunic, the turban, and the sash. The colors of the priestly garments were the same as those in the Tabernacle cloth (blue, purple, scarlet, and fine linen), with the addition of gold, which speaks of purity. The innermost garment, put on first, was the "woven tunic."

According to Exodus 28:39, what materials comprised the tunic? What symbolism do you see? (You may need to look back to previous lessons for the assumed meanings of the different colors and materials.)

The tunic consisted of "fine linen" with a checkered pattern. The checkered pattern was achieved by weaving, not colors, since the linen was white. This whiteness speaks of holiness and purity. This was especially true in the dry, dusty region of Palestine, where a white garment would not stay white without great care and maintenance.

The second piece of apparel is the "robe of the ephod" (29:5). Read 28:31–35 and identify what you can about the robe. Resist the temptation to read too much meaning into it.

Did You Know?

THE PRIEST'S ROBE

The bottom of the High Priest's robe was lined with bells that made noise as he moved about performing his duties. This served for more than mere ornamentation. On the Day of Atonement, he alone would enter the Holy of Holies to sprinkle sacrificial blood on the mercy seat. The bells were an affirmation that he was still alive and well, for entering the very presence of God meant death for those not properly prepared or functioning.

The robe was to be made entirely of blue, and it was to be woven at the neck so that it could not be torn. It was also to be hemmed with golden bells and pomegranates.

Explain in your own words why you feel the robe could not be torn.

According to Scripture, tearing the clothes is a sign of great remorse and/or repentance. In 2 Chronicles 34:27 it is associated with humility before God. The point here might be that the high priest, as a picture of Christ, would have no need for repentance. Remember that at His crucifixion, Christ's outer garments were divided, but His robe was left intact, fulfilling the prophecy of Psalm 22:18.

The third piece the priest would put on was the *"ephod"* or outer covering (28:6). It was to contain all five colors and must have been a beautiful sight. Exodus 39:3 tells us that the gold embroidery was not merely gold coloring, but was actually threads of pure gold. It was held in place on the shoulders with two onyx stones.

📖 Read Exodus 28:9–12 and identify what was written on the stones and the purpose behind this.

Exodus 28:43 indicates that the wearing of the garments guarded the priest from guilt. The garments point to the believer, who is clothed in the righteousness of Christ.

On each stone was engraved the names of six of the twelve tribes. Verse 12 indicates the purpose of these engravings was that Aaron might *"bear their names before the Lord . . . for a memorial."* In other words, when Aaron stood in the presence of the Lord on the Day of Atonement, he represented the twelve tribes as a group.

The fourth piece was the *"skillfully woven band"* (28:8) also called the "sash" (28:4). There is no apparent symbolism beyond the colors.

The fifth piece was the "breastplate" (*"breastpiece"* NASB) which was the centerpiece of the garments. Exodus 28 devotes more time to this one piece (16 verses) than nearly all the other garments combined (19 verses). It was a square piece of the same beautiful material as the ephod, folded in half and open at the top like a pouch. It hung in front of the ephod and must have stood out quite impressively.

📖 Read Exodus 28:15–30 and list what was included with the breastplate.

The essential components were the stones representing the tribes and the "*Urim and Thummim*." While the shoulder stones seem to represent Israel as a nation, here each tribe is represented by its own precious stone, suggesting Israel as individuals and their worth to God. Attempts to describe the *"Urim and Thummim"* (literally, "Lights and Perfection") has led to contradictory opinions, mainly because no specifics about the *Urim and Thummim* are found in Scripture. Some suggest that they were additional names for the rows of stones on the breastplate that represented the twelve tribes. Others believe they were two small images kept in the pouch of the breastplate, by which, in some unknown way, the high priest could give forth his divinely imparted decision when consulted. According to this theory, whichever was pulled from the pouch revealed God's direction. Whatever the *Urim and Thummim* represented, it appears that they were indeed used in times of crisis to determine the will of God. Numbers 27:21 seems to suggest that the *Urim* served a slightly different function than the *Thummim*, with one representing a "yes" decision and the other a "no" decision.

The final component of the high priestly apparel was the turban with its gold plate. The plate was attached with a blue cord and was engraved with the inscription, *"Holy to the Lord."* It reminds one of the seal God will place on the foreheads of the 144,000 in Revelation.

The other priests only wore a tunic and sash with linen undergarments and a cap. Separately, each piece of the apparel is significant, but together they take on further meaning. Verse 43 indicates that the wearing of the garments guarded the priest from guilt. The garments point to the believer who is clothed in the righteousness of Christ.

THE PRIESTLY ACTIVITY

Lesson Six **DAY THREE**

We covered a lot of ground in Day Two. Today's study contains far less detail, so "hang in there." We will look more closely at the priestly activity in a later lesson, so our goal here is only to introduce it and present an overview. The work of the priesthood is summed up in Leviticus 8:35 in the exhortation *"keep the charge of the Lord."* First, we must notice that this charge is *"of the Lord."* In Exodus 28:1 and 29:44, we learned that Aaron and his sons were *"to minister as priests to Me."* It is the Lord who is served in worship. Second, we must recognize that in detailing the service He desired, the Lord divided the tasks of the priesthood into two areas: the **offerings** and the **overseeing**.

📖 Look at Hebrews 5:1 and identify what is said there about the purpose of the offerings.

____

____

____

____

____

____

The priestly offerings could never fully satisfy God's justice or else repeating the offerings would not have been necessary. They merely served to instruct about the seriousness of sin and the coming One who would finally and fully bring together God's justice and love.

We see first that the sacrificial system existed for the purpose of dealing with sin. The **offerings** (gifts and sacrifices) were *"on behalf of men"* but they were *"things pertaining to God."* In other words, it is God's justice that must be satisfied. Of course, as the epistle to Hebrews makes clear, the priestly offerings could never fully satisfy God's justice or else repeating these offerings would not have been necessary. These offerings merely served to instruct about the seriousness of sin and the coming One who would fully and finally bring together God's justice and love.

The second aspect of the priestly activity is the **overseeing**. This involved overseeing the people as well as the process.

📖 Look at the verses below and identify how the priests oversaw the people.

Hebrews 5:2

____

____

Nehemiah 8:1–3

____

____

In Hebrews 5:2 we learn an important principle. One of the responsibilities of the priesthood was *to "deal gently with the ignorant and misguided."* As one who struggles with sin, the priest is in a position to minister to others who also struggle with sin. In Nehemiah 8:1–3 we see Ezra the priest ministering by teaching the people and speaking the Word of God to them.

Of course, the priests also ministered by interceding for the people through the offerings. Not only did the priests oversee the people, but they were also responsible to oversee the process. In overseeing the worship process, Aaron and his sons were responsible for trimming the lamps, burning the incense, arranging and dispensing the showbread, and assigning to the Levites their respective duties. Like the priests, Christians must be purified (Numbers 8:5–6), mobilized (Numbers 3:14–15), and utilized (Numbers 3:25–26; 1 Corinthians 12:11, 18).

Lesson Six **DAY FOUR**

THE PRIESTLY ATONEMENT

Though there were many facets to the priestly ministry, it all culminated one day a year on *"Yom Kippur,"* or the Day of Atonement. Priestly duties were the most important aspect of Aaron's work, for on that day atonement was made for all the sins of the entire congregation (Leviticus 16:16, 21, 30, 33) as well as for the Tabernacle (16:16, 33). *Yom Kippur* took place *"in the seventh month, on the tenth day of the month"* of the Jewish calendar (the month of *Tishri*) and was a "permanent statute" (16:29). It was a special Sabbath, and fasting was required from the evening of the ninth day until the evening of the tenth day.

Read Leviticus 16:29–31 and write down all the attitudes and actions God required on this holy day of *Yom Kippur.*

True Worship

THE HOLY PLACE TODAY

"Since therefore, brethren, we have confidence to enter the Holy Place by the blood of Jesus, by a new and living way which He inaugurated for us through the veil, that is, His flesh, and since we have a great priest over the house of God, let us draw near with a sincere heart in full assurance of faith, having our hearts sprinkled clean from an evil conscience and our bodies washed with pure water." (Hebrews 10:19–22)

The first thing we see about *Yom Kippur* is that the Israelites were called to *"humble* [their] *souls,"* which implies fasting. Leviticus 23:29 prescribed that one who would not humble his soul should be cut off from the people. The next requirement was that no one should work on this day. To the one who would not obey this injunction, God says He would destroy that person. *Yom Kippur* was to be *"a Sabbath of solemn rest."* In other words, what God desired on *Yom Kippur* was an attitude consistent with the goal of verse 30—that *"you shall be clean from all of your sins before the Lord."*

The observance of *Yom Kippur* went like this: first, the high priest brought a sin offering for himself and the other priests. Next, he presented two goats as a sin offering for the people. Lots were cast, and one goat was sacrificed, while the other was sent into the wilderness as a "scapegoat"—picturing the sins being carried away. Then, as all Israel waited in silence, the high priest would enter the Holy of Holies. The bells on the hem of his robe rang as evidence that he had not died in the presence of the Lord (Exodus 28:35). You see, if he was not spiritually prepared, he would die in God's presence. A rope was tied around his ankle because, if anything happened, no one else could come in and get him. Next, he would burn incense so that a cloud would cover the mercy seat picturing a prayer for mercy (Leviticus 16:12–13). Finally, the high priest would sprinkle the blood of the sacrifice on the mercy seat as the golden cherubim gazed down at it. When the high priest exited the tent of meeting alive, the entire nation would cheer in unison, rejoicing at this evidence that their sins had been atoned for. Can you imagine what it must have been like to be a part of that crowd? Can you guess what it was like to wrestle with the uncertainty, wondering if the sacrifice would be accepted, wondering if your sins would be covered? Yet, as Christians, we are part of something even more wonderful! The resurrection of our High Priest is the proof that the sacrifice for our sins was accepted.

Use the chart below to contrast the differences in Hebrews between the old covenant atonement and our atonement in Christ.

	Old Covenant	New Covenant
Where was this atonement done? (9:1, 11)		
What blood was used? (9:12, 14)		
Was this system perfect? (10:1)		
Could it take away sins? (10:10–11)		

"For Christ did not enter a holy place made with hands, a mere copy of the true one, but into heaven itself, now to appear in the presence of God for us."
Hebrews 9:24

	Old Covenant	New Covenant
Were the sacrifices repeated? (10:1–3, 12)	____________	____________
Who could enter through the veil? (9:7, 10:19–20)	____________	____________

Paul's epistle to the Galatians tells us that the Old Covenant, embodied in the Law, was to serve as a tutor to lead us to Christ. As we see in Hebrews, all the glory and majesty of the earthly Tabernacle and Temple (the *"earthly"* sanctuaries), cannot compare with the *"greater and more perfect tabernacle"* in heaven (9:1, 11). The earthly system was incomplete and inadequate because it relied on the blood of bulls and goats, while the heavenly atonement was made with the blood of the sinless Christ (9:12, 14). The imperfect, old covenant system was only a shadow of the *"very form"* we find through Christ (10:1), for it could never take away sins. Yet through Christ, we are sanctified *"once for all"* (10:10–11). Under the old system of atonement, the sacrifices had to be repeated year by year, but in Christ, atonement was made through one sacrifice for all time (10:1–3, 12). In the Old Testament, only the high priest was allowed to enter through the veil—and that with fear and trembling! Now all brethren can enter boldly with confidence through Christ (9:7, 10:19–20). What an awesome, new day dawned with the new covenant of Christ!

Lesson Six **DAY FIVE**

FOR ME TO WORSHIP GOD

You have followed the path of the priest. You have gone from outside the gate, past the brazen altar and the laver, into the Holy Place with the lampstand and table of showbread. You have passed the altar of incense and have gone through the veil into the very presence of God. You have gazed at His throne and experienced the wonder of the angels at His mercy. You have seen the beauty of our atonement. You have worshipped. But you cannot allow these truths to be merely academic. As you finish this week's study, take some time to review and reflect on all the wonderful truths you have learned.

In Day One, we saw the priestly appointment, which ought to remind us of God's calling and choosing us. While it is true that in the exercise of our will we chose Him, it is also true that we were chosen in Him before the foundation of the world. Reflect on all you have learned of the priestly appointment and how that relates to you, then write any observations in the form of a prayer to the Lord.

____

____

____

____

____

____

____

What stood out to you in the priestly apparel? Was it the white linen of holiness? The gold of purity? The scarlet of blood covering sin? The purple of royalty? The blue? Were you affected by the knowledge that wearing the garments of God gives you access to the will of God as pictured in the *Urim* and *Thummim?*

APPLY Think for a moment. Every Christian encounters the need to discern God's will. Eventually, each of us will ask the question, "What should I do, Lord?" Did you realize that hearing God's will is a right of the universal priesthood of all believers?

List an area where you sense the need to hear from God?

While today we don't carry a *Urim* and *Thummim* around with us, we do have the Spirit of the living God within us. While Scripture lays out many principles on how we can put ourselves in a position to hear what God is saying, time and space will not allow us to cover that in full here. But I don't want to leave you empty handed. Let me share with you a process that has served me well in my walk with Christ. What I look for is **desire,** plus **opportunity,** plus the absence of any **red flags**.

DESIRE
+ OPPORTUNITY
+ NO RED FLAGS
= GOD'S WILL

In your decision, what is your **desire**?

While we cannot fully count on what we desire to show us God's will, we cannot dismiss our desires either. Our desires can lead us astray if a surrendered heart does not accompany them, but if we are right with God, He will speak through our desires. Psalm 37:4 tells us, *"Delight yourself in the LORD; And He will give you the desires of your heart."* If we are delighting ourselves in God, He will influence the very things we desire. While we cannot expect this indicator to stand alone, when supported by the other two, it becomes a good leader.

What **opportunity** do you see for your desire?

If what we desire really is of God, He will move heaven and earth to open the doors and opportunities needed. If those doors are not opening, then either it is not God's will, or it is not God's will yet.

Are there any **red flags** as you move in your desired direction?

If our hearts are surrendered to the Lord and His way—that is, if His will really is all we want—then we can trust Him to let us know if we start moving in the wrong direction. We need to keep looking to Him to confirm, for God's will is not a static thing. Paul Little, in his helpful booklet *Affirming the Will of God* (InterVarsity, 1984), expresses it this way:

> The will of God is not like a magic package let down from heaven by a string. . . . the will of God is far more like a scroll that unrolls every day. . . . the will of God is something to be discerned and lived out every day of our lives. It is not something to be grasped as a package once for all. Our call, therefore, is basically not to follow a plan or a blueprint, or to go to a place or take up a work, but rather to follow the Lord Jesus Christ.

"...the will of God is something to be discerned and lived out every day of our lives. It is not something to be grasped as a package once for all."
—Paul Little

If we are making a wrong turn but have a heart to follow the Lord, He will put warning flags in front of us to get our attention. Have you come to the place in your walk with Christ where you recognize how great and awesome it is to have your sins forgiven?

Take some time to express a prayer in writing to the Lord. List some things for which you are grateful as you reflect on your atonement.

What you are doing right now is what worship is all about. Worship is far more than attending a church service or having an emotional experience. It is doing business with God, walking in relationship with Him. Hopefully you are already seeing the fruit of this in your own walk with God. Keep doing your homework, for you will get out of it what you put into it!

Notes

Notes

The Debt of Sin

Dealing with Sin God's Way

In Lessons One through Six, we have seen God's call to true worship, the call of His heart for us to come near, to follow closely, and to walk in oneness with Him. For the next two lessons, our focus will be on the actual offerings that the people and the priests brought. Each offering was a touch point in the people's relationship with God. Each offering carried a special significance and meaning. That significance and meaning did not stop when the earthly Tabernacle was torn down or when the Temple in Jerusalem was destroyed. The offerings of the Old Testament (or the Old Covenant) have meaning for us in the New Covenant because they are fulfilled in the Lord Jesus. They speak to us about our relationship to God through Jesus Christ. God has a message for us and to us in each of the offerings. He commanded these offerings—they were not the invention of man. He had something vitally important to teach His people then, under the Old Covenant, and those same truths apply to us today under the New Covenant.

JESUS PAID THE DEBT

We were enslaved to sin, carrying a debt of death for sin we could in no way pay. With His own blood, Jesus purchased us, which included our debt of sin, a debt He did not owe but which He willingly paid out of His great love.

In the Garden of Eden, the Lord told Adam that the payment for sin must be death. Death had to be paid, but death was not the purpose for which God created man. He made man to experience life. Through the years of man's existence, sin has continued and death has remained constant. The

The Offerings—Offered Year by Year

BURNT OFFERING Leviticus 1:13–17	GRAIN/DRINK OFFERINGS Leviticus 2; 6:14–23; Numbers 15:1–10	PEACE OFFERING Leviticus 3; 7:11–36	SIN OFFERING Leviticus 4:1—5:13	GUILT OFFERING Leviticus 5:14—6:7; 7:1–10

Jesus Our High Priest—Offered Himself Once for All

BURNT OFFERING John 1:29; Ephesians 5:2; Hebrews 10:5–10	GRAIN/DRINK OFFERINGS Isaiah 53:12; Matthew 26:26	PEACE OFFERING Romans 5:1; Ephesians 2:14	SIN OFFERING Galatians 1:4; Hebrews 9:14, 26, 28; 10:5-10, 12, 17–18	GUILT OFFERING Isaiah 53:4–11; I Peter 2:21–25

We Can Walk by Faith in Christ's Finished Work

We Can Walk Yielded as Christ Was in His Surrender to the Father.	We Can Walk Knowing Him as Our Sustenance and Provision.	We Can Walk In Satisfaction with Him Who Is Our Peace.	We Can Walk Forgiven Because Sin Was upon Him and Paid for by Him.	We Can Walk Restored as Sin-Damaged Relationships Are Restored by Him.

debt of sin was particularly evident in the offerings of the Tabernacle. In the offerings for sin, the Lord provided a picture of the final and eternal payment for sin that would be made by the Lord Jesus Himself. Christ's death and payment of our sin debt not only provides us with forgiveness, but allows us to live our lives to the fullest, as God intended. This week, as you look at the debt of sin and the offerings for sin, think of your own life, your sin, and the payment the Lord Jesus has made. The Lord has a message for each of us.

Lesson Seven DAY ONE

DEALING WITH SIN

The detailed instructions for building the Tabernacle were for the purpose of bringing man to God in a holy relationship. God wanted to dwell with His chosen people—to be involved in every detail of everyday life. He wanted to show them holy love, and through them show holy love to the world. But His people had a problem—sin. Sin had to be dealt with, both fully and continuously. Relationship and fellowship with a holy God required holiness in His people, but the people, with their sinfulness, could not produce that holiness.

Sometimes it is hard for us to understand the wretchedness of sin and the insult sin becomes to a holy God. The Tabernacle and the offerings help us understand the awfulness of sin. As we come to understand sin's wretchedness, we will gradually come to experience and know the kindness of God's love as well as the severity of His just and pure holiness. His justice requires a full payment of the sin debt, the offense against Him. God is always just and therefore must see justice carried out. The just penalty for any sin is death—separation from God and from eternal life with God. There are many ways that man sins unknowingly, ways that offend God, because man's nature is contrary to God's nature, His thoughts, and His ways. In His justice mixed with mercy, God provided a way for sin's debt to be paid for or covered (atoned for). It was through the death of a substitute. However, even the substitute had to be acceptable to God. In God's revelation to Moses, He made clear which substitute was acceptable. Through this revelation to Moses, the various offerings were established. Each offering dealt with some aspect of the people's relationship with God. A quick and general overview of each offering will give us a clearer picture of Israel's walk with God in the Old Testament and will give us specific applications for our day-by-day walk with Him today in the New Covenant. At the closing of our Day One study and throughout Day Two, we will study in closer detail two of the Old Testament worship offerings, the **sin** and the **guilt** offerings.

"... without shedding of blood there is no forgiveness"
Hebrews 9:22

📖 Look at Leviticus 1:1 and 7:37–38. Who initiated the offerings?

____

____

____

The offerings were not the invention of Moses or of the people in the land of Egypt. The offerings did not originate from any of the people in and around the land of Canaan. **God** gave specific directions for the offerings He wanted from His people. Everything He gave them was designed to reveal something about His character, His holiness, His ways, and about their relationship and fellowship with Him. God wanted them to follow Him and walk with Him **His way.**

To help assure that the people understood the character and nature of the Lord, as well as the truth about His holiness and their sinfulness, the Lord revealed Himself in many ways. He revealed Himself to the children of Israel in Egypt; in their deliverance through the Red Sea; at Mount Sinai with the giving of the Law; and in all He did in giving them the Tabernacle, the priesthood, the feasts, and the offerings. Just before Moses died, the Lord gave further instruction through him to the people.

📖 Read Deuteronomy 31:9–13 and note **what** they were to do and **why.**

____

____

____

Did You Know?

THE REGULAR OFFERINGS

Various offerings were offered at least twice daily, weekly on the Sabbath, monthly at the New Moon, and in each of the seven yearly feasts (Passover, Unleavened Bread, Firstfruits, Pentecost, Trumpets, Day of Atonement, and Tabernacles).

Every seven years at the Feast of Tabernacles (in our October), the priests were to read the entire law to the people gathered—men, women, and children, as well as any foreigner present. They were to hear the law *"that they may learn to fear the Lord … and carefully observe all the words of this law"* (NKJV), both they and all their children who had not yet heard the law. God made ample provision for the people to know Him and His will, what was right in His sight and what was sin in His sight. The offerings He commanded were regular reminders of these truths.

List the 5 main offerings God required as found in Leviticus 1—5, as well as the accompanying offering found in Numbers 15:1–10. Fill in the chart below.

SCRIPTURE	OFFERING
Leviticus 1:1-3	
Leviticus 2:1	
Leviticus 3:1	
Leviticus 4:1-3, 13–14	
Leviticus 5:1-6	

God gave His people instructions concerning a **burnt** offering, a **grain** offering, a **peace** offering (also known as the fellowship offering), a **sin** offering, and a **guilt** offering (also called a trespass offering). The **drink** offering was always offered with the burnt offering, and the peace offering along with the grain offering. These offerings were to be offered in a certain way, for certain reasons, and in a certain order. While the five main offerings are given in one order, the order in which they were offered is different. When we look at the record Moses penned, we find that the order was first a sin offering, then a burnt offering accompanied by a grain and drink offering. That was followed by a peace offering. The guilt offering was closely associated with the sin offering. When an individual had a particular sin to address or an offense to make right with God, he offered a guilt offering.

True Worship

THE CALENDAR OF THE SIN OFFERING

The Lord required that a sin offering be presented once a month (the New Moon offering) and at the Feasts (Passover, Unleavened Bread, Firstfruits, Pentecost, Trumpets, Day of Atonement, Tabernacles). On the Day of Atonement there were two sin offerings, one for the priest and one for the people, plus a scapegoat who bore away the sins of the people.

Did You Know?

THE HORNS OF THE ALTAR

The horns of the altar were four projections on each corner of the golden altar of incense and on the bronze altar. A horn was a strong point in an animal, a weapon of strength. It symbolized strength to the Israelites and on the altar symbolized the strength or the power of the altar, the place where sin could be dealt with.

Now let's look at two of these offerings in more detail. Leviticus 4 gives instructions concerning the **sin offering.** What was brought differed according to who had sinned: the priest brought a bull for his sin; the whole congregation also brought a bull for their sin; a ruler brought a male goat; and the people of the land brought a female goat or lamb. The procedure was basically the same for each. Note the common steps in the verses below.

When was the sin offering to be offered? (Leviticus 4:3, 14, 23, 28)

____

____

What was done **first**? (4:3–4, 14–15, 23–24, 28–29, 33)

____

____

What is the one thing **common** to each sacrifice listed in Leviticus 4 (4:3, 23, 28, 32)? Why would this be important?

____

____

____

What was done **after** the animal was slain? (4:5–7, 16–18, 25, 30, 34)

____

____

____

What came next? (4:8–10, 19–20, 26, 31, 35)

____

____

What was the **final** step? (4:11–12, 21)

____

____

Final words are important. What are the final words of Leviticus 4:20, 26, 31, 35?

____

____

The basic steps involved in the sin offering began when sin became known to a person or to the congregation. First, the person or group had to recognize and admit they had sinned. Then one brought an animal without defect to the doorway of the Tabernacle. The Lord's holiness and honor required that no animal maimed, aged, diseased, or in any way defective could be offered. At the doorway of the Tabernacle, the transgressor placed his hands on the head of the animal, pressing firmly. This was to show his identity with the animal and to symbolically place his sin on that animal. The sin offering was for any breaking of God's commands. When a person laid his hands on the head of the animal, he also pictured taking personal responsibility for the sin. He was seeking restoration of fellowship with the Lord through that innocent sacrifice and the shedding of its blood.

After the animal had been killed, the priest gathered some of the blood and took it into the Holy Place, where it was sprinkled before the veil and placed on the horns (corners) of the altar of incense. In some cases, the blood was placed on the horns of the bronze altar. The remainder was poured at the base of the bronze altar. The priests took the fat portions and entrails of the animal and offered them on the bronze altar. The remainder of the animal was then taken outside the camp to a clean place and burned completely, symbolizing full judgment for sin. When all steps of the sin offering were completed, the promise of forgiveness was fulfilled, for the final words of verses 20, 26, 31, and 35 are the words of God, promising that each person *"shall be forgiven."*

APPLY There are two applications at hand here. First, is the Lord convicting you of some sin that needs to be confessed and forsaken (1 John 1:9)? If so, do so. Second, you can be assured that you too can experience the reality of God's forgiveness. Stop and apply these principles of confession and forgiveness. The Lord is willing, ready, and able to forgive all those who come to Him as He commands.

True Worship
WITHOUT DEFECT

The animals for sacrifice had to be without defect. The priests thoroughly examined each sacrifice, even looking at the eyelids. After the animal was slain the priests skinned and cut up the animal in a precise manner again watching for any defects on the inside. Without and within the animal had to be whole, without defect. Jesus is the Lamb of God, "unblemished and spotless" (1 Peter 1:19). Before His crucifixion, His enemies could find no fault in Him (Luke 23:4, 13–15), even after three Jewish trials and three Roman trials (Matthew 26:57–68; 27:11–26; Mark 14:53—15:15; Luke 22:63—23:25; John 18:12—19:16).

MAKE IT RIGHT

Lesson Seven **DAY TWO**

We have seen the importance and emphasis of the sin offering. Of a similar nature was the **guilt offering** (Leviticus 5:1–19; 6:1–7). The guilt offering was offered for sins against the *"holy things"* (perhaps not giving tithes or some prescribed offering for the service of the Tabernacle and the priests) or for some sin against a neighbor (deceiving or cheating a neighbor in some way, etc.). God required that the guilty one make it right. In addition to a sacrifice, the guilty person was required to make restitution. As you study this offering, look for any additional insights into the character of God. What does this offering say about His view of wrong? What does it say about your relationship with Him?

The guilt offering was a sin offering with the addition of restitution for certain wrongs. What kinds of wrongs did this include? Fill out the chart below listing the various wrongs given in Leviticus 5:1–4, 15–17; 6:2–3.

SCRIPTURE	OFFERING
Leviticus 5:1	
Leviticus 5:2	
Leviticus 5:3	
Leviticus 5:4	
Leviticus 5:15, 17	
Leviticus 6:2	
Leviticus 6:2	
Leviticus 6:2	
Leviticus 6:3	

THE BURDEN OF A GUILTY CONSCIENCE

There is nothing quite so burdening as a guilty conscience. It robs one of peace, of joy, often of sleep, and certainly of relationships. The only thing more burdening is a seared conscience that can lead to deeper sin and destruction. There is nothing quite as liberating and peaceful as a cleansed conscience, cleansed by the blood of Jesus.

There are ten offenses given in Leviticus 5 and 6: failure to testify when one has been a witness or knows something about a wrong done, touching any unclean thing, touching any human uncleanness, swearing thoughtlessly for good or evil, sinning against the Lord's holy things, deceiving someone about a deposit or security entrusted to him, robbing someone, extortion, lying about something found that was lost, and swearing falsely. Each of these brought guilt and required a guilt offering and restitution where prescribed or possible.

Did You Know?

WHAT IS AN "EPHAH"?

An ephah was equal to about two-thirds of a bushel or almost 21 quarts.

The procedures for the guilt offering given in Leviticus 5 were very similar to those of the sin offering. The person confessed his specific sin, then brought his sacrifice to the priest according to what he could afford. For instance, a wealthier person would bring a lamb or a goat without defect. Those with lesser means might bring two turtledoves or two pigeons, or, if very poor, one tenth of an *ephah* of fine flour (see sidebar). Then the priest offered that sacrifice on the altar. The Lord required that wrongs be righted in a sacrificial way in accordance with what the offender could financially afford. This sometimes included more than a sacrifice.

What do you observe in Leviticus 5:16 and 6:4–5?

____

____

____

Generally, the guilty party brought an offering to the priest for sacrifice and, if possible, restored what was originally taken (lost, stolen, or damaged). In addition, a twenty percent fine, or a fifth of the total value of restitution was paid by the offender to the priest for offenses against *"holy things."* In case the wrongs committed were against an individual, an additional twenty percent of the total value of restitution went to the offended person. When the offering and payment were made, the Lord promised that the offender would be forgiven (5:10, 16, 18; 6:7).

In understanding the guilt offering, we must remember that when a person sinned against the law of God, he was considered guilty of breaking the law even though he may have been unaware of the law. (Actually, God made ample provision for them to know His law.) However, a broken law, no matter how misunderstood, is still a broken law. Leviticus 5:19 says, *"he was certainly guilty before the LORD."* It is the Lord's view of sin that we must accept. God commanded and required a guilt offering and proper restitution. The Israelites would have heard the law and its requirements. Remember that there was a provision for the entire law to be read to the people every seven years (see Deuteronomy 31:9–13). There were no secret or "surprise" laws with unexpected penalties for disobedience. Obedience to God was (and still is) a matter of walking with Him daily and intentionally seeking to know His Word and to obey Him—to follow Him and His ways.

Compare Matthew 5:23–24 with the truths found in this guilt offering. What applications do you see?

____

____

____

____

Jesus made it clear that He wants us in a right relationship with others. If we have offended someone, we then need to make it right before we presume to be in a position of worship. We are presumptuous when we appear to be submitted to God and His will yet refuse to make things right with a brother or sister, someone who has the same Heavenly Father we have. After we have made things right, then we can enjoy our walk in worship.

"... first be reconciled to your brother. . . ."

Matthew 5:24

📖 Look at what Paul said in Acts 24:14–16 (especially verse 16). Though Paul knew God's Word and was assured of the resurrection to come, how did he seek to live before God and before others?

____

____

____

Paul's heart desire was to maintain a clear conscience toward God and others especially in light of eternity. He wanted no offenses between himself and God, nor between himself and any man. He states in verse 16, *"I exercise myself, to have always a conscience void of offence toward God, and toward men."* That term "exercise" or "practice" is from the Greek word *askeo,* meaning "to labor or to take pains" and is the root of the English word "ascetic." Paul did everything he could to maintain a clear conscience towards God and towards others. He did not want to stumble, nor did he want others to stumble over him. That meant he dealt with any sins or offenses very quickly.

APPLY Pause for a moment and ask the Lord to show you any sin you have committed against Him or against a "neighbor" for which you need to make restitution in some way. If He convicts you, make plans now to deal with it and make it right. You may need to stop reading this lesson right now and make a phone call. Confess whatever the Lord leads you to confess. Don't be tricked into the "it's just a little thing" excuse. Make it right. It may be uncomfortable, and you will probably have to humble yourself before the person you wronged. However, it will be well worth the effort. The alternative is lack of fellowship with the Lord and with others. Even worse, you may be an obstacle to someone else. Why carry around the heavy weight of guilt and pride, especially when you can know the light-hearted joy and peace of having made a wrong right. A restored, guilt-free relationship is worth more than money can buy.

CIRCLE OF CONFESSION

The circle of confession is to be no bigger than the circle of the offense. If the sin is against God alone, then make things right with Him. If you have offended an individual, make it right with that person. If you have offended a group, make it right with the group.

The Sin Offerings on The Day of Atonement

Lesson Seven **DAY THREE**

The Lord used several pictures in the Old Testament to communicate His heart and His will for His people. God knew it was essential that His people understand their sin and know how to deal with it. He wanted them to know His remedy for their sin. That is why He taught them about the offerings, especially the sin offering and the guilt offering. The repetition of these offerings served as a teacher to the people. God commanded they offer a sin offering monthly (the New Moon offering), and during the seven feasts (Passover, Unleavened Bread, First Fruits, Pentecost, Trumpets, Day of Atonement, and Tabernacles). The Day of Atonement focused especially on dealing with sin, specifically the atonement or covering for sin. Sin offerings played a central role on this all-important day. We have seen the High Priest walk through the Day of Atonement in Lesson Six. Today, we will look more closely at those events to see a picture of how carefully and thoroughly the Lord deals with our sin.

"By those who come near Me I will be treated as holy, And before all the people I will be honored."
Leviticus 10:3

The Lord wanted His people (Israel) to walk with Him. He wanted them to live in His presence, but they had to live with proper regard for His holiness. Two sons of Aaron, Nadab and Abihu, used common coals from a fire they had kindled instead of coals from the fire God kindled in the altar. In so doing, they did not honor the Lord and were struck dead in His presence (Leviticus 10:1–7). In Leviticus 16, in light of the offense of Nadab and Abihu, the Lord gave specific instructions about how the high priest was to approach the Lord at the mercy seat in the Holy of Holies.

Read Leviticus 16 and answer the exercises below concerning that chapter.

What warning did the Lord give in Leviticus 16:2?

How was Aaron to come before the Lord according to Leviticus 16:3–4?

True Worship
WHITE LINEN GARMENTS

What is the significance of linen? First of all, the linen was white, symbolic of purity and holiness. Linen was also a cooling garment unlike wool. In Ezekiel 44:17–18, the Lord gave specific instructions that the priests wear linen and not wool in the service of the Temple. He wanted no sweat involved in service to Him. No fruit of the fall and the flesh was to be a part of worship. The priests changed into linen garments to take the ashes of a sacrifice out to a clean place or to take the sin offerings out to that place for burning. Christ was buried in linen cloth in an unused tomb (a clean place) outside the city (Matthew 27:57–60; John 19:38–42; Isaiah 53:9).

The Lord warned Aaron that he could not enter the Holy Place inside the veil (Holy of Holies) at just any time of his own choosing or in any way other than God's way. Disobedience to this mandate would result in the penalty of death. There was a specific way Aaron could enter and that was through the shed blood of a sin offering after a ram was sacrificed as a burnt offering. First, Aaron had to bathe his body in water and put on certain clothing—a linen tunic set aside for that purpose, holy to the Lord, along with a linen sash and linen turban.

The Lord required that Aaron offer a bull as a sin offering for himself and his household first (16:6). What **steps** did Aaron take in this first duty on the Day of Atonement? Read Leviticus 16:11–14, and note these steps.

Aaron (or whoever occupied the role of High Priest in later years) was to slay the bull for the sin offering and collect some of the blood. He was to gather some coals from the altar of incense, place them in a firepan, and take the coals and the blood inside the veil into the Holy of Holies. There he was to place incense on the coals so that first a cloud of smoke filled the Holy of Holies covering the mercy seat. Then he was to sprinkle the blood of the bull once upon the mercy seat and seven times down in front of the mercy seat. In these exercises is exhibited the symbolism of a blood substitute that covered sin, averted the judgment of death for Aaron, and opened the way to fellowship in the presence of the Lord.

Then, Aaron was to take two male goats from the congregation and offer one of them as a sin offering. He presented the goats before the Lord at the doorway of the Tabernacle (16:7). How was he to choose which goat was to be the sin offering according to Leviticus 16:8–9?

Aaron was to cast lots to determine which goat was offered for a sin offering and which goat became the scapegoat. He did this trusting the Lord to sovereignly oversee the outcome of the lots as they were cast. The goat designated by the lots as the Lord's was then offered as a sin offering.

Describe what the priest did with the goat for the sin offering in Leviticus 16:15–19.

Doctrine

THE FULFILLMENT OF THE DAY OF ATONEMENT

On the Day of Atonement, the blood of a bull and a goat went into the Holy of Holies, where the high priest placed the blood on the mercy seat. The bodies of the bull and the goat for the sin offering were burned outside the camp. The scapegoat was sent into the wilderness carrying away the sin—Jesus is our Sin Offering, our High Priest, our Mercy Seat, and our Scapegoat.

The high priest slaughtered the goat of the sin offering and brought its blood inside the veil into the Holy of Holies as he had done with the blood of the bull. The blood of the bull was for the sin of the high priest and the sin of his family, while the blood of the goat was for the sin of the people. He sprinkled the blood once on the mercy seat and seven times in front of the mercy seat. Then, the blood of both animals was to be placed on the horns of the golden altar of incense that stands before the veil. This cleansed the holy place first and then covered the sins of the people. The high priest had to go in alone to make atonement for himself and the people, showing this to be a very serious and holy moment.

All that occurred on this day was to atone for or cover the "impurities," "transgressions," and "sins" of the people. "Impurities" refer to any uncleanness whether ceremonial, moral, or physical. "Transgressions" are actions where we step aside from the right path. To transgress is to go outside the laws or boundaries set by the Lord. The word "sin" carries the idea of missing the mark. All aspects of sin were addressed in these offerings.

What steps were taken with this second goat according to Leviticus 16:10, 20–22?

The scapegoat was presented before the Lord, and the high priest laid his hands on the head of the goat symbolically placing the sins of the people upon that animal. This goat was then led into the wilderness and released. This pictured the people's sins being carried away never to be remembered or brought before the Lord again. The scapegoat became a picture of the forgiveness and the covering for sin the Lord provided for His people.

After Aaron sent out the scapegoat, he bathed, changed his garments and offered a burnt offering for himself and for the people, and then he offered the fat of the sin offering. The bodies of the bull and goat sin offerings, whose blood had gone inside the Holy of Holies, remained at the bronze altar area. After the fat was offered, the bull and the goat were taken outside the camp and totally burned. What is the significance of this?

THE BODY AND THE BLOOD

The blood and the body of the Lord Jesus were pictured in the events of the Day of Atonement. His blood was taken into the heavenly Holy of Holies, signifying our eternal redemption. His body was taken outside the city to bear the full judgment for our sin.

📖 Read Hebrews 13:11–12 with Hebrews 9:11–14 and note the full meaning of this offering. What do you find?

____

____

____

____

Jesus is our sin offering, whose body was offered outside the camp—outside the city of Jerusalem. Jesus took upon Himself the complete judgment for sin, just as the bodies of the bull and the goat were completely consumed in the fire—the fire of judgment on sin. His blood bought our eternal redemption, and through that blood He entered the heavenly Holy of Holies, where He guarantees our forgiveness and cleansing. The way is now open for us to fellowship with Him and to serve Him with a cleansed conscience.

Lesson Seven **DAY FOUR**

JESUS, THE LORD'S SERVANT, OUR GUILT OFFERING

Isaiah 52:13–15 and 53:1–12 present to us one of the clearest pictures of God's view of sin and the remedy for it. This passage also paints a portrait of the Lord Jesus as He died for our sins. In this prophecy of the suffering servant of the Lord, we clearly see the one who would die as a substitute for the people, a guilt offering for the guilt of our sin.

📖 Isaiah 52:13–15 introduces us to the servant of the Lord by telling us that this servant will prosper and be greatly exalted. However, these verses also reveal that this servant will face severe agony first. What are the details of his agony?

____

____

____

____

📖 Read Isaiah 53, and answer the exercises devoted to the chapter below.

Look first at Isaiah 53:1–3, and record what you find.

____

____

____

This servant was born in simple conditions as a shoot out of dry ground. He grew up before the Lord. He was not outwardly impressive and was actually despised and forsaken by men. He faced many sorrows and was well acquainted with grief and pain.

This servant took our place. Note every reference to the pronouns "our," "we," and "us" in Isaiah 53:2–6. You may want to circle them with a pencil. List the words connected to each of these pronouns. What do these verses tell you about what this servant did?

____

____

____

This passage speaks of our griefs, sorrows, transgression, iniquities, as well as our going astray like sheep, each one of us turning to our own way. We did not care to look upon him; were not attracted to him; nor did we in any way honor or esteem him. This servant endured this rejection and bore all the sin of all the people, all kinds of sin.

What did this servant actually face? Note all the words and phrases in Isaiah 53:4–12 that speak of what happened to him, especially the phrase *"guilt offering."* Using those words, describe what the servant did and what he faced.

____

____

____

____

This servant bore our griefs. The word "bore" (Hebrew: *nasa*) means to lift up or to take away. It is the same word that was used of a person bearing the guilt of sin (Leviticus 5:1) or of the scapegoat bearing away the iniquities of the people on the Day of Atonement (Leviticus 16:22). The servant also carried our sorrows and was stricken, smitten, and struck down of God. He was afflicted; He was pierced through because of our transgressions and crushed for our iniquities. He took our chastening and scourging so that we might receive peace and wholeness. We were the sheep who turned to go our own selfish way, but the iniquity of each of us fell on him. When the servant faced the oppression and affliction caused by our sin, he did not open His mouth, but bore it as a silent sacrificial lamb. He took our judgment, dying as the innocent one, the one with no deceit in his mouth nor any violence in his actions. He was crushed by the Lord and put to grief, dying as a *"guilt offering"* (v. 10). He paid the full price for our sin. He was our perfect substitute, taking our sin upon himself, dying in our place so that we would not have to face judgment for sin.

THE SUFFERING SERVANT

"I gave My back to those who struck Me. And My cheeks to those who plucked out the beard; I did not hide My face from shame and spitting. For the Lord GOD will help Me; Therefore I will not be disgraced; Therefore I have set My face like a flint, And I know that I will not be ashamed." (Isaiah 50:6–7 NKJV)

Jesus was our perfect substitute, taking our sin upon Himself, dying in our place so that we would not face judgment for sin.

What were the results of the death of this servant according to Isaiah 53:11–12?

Because of what he did, bearing the iniquities of the people and pouring out himself to death, the servant brought justification to *"the many."* His intercession for the transgressors proved effective in bringing them salvation. Verse 10 speaks of him prolonging his days and points to the resurrection of this servant.

"... he preached unto him Jesus...."
Acts 8:35

📖 Who is this servant? The Scriptures tell us very clearly. Read the story of Philip the evangelist in Acts 8:26–40. What do you find in verses 32–35 that would identify the servant of Isaiah 53 (quoted in verses 32–33)? What insights do you see about this servant of Isaiah 53?

The Ethiopian official had been reading the scroll of Isaiah the prophet and was reading Isaiah 53:7–8 when Philip joined him. Acts 8:35 tells us that beginning with that Scripture *"he preached Jesus to him."* All that we find in Isaiah 53 points to the Lord Jesus in His birth and upbringing, then His death and resurrection. Jesus was **the guilt offering** for the sins of all mankind. Because He interceded for us; because He was willing to bear our sins and pay the full price in dying for us, we can know His forgiveness and the presence of His Spirit in our lives.

Lesson Seven **DAY FIVE**

For Me to Worship God

This week we have looked at the meaning and significance of the **sin offering** and the **guilt offering**. Why are these offerings so important? Why does God want us to walk with Him in a right relationship, dealing with sin promptly and fully? One reason is that we know where sin is allowed to stand, it always causes a stench. As someone has said, not dealing with sin is like waiting to take the garbage out, the longer one waits the more it stinks. Sin is offensive to God, to His nature. As we become more like Him, sin becomes increasingly offensive to us. We then become increasingly sensitive to sin and want to deal with it His way. The only way to deal with sin God's way is to take it out or to take it away. Jesus has dealt with sin on the cross. He did that as *"the Lamb of God who takes away the sin of the world"* (John 1:29).

Jesus has provided forgiveness and cleansing, but He provides us another blessing that goes beyond forgiveness and cleansing. We see this extra blessing in the Tabernacle and in the work of Christ. Jesus not only takes sin away—He comes near and draws us near to Himself. Forgiveness is pictured at the brazen altar in the outer court, but the Lord wants His people to join Him in the Holy of Holies where His merciful presence is fully known.

Just as we desire to provide a clean, attractive, warm and inviting place for guests or family, so the Lord wants to fellowship with us in a clean place, a place of beauty, a place where there is freedom from sin and guilt. Just as we would want nothing offensive in our homes for family or guests, so He wants nothing offensive in the place of worship and fellowship. He wants us to walk in the fullness of His presence. We will see that today. Ask Him to show you personal applications as you look at the Scriptures.

Word Study

"THE PRESENCE OF THE LORD"

The "presence of the Lord" is often a translation that literally refers to the face of the Lord (Greek, *prosōpon*—Acts 3:19; 2 Thessalonians 1:9). It pictures a very personal, intimate closeness for His children and a personal, severe judgment for those who do not know and obey Him.

What marks the presence of the Lord? Read the following Scriptures and write your insights. (Some translations use the word *"presence of the Lord"* and others use *"before the Lord"* or *"before Him,"* or picture His presence in some other way, but each translation should essentially convey the same truth.)

Exodus 13:21–22

Exodus 33:14–15

Deuteronomy 12:5–7, 11–12, 18 (speaking of where they would eventually place the Tabernacle and then the Temple)

1 Chronicles 16:27

Psalm 23:1–6; 16:11

These verses and several others show us that the presence of the Lord is a wonderful reality. There is guidance in His presence, as well as rest, joy, and peace. In His presence, we gladly surrender and give ourselves to Him, just as the Israelites brought their offerings to Him. When we are surrendered to the Lord, resting in His presence, obeying Him, we can rejoice in all our activities. In His presence, we can know something of His splendor and majesty and can experience His strength and joy. David knew the peace of *"Thou art with me"* (Psalm 23:4). In eternity, there will be the fullness of joy and pleasures forever. In His presence is life in all its fullness.

Word Study

WHAT IS SIN?

The Greek word for "sin" is *hamartía,* which means to miss the mark or to come short of the goal. It was used of a Greek archer coming short of his target. Sin is a choice that comes short of what God wants and fails to fulfill the command or reach the goal God has set. Such a choice is an offense to God.

📖 What does God want people to experience in His presence (now and forever)? Read the Scripture passages listed below and write down the desires of God for us that are listed in each passage.

Acts 3:18–19

____

____

____

John 14:16–17, 26–27; 16:7–15; Ephesians 1:13–14

____

____

____

2 Thessalonians 1:10

____

____

____

Jude 24

____

____

____

God wants people to know times of refreshing from His presence in their lives. That comes through repenting of sin and believing in Jesus as Lord and Savior. Those who do that experience the presence, peace, and encouragement of the Holy Spirit as well as His guidance and instruction as He illumines the Word of God. One day, we will marvel at His fully-revealed presence when He returns. We will stand in His presence blameless and with great joy because He has saved us.

📖 Read the Scriptures listed below and answer the following questions: How does sin impact our experience of, or enjoyment of, the presence of the Lord? How does it affect God's actions toward His children, and how does it affect His actions toward those who do not know Him?

Genesis 3:8

____

____

Leviticus 10:1–3

____

____

Jeremiah 5:21–29 (note verse 22)

____

____

Ephesians 4:29–30

____

____

1 Thessalonians 5:19–22

____

____

2 Thessalonians 1:7–9

____

____

Extra Mile

WHAT THE BIBLE SAYS ABOUT SIN

The Scriptures paint several pictures of what sin is. Look at Matthew 13:41; John 8:24 and 16:8–9; Romans 3:9–18 and 14:23; James 3:13–17; and 1 John 3:4; 5:17. Record your insights.

When Adam and Eve sinned, the Lord came walking in the Garden of Eden, calling to Adam. Genesis 3:8 says they *"hid themselves from the presence of the Lord God."* What an impact sin made! When Nadab and Abihu offered incense on ordinary coals, coals that were not set apart by the Lord as holy, they offended Him. They disregarded His holiness, and God immediately struck them dead. The people of Jeremiah's day continually disregarded the Lord and His commands. Their sin made them insensitive to God's presence and caused them to continue to live their lives without the appropriate fear and respect for God that He deserved. Paul exhorted the Ephesian believers to do nothing that would grieve the Spirit, especially speaking ugly words to one another. When we fail to walk wisely or reject the clear Word of God, we can quench the Spirit. Sin affects how we follow and fellowship with God; it disrupts that fellowship and hinders our enjoyment of His presence. Those who do not know God or obey the gospel of Jesus will be banished from the presence of the Lord in judgment.

When we see what the Bible says about sin and how God longs for us to know His forgiveness, we realize how important it is that we apply these truths. One of the greatest needs in individuals, churches, and communities is the need to admit sin and experience the forgiveness and peace God longs to give. Many are allowing the offenses of others and their own offenses against others to spoil their walk with God, to cause discord in their church, and to cripple their witness in their community. In the Welsh Revival of 1904, a young man named Evan Roberts preached a message that God used to bring great awakening and revival to that small land and beyond. His message was simple in addressing the issue of sin and obedience. Read these four statements that summarize his message and allow the Lord to show you anything you need to do personally:

1. Confess any known sin to God, and make right any wrong against man.
2. Forsake any questionable habit in your life.
3. Obey the Holy Spirit promptly. (The Spirit always agrees with the Word of God. He never contradicts it.)
4. Confess your faith in Jesus Christ before men.

Doctrine

OUR RESCUE

Jesus died to *"deliver us out of this present evil age."* (Galatians 1:4). He rescued us as He rescued the Israelites from the Egyptian bondage (Acts 7:10, 34); as He rescued Peter from prison (Acts 12:11); and as the Roman commander rescued Paul from the angry mob in Jerusalem (Acts 23:10, 27)—each from certain death and destruction.

APPLY Read through these four items once again, and pause for some time in prayer. Obey what the Lord is saying to you.

One more verse of Scripture needs mentioning. Some people still struggle with the idea that **their** sins can be forgiven. However, the Scriptures are clear about forgiveness. What does 1 Peter 3:18 tell us about what Jesus did? Why did He do this, and what does His action mean to each of us?

Jesus Christ died for sins once for all. He did not need to offer Himself more than once, since His death as the Holy One was fully sufficient to pay for the sins of any of us. Jesus obeyed His Father in every detail—in thought, word, and deed, He fully obeyed the Law of God. He walked in faith and dependence on His Father every day. He trusted His Father in all of life and gave the Father and every man what was due them. He was and is the Righteous One. Compared to Jesus, each of us is unjust and unrighteous. He died for us, the unjust, to bring us to God, that we might be reconciled—made right—with God. This means that regardless of the amount of sin or the depth of sin, the Just One has died for that sinner and his or her sin. Each of us can now be brought to God, knowing our sin has been fully taken care of.

"He Himself bore our sins in His body on the cross, that we might die to sin and live to righteousness. . . ."

I Peter 2:24

Spend some time in prayer with the Lord right now.

Lord, thank You for dying for me and for paying for my sins once and for all. Thank You that You gave Your life willingly and that part of the joy set before You was in calling me to come to You for forgiveness, cleansing, and new life. Thank You that The Way is now open for me to come with confidence into the Holy of Holies where I can fellowship with You, unhindered by the guilt of sin and blessed by the peace of Your forgiveness. I praise You that You have provided The Way to make things right with You and with others, that I can enjoy fellowship with You and with my brothers and sisters in the Body of Christ. Thank You that I can walk in harmony and peace with You and one another. Thank You for the joy of Your presence. In Jesus' name, Amen.

Write your personal letter of thanksgiving to Jesus for what He has done for you in His death and resurrection.

General Overview of the Tabernacle and Temple Offerings

Offering	Burnt Offering	Grain Offering	Drink Offering	Peace Offering	Sin Offering	Guilt Offering
	"Sweet Savor" Offerings				Offerings That Dealt with Sin	
Scripture	Leviticus 1:3–17 6:8–13; 8:18-21; 16:24	Leviticus 2; 6:14–23	Exodus 29:40–41 Numbers 15:1–10 Leviticus 23	Leviticus 3; 7:11–36	Leviticus 4:1—5:13; 6:24–30; 8:14–17; 16:3–22	Leviticus 5:14—6:7; 7:1–10
What Was Offered?	Bull, ram, lamb goat, turtledove, or pigeon according to what one was able to offer. All of the offering was burned except for the skin of the animal.	A memorial portion, a handful of flour or oven-baked, fried, or roasted grain mixed with oil and salt of the covenant. No leaven or honey. Each portion burned with a full measure of frankincense and a measure of wine.	A different measure of wine was offered for each of the offerings.	Fat and entrails of a ram, bull, lamb, or goat. The remainder of the grain offering that accompanied the peace offering were eaten by the worshiper and his family in a fellowship meal.	Bull (for priest or nation), male goat (for a leader), female goat or lamb (for any of the people), turtledove, or pigeon (for a very poor person). On the Day of Atonement, the sin offering consisted of a bull, a male goat, and a scapegoat.	The fat and entrails of a ram, male or female lamb, or goat, plus restitution and an added 20 percent to the offended party
When Was It Offered?	Twice daily, Sabbath, New Moon, and at all the Feasts	Twice daily, Sabbath, New Moon, and at all the Feasts	Twice daily, Sabbath, New Moon, and at all the Feasts	Feast of Weeks (Pentecost). Anytime as Thank Offering, Votive, (vow) offering or Freewill Offering of devotion.	New Moon and at all the Feasts. Sin offering was the special focus on the Day of Atonement.	Anytime there was an offense that required a guilt offering with its restitution.
Priest's Portion	All parts of animal burned except skin, which went to the priest	The remainder of flour and oil or remainder of cakes or grain.	Nothing	Breast and shoulder of the animal	Portion of certain offerings	Certain portions burned. Priest received remainder.
Offerer's Portion	Nothing	Nothing	Nothing	Remainder eaten by the offerer and family in a fellowship meal	Nothing	Nothing
Significance	A picture of surrender, one totally yielded to the Lord	A picture of dependence on the Lord for our daily sustenance	A picture of one pouring out himself to the Lord	A picture of fellowship with the Lord, having a common meal in the peace of reconciliation	A picture of a substitute, dying in our place for our sin	The restoration of one person to another as brothers and sisters. All offenses cleared.
Fulfillment in Jesus Christ	Jesus, the Lamb of God, totally yielded Himself to the Father as our sacrifice.	Jesus was the grain of wheat crushed and offered on the Cross.	Jesus poured Himself out in death.	Jesus is our Peace Offering, who made peace by the blood of His cross.	Jesus offered Himself once for all to take away sin.	Jesus offered Himself, paying our debt in full to restore us to God and to one another.

Notes

lesson 8

The Devotion of Surrender

Walking in the Joy of Surrender to Jesus Christ

When someone is devoted to another, he or she delights to please the other. Gifts are given, and love is expressed in many ways. When we look at our devotion to the Lord, it is the same. We delight to please Him, to express love to Him, and to give to Him. The greatest gift we can give is a surrendered heart, yielded to Him first for cleansing and forgiveness, then for a life of worship. A worshiping heart is a heart surrendered to what the Lord wants. That surrendered heart will reveal itself in outward acts of love and service, but the outward acts alone are not what the Lord is looking for, just as outward sacrifices and offerings were not the only things He desired in Tabernacle worship. What God longs to see day by day is the devotion of surrender, a heart that bows to Him and His ways. In the offerings of the Tabernacle and the Temple, God gave His people opportunities to show their submission and surrender.

True Worship

A SURRENDERED HEART

God is always looking at the heart. He rejoices over a heart that gladly receives His forgiveness and eternal life. He died to give us that life so that we would belong to Him and gratefully worship Him forever with a surrendered heart.

Some of the offerings closest to His heart were the burnt offerings, the grain and drink offerings, and the peace offerings. These were known as the "sweet savor" offerings, or the "soothing aroma" offerings. They speak of the joy He experienced and the joy of surrender and fellowship His people could experience with Him. We too can know that joy of surrender and a

The Offerings—Offered Year by Year

BURNT OFFERING	GRAIN/DRINK OFFERINGS	PEACE OFFERING	SIN OFFERING	GUILT OFFERING
Leviticus 1:13–17	Leviticus 2; 6:14–23; Numbers 15:1–10	Leviticus 3; 7:11–36	Leviticus 4:1—5:13	Leviticus 5:14—6:7; 7:1–10

Jesus Our High Priest—Offered Himself Once for All

BURNT OFFERING	GRAIN/DRINK OFFERINGS	PEACE OFFERING	SIN OFFERING	GUILT OFFERING
John 1:29; Ephesians 5:2; Hebrews 10:5–10	Isaiah 53:12; Matthew 26:26	Romans 5:1; Ephesians 2:14	Galatians 1:4; Hebrews 9:14, 26, 28; 10:5-10, 12, 17–18	Isaiah 53:4–11; 1 Peter 2:21–25

We Can Walk by Faith in Christ's Finished Work

We Can Walk Yielded as Christ Was in His Surrender to the Father.	We Can Walk Knowing Him as Our Sustenance and Provision.	We Can Walk In Satisfaction with Him Who Is Our Peace.	We Can Walk Forgiven Because Sin Was upon Him and Paid for by Him.	We Can Walk Restored as Sin-Damaged Relationships Are Restored by Him.

depth of fellowship with Him and with one another. As you search the Scriptures this week, listen to what the Lord says to you about surrender to Him and the joy and freedom He can bring.

Lesson Eight **DAY ONE**

The "Sweet Aroma" of The Burnt Offering

In Lesson 7, we introduced the six main offerings (sin, guilt, burnt, grain, and peace offerings, plus the drink offering) and looked specifically at the sin offering and the guilt offering (also known as the trespass offering). We also saw how the Lord Jesus is the fulfillment of the sin and the guilt offerings. This week we will look at the other offerings as they were observed in the Tabernacle. All of these teach us about who the Lord is and about His ways and His will. They also teach us about our hearts and how we can walk in right relationship and joyful fellowship with God.

📖 The burnt offering was one of the most significant offerings in the Old Testament. Read Leviticus 1:1–17. What were the first requirements for this offering as given in Leviticus 1:3? Who is the focus of this offering in that verse?

___

___

___

___

📖 Look at Leviticus 1:5, 10, 14, and list the different types of burnt offerings. Do you see any significance in the three different types of offerings? (Compare what is said in Leviticus 5:7 about the guilt offering.)

___

___

___

___

___

___

Wealth or poverty was neither a help nor a barrier in worshiping God; any person could offer a burnt offering.

The burnt offering was offered *"before the LORD."* The Lord was the focus of this offering. To be acceptable to the Lord, the burnt offering had to be a male animal without defect, just as we saw in the sin and guilt offerings. A person could offer **1)** a bull from the herd (1:3); **2)** a male sheep or goat (1:10); or **3)** a turtledove or young pigeon (1:14). The three types of offerings were different in cost and represented what one was able to give. Some could afford to give a bull, some a sheep or goat, and some only a small bird. Wealth or poverty was neither a help nor a barrier in worshiping God, for any person could offer a burnt offering. The Lord simply wanted a wholehearted sacrifice from each person regardless of his or her wealth or poverty.

📖 What procedures were required for each type of burnt offering according to Leviticus 1:3–9, 11–13, 14–17? Think through each step and list them.

The sacrifice was brought to the doorway of the tent of meeting. The man who offered it would lay his hand on the head of the sacrifice, which represents the giving of the burnt offering as a substitute for the individual, *"to make atonement on his behalf"* (1:4). The sacrifice was a picture of one's surrender to the Lord and always included the idea of atonement, which points to the need of sinful man to have his sin covered. After the man slew the animal, the priests offered up the blood and sprinkled it around the brazen altar. If the sacrifice was a sheep or goat, the man was to slay it on the north side of the altar. Then the priests sprinkled the blood around the altar. If the sacrifice was a bird, the priest was to slay the bird by wringing off its head and draining its blood on the side of the altar. The man skinned the animal and cut it into its proper pieces. After this step, Aaron's sons arranged the fire and placed the pieces of the sacrifice on the altar. The entrails and legs were washed with water and then placed on the altar. As a final step, all of the sacrifice except the skin was burned as "a soothing aroma to the Lord" (1:9, 13, 17).

Did You Know?

SACRIFICES AT THE TABERNACLE

The number of sacrifices offered yearly in the Tabernacle would include at least 113 bulls, 32 rams, 1,086 lambs, over 2,000 pounds of flour, and hundreds of gallons of wine. The activity at the Tabernacle altar was endless.

📖 Think about the focus of this offering and how the Lord viewed it. What do you find in Leviticus 1:2, 3, 5, 9, 11, 13, 14, 17 along with Numbers 28:2? What is the significance that all of the sacrifice was burned up? Notice what this offering is called in Leviticus 1:9, 13, 17.

This was a whole offering given solely to the Lord, burned completely before Him. It symbolized a whole-hearted surrender to the Lord. The phrases *"to the Lord"* and *"before the LORD"* are repeatedly used. In Numbers 28:2 the Lord points to the offering as *"My offering*[s]*"* and *"My food"* offered *"to Me."*

Leviticus 1:9, 13, and 17 show this offering was one of the "sweet savor" or "soothing aroma" offerings to the Lord, offerings that pleased Him.

What do you discover about the burnt offering in Exodus 29:38–46? When was it to be offered? What was always included with the burnt offering? What is the Lord's focus in verses 42–46?

____

____

____

____

____

____

____

____

____

The Lord desires a personal relationship and an ongoing fellowship with His children marked by His children's acknowledgment of sin and active surrender.

For the daily burnt offerings in the Tabernacle, the priests were to offer two one-year-old lambs, one in the morning and one at twilight. This daily offering was to be offered continuously throughout the generations of Israel. With it were offered a grain offering and a drink offering. The combination of these offerings were a sweet aroma to the Lord and serve as a picture of the people's relationship with the Lord. The Lord's focus in verses 42–46 was on that relationship, specifically on His dwelling with His people as their God, His speaking with them, fellowshipping with them, and guiding them. The burnt offering, with its blood poured out, always acknowledged sinful man's need for an atoning sacrifice, but it also spoke of the joyful expression of surrender to the Lord. He desires a personal relationship and ongoing fellowship with His children marked by His children's acknowledgment of sin and active surrender. One reason the burnt offering was continual is that it was a picture of God's continual love for us. God continually focuses His love, attention, and provision on His people and wants them to ever focus their love and surrender to Him.

Have you come to realize how much there is to see in the offerings of the Tabernacle? When Aaron and his sons began their ministry as priests, Leviticus 9 (verses 3, 7, 15 and 16) records the proper order (or sequence) for the burnt offering in relationship to the other offerings. This is significant in what it pictures. The sin offering was to come first, then the burnt offering. With the burnt offering there had to be a grain and a drink offering. A peace offering often followed the burnt, grain, and drink offerings. This occasional peace offering serves to remind us that we must deal with sin before we can offer ourselves to the Lord and experience fellowship with Him. The Lord does not want us simply to move the offense out of the way. He wants us to come to Him in surrender, to know and enjoy the relationship of surrender to Him. In the sin offering, the offerer focused mostly on God's holiness and recognized God as Sovereign Creator and Lord to whom one is accountable. In the burnt offering, the offerer focused on who God is in the fullness of His love, mercy, and kindness, as well as who God is in His purity and holiness. We will look at more aspects of the "sweet savor" offerings in Days Two and Three of this lesson.

THE "SWEET AROMA" OF THE GRAIN OFFERING AND THE DRINK OFFERING

Lesson Eight **DAY TWO**

With each burnt offering, the Lord required that a grain offering and a drink offering be made. Today we will carefully and extensively look at the grain offering and the drink offering. The Lord used both offerings in the Old Testament to teach some valuable lessons about Himself and His relationship to His people, and we find them pictured in the New Testament revealing even more about what it means to follow God.

Grain represented the basic daily sustenance of the people. The grain and drink offerings acknowledged the Lord as the provider of that sustenance.

📖 Describe the grain offering as given in Leviticus 2:1–7, 12, 14–16. List the five ways one could bring this offering.

____

____

____

____

____

The grain offering could be brought in one of five ways: **1)** as flour with oil and incense (2:2); **2)** as oven-baked cakes (2:4); **3)** as griddle-cooked cakes broken into bits (2:5–6); **4)** as pan-cooked cakes (2:7); or **5)** as first fruits of grain (fire-roasted) along with oil and incense (2:12, 14–16). The grain offering was an offering to the Lord. Using the first kind as an example, the offering of fine flour mixed with oil was brought to the priests. He offered a memorial portion, a handful of the flour with some oil and all of the frankincense that was brought. The remainder of the offering (flour and oil) went to the priests as a holy offering for their use.

📖 There are some significant regulations about the grain offering given in Leviticus 2:11, 13. What do you find there?

____

____

____

____

____

No leaven could be offered in any of the grain or baked cakes. No honey was to be offered up in or with the offering. Every grain offering was to be seasoned with salt, *"the salt of the covenant"* (v. 13). One significant aspect about both the leaven and the honey is found in the fact that each can be an object of corruption. Yeast is associated with corruption and fermentation. It has been known to cause dough to sour. Honey is also capable of fermenting and is a potential corrupting influence. The Lord wanted no evidence of corruption in this offering. Salt, on the other hand, is known for its preserving, purifying, and non-corrupting influence. The concept of salt's incorruptibility carries with it the idea of continual faithfulness because it does not decay.

Perhaps that is why salt is called *"the salt of the covenant"* in verse 13. The essential idea of a covenant is faithfulness, loyalty, and consistency with no corruption or deceit of the flesh. The grain offering was a picture of daily sustenance, of God's day-by-day faithfulness, and of the promise of day-by-day faithfulness on the part of His people.

The drink offering or *"libation"* is described in Numbers 15:1–10. The specifics of this offering can be summed up as follows: For each burnt offering, vow offering, freewill offering, or peace offering there was to be a grain offering and a drink offering. For a lamb, this "libation" was to be one fourth of a "hin" (about one quart) of wine; one third of a hin (about one and a half quarts) for a ram; one half of a hin (about two quarts) for a bull. Think of this offering being totally poured out on one of these sacrifices. Picture the smoke ascending from the altar. What insights do you see? What is the result in verses 7 and 10?

True Worship

THE DRINK OFFERING

The drink offering was poured around the sacrifice as it was burning on the altar. The sacrifice was completely surrounded, enveloped by the vapors of the drink offering—a beautiful picture of pouring our lives unto the Lord in complete surrender.

The drink offering, or libation, was *"a sweet savor"* or *"a soothing aroma to the LORD."* This offering was totally consumed in the fires of the altar. It was poured on the altar and served to enhance the sacrifice that was already present. In this offering, as in all the other offerings, we see the Lord pleased with obedience to His will. In the drink offering, we see a picture of the heart that is willing to pour itself out to Him, in surrender, in dependence, in love, and in service.

Remembering that the drink offering enhanced the sacrifice given, look at Philippians 2:12–18 (especially verse 17). What insights do you glean from Paul's statement?

The drink offering poured out made the sacrifice a richer offering, a more fragrant aroma to the Lord. In Philippians 2, Paul is content to see himself as a drink offering—poured out before the Lord. Here is a man surrendered to the Lord, seeking to be and do all God wants, desiring for the Philippians to be all God wants them to be. If his life and service on their behalf were a simple drink offering poured out, he was confident it would enhance the offering of their lives, the offering growing out of their faith. With that, he could rejoice knowing the Lord was pleased. Paul urged the Philippians to rejoice in like manner.

Philippians 2 is a chapter about unselfish living, about giving away one's life with a servant's attitude. Paul knew and rejoiced that Christ had poured out Himself in obedience to the Father (Philippians 2:5–11). He also rejoiced in the service of his fellow workers, Timothy and Epaphroditus (Philippians 2:19–30).

APPLY Is your life a drink offering in some way? Are you willingly serving to enhance the faith walk of others? Are you encouraging someone in his or her life and service?

THE "SWEET AROMA" OF THE PEACE OFFERING

Today we will look more at the **peace offering** or the fellowship offering. The procedures in Leviticus 3 for the peace offering were similar to those of the burnt offering in that the offerer placed his hands on the head of the offering, identifying with the sacrifice. Then the animal was slain, and the blood was sprinkled on the altar. After that, the similarities between the peace offering and other offerings cease. What is different about the peace offering? What is its significance?

Read Leviticus 3:3–5, 9–11, 12–17. What was offered to the Lord?

The peace offering could be a male or female from the herd, from the flock of sheep, or from the goats. Unlike the burnt offering, the sacrifice of the peace offering was not wholly consumed on the altar. Only certain portions were burnt. Leviticus 3 specifies that the fat and certain entrails were to be offered on the altar. Yet no fat, nor entrails, nor any blood was to be eaten by the priests or by the people.

What additional regulations are found in Leviticus 7:11–18?

With the peace offering, a person was to offer three types of grain offering mixed with oil (unleavened cakes, unleavened wafers, and cakes of fine flour). In addition, he was to offer leavened bread. The offerer gave the priest one of each of these for his use. After the priest offered certain portions of the sacrifice on the altar, the offerer (and his family) ate the remainder of the sacrifice. For a votive or freewill offering, some could be eaten the next day, but none could be eaten on the third day. On the third day, all remnants of the offering were to be burned with fire.

In Leviticus 7:11–12, 15–16 the peace offerings or fellowship offerings could be one of three kinds of offering: **1)** a thanksgiving offering to express thanks to God for some blessing or deliverance of some sort; **2)** a votive offering (offering in fulfillment of a vow); or **3)** a freewill offering as an expression of worship, devotion, and fellowship. Think about each of these offerings and what significance each had. Write your insights.

Each offering served a specific purpose in expressing one's heart to the Lord. Each offering served to honor and acknowledge the Lord as the provider of all blessings and also served as a celebration meal in His presence. The thanksgiving offering emphasized some gift or provision God had given, and it allowed an offerer to express his heart of thanks. The votive offering emphasized the fulfillment of a vow and thus some aspect of one's faithfulness to the Lord and the Lord's faithfulness to the worshiper. The freewill offering emphasized one's devotion to the Lord and pointed to His graciousness. It was an opportunity to express worship.

APPLY Think of a family coming to the Tabernacle to offer a peace or fellowship offering, knowing this was a special meal in the presence of the Lord. What do you think their attitude would be? What would go through their minds as they approached the Tabernacle? What would you think if you were about to eat a meal in the presence of the Lord?

". . . you shall eat . . . before the Lord your God in the place which the LORD your God will choose . . . and you shall rejoice before the LORD. . . ."

Deuteronomy 12:18

In the peace offering and the meal that followed, the Lord was the host in a sense—with the priest acting as His representative. This was a time of great fellowship following the sin offering and the burnt offering. All sin and guilt had been dealt with. Relationships had been made right. This was a time for offerers to fellowship in the presence of the Lord, knowing His forgiveness and enjoying that peace with Him. It was truly a time for the people to celebrate with their Lord.

📖 Jesus is the fulfillment of the peace offering. Think of all the peace offering means to you as you picture a family enjoying their meal together in the presence of the Lord. Now read Ephesians 2:11–18 and summarize what you find about the peace Jesus brings and what it means.

____

____

____

God sent Jesus to shed His blood to pay for the sins of Jews and Gentiles. When He died and rose again, He made peace between God and man and made peace possible between Jew and Gentile. He did that by breaking down all the barriers between man and God, especially the Law of commandments that judged man for his sin, his coming short of the standards of God. Christ fulfilled that Law and paid the sin debt for all who could not fulfill it (none but Christ could fulfill it as God wanted and required). We can know peace with God and peace with one another, and in that peace we can all draw near to the Father. He enables us to walk in oneness with the Father as He desires and as the peace offering portrays. Just as the peace offering was continually offered, God wants us to enjoy a continual fellowship with Him.

APPLY Two questions: First, do you have peace **with God** (Romans 5:1–2)? In other words, have you placed your faith in Christ so that you can receive the forgiveness of your sins and new life in Him? Second, do you have the peace **of God**? (John 14:27; Philippians 4:6–7; Colossians 3:15) Is God's peace ruling in your heart, or are you filled with anxiety and worry over something?

Jesus, Our "Sweet Aroma" Offering

When Jesus walked on this earth, He perfectly understood the various offerings we find described in the Word of God. What He taught and did about those offerings is vitally important for us to understand if we are to follow Him day by day. The Lord Jesus told His hearers in Matthew 5:17: *"Do not think that I came to destroy the Law or the Prophets. I did not come to destroy but to fulfill"* (NKJV). He fulfilled the Law and the message of the Prophets in the way He lived, in all that He said, and finally in His death and resurrection. He also became the fulfillment of all the Old Testament offerings. Jesus understood and fulfilled them perfectly. Today we will see how Jesus fulfilled the Law, the Prophets, and all offerings and what that fulfillment means to us.

"Do not think that I came to destroy the Law or the Prophets. I did not come to destroy but to fulfill."
Matthew 5:17(NKJV)

Though Jesus fully understood everything that was written in the Old Testament, what was most important to Him? One incident in His life reveals much. He had an encounter with a scribe, one who was well versed in all the Law of Moses and the prophets, including all the sacrifices and offerings. That encounter gives us some wonderful insights into the heart of those offerings and into the heart of the offerers.

📖 Read Mark 12:28–34 and record what you find.

____

____

____

____

A certain scribe asked Jesus what was the most important commandment, and Jesus responded that the commandment to love God with all heart, soul, mind, and strength was indeed the greatest commandment (see Deuteronomy 6:4–5). The scribe agreed with Jesus and then added that this commandment was even more important than all the burnt offerings and sacrifices. Jesus saw the wisdom in the scribe's answer and declared that this man was not far from the kingdom of God. Jesus pointed out that loving God and one's neighbor is at the heart of the kingdom, far more than any number of outward temple offerings and sacrifices.

Jesus knew the Law and the prophets and often quoted them. He quoted at least twice from the prophet Hosea. What insights do you find from the writings of the prophet Hosea in Hosea 6:6?

____

____

____

____

KING DAVID ON THE OFFERINGS

King David spoke about the offerings—*"For You do not desire sacrifice, or else I would give it; You do not delight in burnt offering. The sacrifices of God are a broken spirit, A broken and a contrite heart—These, O God, You will not despise."* (Psalm 51:16–17 [NKJV])

God sent Hosea to a people who were fulfilling the sacrifices at the Temple but not faithfully following the Lord. To them the Lord declared what was most important to Him. More than legal fulfillment of the sacrifices, He wanted people with hearts like His, hearts of mercy (acting right toward others). The word "mercy" is a translation of the Hebrew word *hesed,* which

Extra Mile

WHAT GOD DESIRES

Read Matthew 9:10–13, where Jesus quotes Hosea 6:6. Find the main points on which He focused.

refers to covenant faithfulness or loyalty shown to others or to the Lord. The people of Hosea's day were neither faithful to the Lord nor faithful to His commands. In addition, the Lord instructed them in the importance of knowing Him, interacting with Him, and walking in obedience to Him. He wanted people to follow Him from the heart. He wanted them to obey His Law because the Law reflected His heart, His holiness, His forgiveness, and the opportunity to receive mercy from Him as well as show mercy to others. Granting mercy was of a higher priority than any number of ritualistic burnt offerings.

When Jesus quoted Hosea 6:6, He revealed the heart of God. Read Matthew 12:1–8 and record what you find. What is more important to Him—showing compassion or offering sacrifices? What insights do you gain about the offerings?

Jesus and His disciples walked through the grain fields on the Sabbath and picked some of the grain to eat. This was considered by the Pharisees as "work" and violated their interpretation of the law that said no work was to be performed on the Sabbath. Jesus rebuked their understanding of the Sabbath law. Jesus explained that David and his men ate the *"consecrated bread"* (showbread) in the *"house of God"* during a time of great need, yet the Lord did not rebuke them. Instead, He showed mercy and kindness to them (see 1 Samuel 21:1-6). The Sabbath was given for the benefit of man, not for the sake of religious regulations. When Jesus and His disciples were hungry and picked grain, they were not guilty of any violation. In addition, the priests worked on the Sabbath in the Temple in fulfillment of God's will. The Pharisees also failed to consider that Jesus Himself was Lord of the Sabbath, God in their midst. He lived among them and was far greater than the Temple where God had only occasionally revealed Himself. Of even greater significance is the fact that the One who is greater than the Temple would also be greater than all the sacrifices and offerings brought to the Temple. Quoting Hosea 6:6, Jesus pointed the Pharisees back to the real significance of the Law and the offerings; He wanted a people marked by mercy and faithfulness to Him, not empty ritual and merciless regulations.

Jesus said, ". . . I lay down My life that I may take it again. No one takes it from Me, but I lay it down of Myself. I have power to lay it down, and I have power to take it again. This command I have received from My Father."

John 10:17b–18 **NKJV**

Though the offerings provided temporary atonement for sins, Jesus knew that they were also pictures or signs that pointed to the reality found in Him. He came to fulfill **all** the offerings.

Read Hebrews 10:1–10, then summarize what is written there.

The Law provided for sacrifices that could not permanently take sin away. The Law served as a temporary provision until the perfect sacrifice came. *"Bulls and goats"* mentioned in Hebrews 10:4 refer primarily to the animals slain as the sin offerings on the Day of Atonement. Those sacrifices reminded men of their sin year after year. When the Lord Jesus came, He knew that sacrifices for sin and burnt offerings were not ultimately what the Father wanted. He wanted a perfect sacrifice, and that sacrifice was found in the God-Man Jesus Christ, God in human flesh. He came to do the will of the Father, to die as the sacrifice for sin *"through the offering of the body of Jesus Christ once for all"* (10:10) .

📖 Read Ephesians 5:1–2 and record your insights about what Christ did and why He did this. What does Paul call this act? What does this show about Jesus' fulfillment of the offerings?

____

____

____

____

Word Study
SURRENDER

Ephesians 5:2 says Jesus *"gave Himself up."* The Greek word used for this phrase, *paradidomi* carries the idea of "giving over to" or "surrender to" (with a specific purpose in mind). Jesus gave Himself up as a sacrifice and offering to bring salvation to us.

Christ gave Himself up **for** us on the cross as an offering and a sacrifice **to** God. He did that because of His love for each of us and because of His surrender to His Father. True love gives sacrificially. What Jesus did was both an offering and a sacrifice. As the grain and wine were offerings, Christ was an offering to God. Jesus was also a sacrifice, slain and placed on the altar—the cross. He died in giving Himself. This act of sacrifice was as a *"sweet-smelling savor,"* (KJV) a *"sweet-smelling aroma,"* (NKJV), or a *"fragrant aroma"* (NASB) acceptable to the Father (Ephesians 5:2). Through sacrificing His life, Jesus showed His love and fulfilled all the "sweet savor" offerings—the burnt offering, the grain offering, the drink offering, and the peace offering—and became a complete and perfect offering and sacrifice that was well pleasing to the Father.

For Me to Worship God

Lesson Eight **DAY FIVE**

We have seen that Jesus Christ is the fulfillment of all the sacrifices and offerings. He truly came to fulfill **all** the Law and the Prophets (Matthew 5:17). His precious blood was shed to pay for our sin, to buy us out of its slavery, and to bring us into oneness and fellowship with the Father. What an awesome salvation He has purchased and given to us. How should we live and worship in light of that? What do the Scriptures say? Today we will look at how we are to worship Him in light of the mercy He has shown us.

Jesus Christ is the fulfillment of all the sacrifices and offerings. He truly came to fulfill all the Law and the prophets.

📖 What does Romans 12:1–2 show us about how we are to live before the Lord? Read those verses and record your insights about worship and about our offerings.

____

____

____

After revealing the mercies of God in Romans 1–11, Paul gives the Lord's call to present ourselves to Him as a living sacrifice—always yielded and available every day. He wants us to be a holy sacrifice, set apart to Him and for Him. This is an acceptable or well-pleasing sacrifice to Him. It is true

"Grace to you and peace from God our Father, and the Lord Jesus Christ, who gave Himself for our sins, that He might deliver us out of this present evil age, according to the will of our God and Father, . . ."

Galatians 1:3–4

worship, continuous worship. With this attitude and this action, He commands us to be transformed in our thinking, no longer surrendering to the thinking of the world system in this evil age. As we are transformed by the renewing of our surrendered hearts and minds, we will know and experience the full range of His will. We will experience how good and beneficial His will is for us and for others. We will see how well pleasing His will is and how it brings us to the goal God has for us—to know and experience Him and to make Him known to others.

📖 In light of what Christ did for us, what is Paul's call to believers in Ephesians 5:1–2? (In answering this, you may want to look at how Jesus walked in John 5:19; 8:28–29.)

____

____

____

____

As the very deeply-loved children of God, we are to be imitators, or "mimics," of God. Just as God the Father loved us and as Jesus Christ walked in the Father's love and gave his life for us, so we are to walk daily in love, giving ourselves for the benefit of others. This is as if we were offering a "sweet aroma" to the Lord—not a perfect sacrifice like Christ offered when He took away our sins, but rather an example of Christ's surrender. He yielded Himself day after day, always doing the things that pleased His Father. In daily surrender and dependence, Jesus' actions and words were those that were guided by His Father. We too must daily surrender our lives to the Father, trusting His Spirit within to empower us and give us wisdom in the things we say and do. As the Holy Spirit enables us, we can love as God loves, revealing the presence and the fruit of His Spirit in our lives.

The Lord wanted the offerings of the Old Testament to come from hearts that loved Him. The offerings were part of the devotion of surrender to Him. They were part of showing love to Him. God's desire to be loved did not end with the arrival of the New Covenant. There are "offerings" the Lord wants from us even today.

📖 Read the following verses and note what kind of "offering" you find in each reference.

Matthew 15:32–36

____

____

Acts 27:33–35

____

____

1 Timothy 4:4–5

____

____

Hebrews 13:15–16

The Lord desires a continual sacrifice of praise, praising Him for who He is and thanking Him for all He has done.

In Matthew 15 Jesus saw the physical needs of the people and offered thanks to the Father for His provision of that need. In Acts 27, Paul was in the middle of a storm, the fourteenth day of being battered by a "Northeaster" in the Mediterranean Sea. Even in that circumstance, He was quick to give thanks for the food in the presence of all the people and then gratefully partook of that food. Paul wrote to Timothy that everything created by God should be received with gratitude. That includes offering a prayer of thanksgiving from a heart of thanksgiving. With our access to God through Jesus, the Lord desires a continual sacrifice of praise, praising Him for who He is and thanking Him for all He has done, for all He is doing now, and for all He has promised to do. In addition, He wants us to do good for others, sharing our lives with them and giving to them as needs arise.

We have seen in Lessons Seven and Eight that the offerings in the Tabernacle were of great importance to God and to the people. They were a daily reminder to the people of their covenant relationship with God. As we think back over the offerings—burnt, grain, drink, peace, sin, and guilt offerings—it is vital to think of the significance of each of these for the people as they worshiped God. It is also vital for us to think of these offerings as we apply them in our daily walk and worship.

APPLY Read the summary statements below. What might God be saying to you?

1) Worship cannot be separated from sacrifice and surrender.
2) God is only interested in acceptable sacrifices.
3) God must always remain the focus of our worship. We must guard ourselves from the temptation to worship the things of earth, the approval of man, or the temporary pleasures of the flesh
4) We must realize the depth and the debt of our sin and the holy price God paid to atone for that sin—the very life and blood of His Son, the Lord Jesus.
5) God is pleased when we agree with Him about our sin, about His remedy for our sin, and about our walk of fellowship with Him.
6) God wants us to be a people . . .
   - who acknowledge our sin and trust the provision of His Son as our sin and our guilt offerings
   - surrendered as a burnt offering
   - broken and yielded as a grain offering
   - poured out to Him as a drink offering
   - who fellowship with Him as the Israelites did in the peace offering:
     - ✓ with a heart of thanksgiving to Him,
     - ✓ with a walk of faithfulness to Him,
     - ✓ with a moment-by-moment, willing surrender to His will.

Extra Mile

OUR OFFERINGS

Look at the offerings mentioned in Romans 15:16 and Philippians 4:18 and record your insights.

The offerings point us to Jesus Christ. When we have our sin forgiven through Christ and our hearts yielded to Him, we can enjoy a walk of fellowship with Him and with one another. We can also reach out to bring others to know Him in that forgiveness and fellowship.

APPLY After reading the statements given above, write your application points in the space below.

____

____

____

____

____

Every offering points us to Jesus Christ.

Lord, I Thank You that You surrendered all of Your life to the Father and were willing to be that "sweet aroma" offering. In offering Yourself willingly for me, You showed the depth of Your love and mercy. Thank You for calling me to come to You, to admit my sin, and to surrender my life to You. Thank You for forgiving and cleansing me and for the presence of Your Spirit in my life. May I come to know and understand the full meaning of surrender to You more and more each day. Thank You for the fellowship I can enjoy with You and for the peace You give, even in the difficult days. May my life be more and more a well-pleasing sacrifice as I die to my self and my selfish ways and allow You to fill me, guide me, and empower me to do Your will. I love You, Lord. In Jesus' name. Amen.

Write your own prayer to the Lord or make a journal entry in your walk with Him.

____

____

____

____

____

____

____

____

____

____

Notes

Notes

lesson 9

Positioning for Worship

God's Order for Transporting and Positioning the Tabernacle

God is a God of order and purpose. Everything He does is significant. Nothing is random or meaningless. So far, we have studied the Tabernacle from the standpoint of why it was needed; we have studied its construction, its furniture and coverings, and we have looked at the many pictures of the Lord Jesus in this beautiful building. We have looked at the priesthood that ministered there and the significance of the offerings. However, there is still more to be seen. There is truth to be gleaned from the order He gave to the positioning of the Tabernacle. The positioning of the camp was always to be the same, with the Tabernacle in the same place as well. Each time it was erected, it was to face the same way. Each time the pieces were positioned the same within the fence. There was even a prescribed order to how the Tabernacle was to be carried as it was moved. The thought of transporting the Tabernacle seems like a simple concept, yet it is very profound, for the positioning of the Tabernacle relates directly to the positioning of ourselves in worship.

The positioning of the camp and Tabernacle was always to be the same.

Lesson Nine **DAY ONE**

THE TABERNACLE'S POSITION IN THE CAMP

The nation of Israel lived as nomads during the first forty years of their liberation from Egypt. Wherever they were, the Tabernacle always sat in the same place. It was attended to by the very presence of God, manifested in a pillar of cloud by day and a pillar of fire by night. It was an uncertain existence, for the Israelites never knew when the pillar would move and indicate when it was time to pack up and follow. Neither did they know where the pillar would stop once they began moving. Yet in the midst of such disorder and chaos, theirs was an orderly existence. Every time they broke camp, the same pattern was followed. Wherever they moved, the progression followed the same order. And each time they settled, the structure was to be the same. Every morning when they awoke, the landscape might be different, but as they looked from their tent, the Tabernacle would be sitting in the same position and facing the same direction. They were learning to follow God moment by moment, and they were learning to keep Him at the very center of their lives.

Did You Know?

THE TWELVE TRIBES

The twelve tribes of Israel were twelve divisions of the nation who were direct descendants of the twelve sons of Jacob, whom the Lord renamed "Israel." At first, the actual sons served as representatives of their extended families, but after their deaths, a patriarch was appointed to represent each tribe.

📖 Read through Numbers 2:1–16 and using the diagram and space below, fill in how the Tabernacle was positioned in relation to the rest of the camp. You will want to place each tribe in the order you think they might have camped, along with that tribe's population. Also, take time to add up the total numbers for each direction of the Tabernacle.

NORTH

	Tribes	*Population*
1.	______________	______________
2.	______________	______________
3.	______________	______________
4.	______________	______________
	TOTAL	______________

SOUTH

	Tribes	*Population*
1.	______________	______________
2.	______________	______________
3.	______________	______________
4.	______________	______________
	TOTAL	______________

EAST

	Tribes	*Population*
1.	______________	______________
2.	______________	______________
3.	______________	______________
4.	______________	______________
	TOTAL	______________

WEST

	Tribes	*Population*
1.	______________	______________
2.	______________	______________
3.	______________	______________
4.	______________	______________
	TOTAL	______________

The positioning diagram below is not inspired. Scripture does not tell us exactly how the tribes were positioned, but when factored with the rectangular shape of the Tabernacle, the numbers suggest the possibility that the camp took the shape of a cross. The population figures listed are of all the males who could participate in battle (excluding the Levites). These numbers suggest that the population of the nation as a whole was between two and three million at this time.

^^
^^^
^^^ Manasseh (32,200)
^^^ Ephraim (40,500)
^^^ Benjamin (35,400)
^^^ Levites (Gershonites) (7,500)
^^^ TOTAL = 115,600
^^^

Simeon (59,300) Reuben (46,500) ^^^^^^^^^^^^^^^^ ^^^^^^^^^^^^^^^^ Gad (45,650) Levites (Kohathites) (8,600) TOTAL = 160,050	Tabernacle Fence and Outer Court	Asher (41,500) Dan (62,700) ^^^^^^^^^^^^^^^^^ ^^^^^^^^^^^^^^^^ Naphtali (53,400) Levites (Merarites)(6200) TOTAL = 163,800

^^^
^^^
^^^
^^^
^^^ Issachar (54,400)^^^ Judah (74,600)
^^^ Zebulon (57,400)
^^^ Moses, Aaron, Priests (?)
^^^ TOTAL = 186,400
^^^
^^^
^^^
^

* LEGEND: each tent symbol (^) = 5,000 people

Did You Know?

EPHRAIM AND MANASSEH

The tribes of Manasseh and Ephraim were actually sub-tribes that later became recognized as full tribes. Manasseh and Ephraim were the two sons of Joseph, and Joseph's tribe was divided between them. Later in Scripture, we see these two referred to as full tribes among the list of twelve, and for uncertain reasons, the tribe of Dan is omitted (see Revelation 7:4–8).

Although the Tabernacle moved often during its nearly five hundred years of use, one thing remained constant. It was always at the very center of the camp and the nation.

APPLY What does the Tabernacle's position in relation to the rest of the camp speak to you about your own worship of God?

____

____

____

____

____

____

The important point here is not just the obvious one that God is to be at the center of our worship. For most people that would only be relevant when they went to church. The greater reality is that for Israel, God was at the center of their lives seven days a week. Anything less than full devotion to the Lord is not true worship, for true worship is how we live, not just how we do church.

What a joy it is to move when God moves and to stay when God wishes to stay!

According to C. W. Slemming in his book, *Made According to Pattern,* the significance and beauty of the Tabernacle's position in the center of the camp is more clearly understood when we look at the cultural context in which the Tabernacle existed. Tabernacle worship was instituted during a time when nomadic Bedouin tribes journeyed about the desert. Every tribe or company had its sheik or chieftain. As a tribe would travel, the sheik would lead the way on his camel or Arabian steed, and in his hand would be his spear—some fifteen to twenty feet in length. When the chieftain wanted to settle his camp for a while, he would just plant his spear into the ground. That was the sign of rest. His servants would immediately erect their master's tent behind the spear and then pitch their own tents around his. The sheik then dwelt in the midst of his people. When he desired to move on, he removed his spear and rode forth.

Do you see the parallels between the nomadic tribes and the Hebrew children? Here we have two to three million people wandering through the wilderness. Their "chieftain" is Jehovah God, whose "spear" is a pillar of cloud and fire. When the pillar moves, they move—when it stays, they stay. His servants, the Levites, pitch their Master's tent (the Tabernacle) and the hosts encamp around Him. What a joy it is to move when God moves and to stay when God wishes to stay! This type of obedience and attentiveness to the Lord's leading is at the heart of living in the center of His will and having Him as the center of our lives.

Lesson Nine DAY TWO

THE TABERNACLE'S COMPASS POSITION

Every time the Tabernacle was erected, it was to be placed with the gate facing the same direction geographically. While Moses probably didn't have an actual compass to determine the position, it would have been a simple task. All he had to do to was identify sunrise (east) and/or sunset (west). There is a spiritual significance to the way the Tabernacle was to face.

📖 Take a moment to read through Exodus 26:18–22. Which direction did the entrance to the Tabernacle always face?

God is, and always has been, the God of order. Every time the Tabernacle was erected, it was with the gate facing east. This emphasis of the compass is not mere coincidence. Take some time to review your notes from Lesson Three (p. 39) on the positioning of the gate facing east, and transfer your significant observations in the space provided below.

Remember that the Tabernacle was a portable building that was moved many times during its 470–year history. Yet God was very specific in His instructions on how the Tabernacle should be moved. Every time the Tabernacle was reassembled, the gate was to be placed toward the east. This meant that the way to approach God was to enter at the east and go west. There is a reason behind this, and we may not fully be able to understand all that God is saying through this, but let's look at the pattern Scripture presents us.

📖 Look at the passages below, and answer the questions that accompany them.

Where was the entrance to the Garden of Eden? (Genesis 3:24)

What direction did Adam and Eve take to go away from Eden, the picture of the presence of God?

What direction did Cain go when he separated from the people of God? (Genesis 4:16)

Where did Ishmael settle in relation to Isaac, the son of promise and father of Israel? (Genesis 16:12)

Did You Know?

NOMADIC CULTURE

It was a fundamental principle of the Bedouin culture that no enemy would be allowed to touch anyone who had been invited by a sheik into his tent. The Bedouin culture placed great value on showing hospitality to guests. A tent for a guest was supposed to be a place of safety and protection.

When Solomon's heart turned away from God, which direction did he go to erect a place to worship other gods? (1 Kings 11:7)

____

Look at Isaiah 2:6, and write what this verse implies about the *"influences from the east."*

____

____

Look at Matthew 2:1–2. Which direction did the Magi travel to see Jesus?

____

It is amazing, when we begin to look at the scriptural significance of going east or west, how many examples there are. With the Tabernacle erected with its gate facing east, that meant to move toward God was to go west and to move away from Him was to go east. The entrance to the Garden of Eden faced eastward (Genesis 3:24), and when Adam and Eve left the garden, they apparently traveled east. Likewise, when Cain separated from the people of God, he went east (Genesis 4:16). In the same way, Ishmael settled east in relation to Isaac, the son of promise and father of Israel (Genesis 16:12). When Solomon's heart turned away from God, he went east to erect a place to worship other gods (1 Kings 11:7). In Isaiah 2:6 we see implied that obviously these *"influences from the east"* were directly opposed to God and His sovereign will. In Matthew 2:1–2, magi from the east traveled west to see the infant Jesus. Virtually every time Scripture speaks of the east, it is in a negative sense. The "east wind" was an ill wind of bad tidings. (If you have time, look up in a concordance all the occurrences of the words "east wind.") It would seem clear that "east" is a type of evil.

We probably do not know all the reasons for God's placing the gate where He did. Yet we do see that, throughout Scripture, heading east is a picture of moving away from God and going west is a picture of pursuing God.

Lesson Nine **DAY THREE**

The Positioning of the Tabernacle's Contents

You have invested a great deal of time studying the Tabernacle, and by now, it should be quite a familiar subject to you. However, our goal in this study is not simply that you understand the facts and figures of the Tabernacle. Our hope is that, through your studies and analysis of the Tabernacle, you have now been moved ahead in your ability to worship God in His way. What we want to focus on today is a review of the components of the Tabernacle from the order in which the high priest approached them. Remember, the path of the priest is not random. It is a reflection of God's order for worship. In the blank lines designated for each tabernacle component below, see if you can jot down applications to your own worship of the Lord. If necessary you can look back over your notes, but write as much as you can from memory.

THE GATE:

The Gate is the **place of entry.** The one entrance pictures the reality that there is no other way to God than through Jesus. To worship Him we must know Him.

THE BRONZE ALTAR:

The Bronze Altar is the **place of reconciling.** It was a place of death where sin could be dealt with. The Altar of the Old Testament is the cross of the New Testament. It is not those in rebellion to God who can worship, but those who have been reconciled. This pictures not only salvation, but the ongoing process of dealing with sin.

THE LAVER:

The Laver is the **place of cleansing.** It speaks of the sanctification which comes from the *"washing of water with the Word"* (Ephesians 5:26). The Word of God is central to the worship of God, for *"God is spirit, and those who worship Him must worship in spirit and truth"* (John 4:24).

THE GOLDEN LAMPSTAND:

The Lampstand is the **place of light.** It speaks of the light of God's leading. To worship God, we must have a lifestyle of seeking and doing the will of God as He leads.

True Worship

TABERNACLE COMPONENTS

- The Gate is the **place of entry.**
- The Bronze Altar is the **place of reconciling**
- The Laver is the **place of cleansing.**
- The Lampstand is the **place of light.**
- The Table is the **place of dining.**
- The Altar of Incense is the **place of prayer.**
- The Ark is the **place of fellowship.**

THE TABLE OF SHOWBREAD:

____

____

____

____

There is no real worship without two-way communication between the Lord and us.

The Table is the **place of dining.** It speaks of finding our sustenance in the Lord and being satisfied with Him. To worship God, we must be seeking Him. If He is what we pursue, then we will always be satisfied, but if something else is our priority, we will always be frustrated.

THE ALTAR OF INCENSE:

____

____

____

____

The Altar of Incense is the **place of prayer.** It speaks of to role of true prayer in worship. There is no real worship without two-way communication between the Lord and us.

THE ARK AND MERCY SEAT:

____

____

____

____

The Ark is the **place of fellowship.** It is the throne of God sitting in the presence of God. Once we have faithfully followed the path of the priest, we are able to bask in the reality of God's presence and worship in the deepest way.

Lesson Nine DAY FOUR

THE TABERNACLE'S POSITIONING AS IT WAS CARRIED

There is one final area to consider in the Tabernacle's positioning. So far we have studied aspects of a stationary Tabernacle. We have seen where it was placed in the camp and the direction it faced according to the compass. We have seen how its contents were to be positioned. Today, we will consider God's order for the movement of the twelve tribes and God's order for transporting the Tabernacle and all its components. The pillar of cloud and the pillar of fire led the Israelites on their journeys.

It must have been an awesome sight to see the pillar of cloud or fire. And what a blessing too! In the cold and darkness of night, there was a warming pillar of fire. In the heat of day there was a refreshing cloud of shade.

📖 Read Numbers 9:15–23, and write your reflections about the pillar.

____

____

____

____

The list below shows the "marching orders" for people and Tabernacle items as related in Numbers 10:11–28.

THE PILLAR OF CLOUD AND PILLAR OF FIRE

JUDAH
ISSACHAR
ZEBULUN

LEVITES (GERSHONITES) WITH 2 WAGONS CARRYING THE FOLLOWING TABERNACLE ITEMS:
CURTAINS, COVERINGS, HANGINGS, GATE, AND **DOOR**

LEVITES (MERARITES) WITH 4 WAGONS CARRYING THE FOLLOWING TABERNACLE ITEMS:
BARS, BOARDS, PILLARS, SOCKETS, PINS, AND **CORDS**

REUBEN
SIMEON
GAD

LEVITES (KOHATHITES) CARRYING THE FOLLOWING TABERNACLE ITEMS:
THE ARK OF THE COVENANT, TABLE OF SHOWBREAD, LAMPSTAND, ALTAR OF INCENSE, BRONZE ALTAR, AND **BRONZE LAVER**

EPHRAIM
MANASSEH
BENJAMIN
DAN
ASHER
NAPHTALI

An application we can draw from the pillar of cloud and pillar of fire is that God is always giving us direction, even if we are not following it.

Obviously, the pillar speaks of God as pre-eminent, leading the way out in front. A key thing to notice is the repeated phrase *"the command of the Lord"* (literally, "by the mouth of Yahweh"). The lesson here is that God is in charge and always should be. Another application we can draw from the pillar is that God is always giving us direction, even if we are not following it.

As you look at the order of wilderness travel, immediately behind the pillar was the tribe of Judah. Why do you think they were first in line?

____

____

____

____

____

An obvious possibility is the fact that Jesus was from the tribe of Judah. Perhaps not so obvious is that Judah means "praise" or "the praise of Jehovah." God always puts praise first, and praise holds a prominent place in worship.

In the order for travel, there were six tribes followed by the ark and then the other six tribes. What significance do you see in the placement of the ark?

____

____

____

The ark, which was the throne of God, speaks again of the centrality of God. No matter where Israel was, stationary or moving, God was always in the center. The ark also speaks of God's dwelling in their midst. Although God led the way in front, He also retained His rightful place in the middle of the tribes.

Lesson Nine **DAY FIVE**

For Me to Worship God

As you can see, we are beginning to take the pieces we have pulled apart to study and are now putting them back together again. We want to make certain that we keep the main truths in view. We have followed the path of the priest. We have gone from outside the gate, past the brazen altar and the laver, into the Holy Place with the lampstand and table of showbread. We have passed the altar of incense and have walked through the veil into the very presence of God. We have gazed at His throne and experienced the wonder of the angels at His mercy. We have seen the beauty of our atonement. We have worshipped. As we finish this week's study, let's take some time to review and reflect on all the wonderful truths we have learned.

In Day One, we saw the positioning of the Tabernacle in relation to the camp that ought to remind us of God's centrality in our lives, not just in our "worship" services. Unless Christ is central to all, He is not really Lord of every area of our lives. Reflect on all you have learned regarding the Tabernacle's position in the midst of the camp and how its position relates to you.

APPLY As you consider the challenges of walking with God today, look at the areas below and identify which ones make it difficult for you to keep the Lord at the center of your life.

___ too busy ___ temptations ___ lack of encouragement
___ selfishness ___ lack of fellowship ___ family discord
___ material wishes ___ other:____________________

Are there any changes you need to make in your worship because of the things you have learned in this lesson?

____

____

____

APPLY As you look at the process of worship (the way of the priest), rate yourself in each of those seven areas.

The Gate is the **place of entry.** Have you entered by way of a personal relationship with Christ?

The Brazen Altar is the **place of reconciling.** As you seek the Lord, do you see any rebellion that needs to be dealt with or any wrongs that have not been corrected?

The Laver is the **place of cleansing.** Considering personal holiness, is God calling you to any areas of separation?

The Lampstand is the **place of light.** Are you drawing the light of God's Word into your life on a regular basis?

The Table is the **place of dining.** Are you bringing the needs of your heart to God and seeing Him meet them?

The Altar of Incense is the **place of prayer.** Are there others who need your support through prayer?

Unless Christ is central to all, He is not really Lord of every area of our lives.

The Ark is the **place of fellowship.** Are you enjoying daily fellowship with God?

Take some time to express to the Lord in writing all the applications He has given you. You may also jot down any confessions you want to make to the Lord.

What you are doing this moment is what worship is all about. As we have stated in earlier lessons, worship is far more than attending a church service or having an emotional experience. Worship is doing business with God, walking in relationship with Him. Hopefully you are already seeing the fruit of this in your own walk with God. Keep doing your homework, for you will get out of it what you put into it!

Notes

Notes

False Worship

Disobedience to God's Order for Worship and its Consequences

> **"By those who come near to Me I will be treated as holy, and before all the people I will be honored."**
> **Leviticus 10:3**

We are nearing the end of our journey. After weeks of labor, we have studied the Tabernacle from the standpoint of why it was needed. We have studied its construction, its furniture and coverings, and we have looked at the many pictures of the Lord Jesus in this beautiful building. We have looked at the priesthood that ministered there and the significance of the offerings given in that place. Most recently, we have gleaned truth from the order He gave to the positioning of the Tabernacle. As we bring our study toward a close, we must remind ourselves of where we began. The foundation of our entire study was not simply to understand the Tabernacle of old, but to use the study as a vehicle through which we might understand the way to worship God. In this lesson we want to define what true worship is **not.** We must look at false worship and that which Scripture shows us God has rejected if we are to rightly appreciate what true worship of God is.

THE GOLDEN CALF

No study of the Tabernacle would be complete without considering the context in which it began. Amazing as it may seem, while Moses was on the mountain getting the instructions for the Tabernacle, Israel was at the bottom (literally and figuratively) worshiping the golden calf. Think about that for a moment. Think of all Israel had experienced in the weeks that preceded this event. After four hundred years of slavery, they had finally been set free in miraculous fashion. God had affirmed His power through ten supernatural plagues. As God's chosen people left Egypt, once again God showed His strength and majesty by parting the Red Sea for them. God then used those same waters to destroy the enemy. Yet only a short time later, these same people that God rescued were bowing before an idol. There is an important lesson for each of us in this. Just because we worshiped God and walked with Him yesterday does not mean we will do so today.

📖 Read Exodus 24:12–18 to get the context for the Tabernacle instructions. Notice verse 14. What were the leaders supposed to do?

Moses instructed the elders to "wait." Aaron and Hur were in charge to settle disputes, but the main instruction was for the elders to wait for Moses to return with God's instructions.

📖 Now read 32:1. What did Israel actually do, and what dangers does this reveal about our worship?

Word Study

"ROSE UP TO PLAY"

The Hebrew word in Exodus 32:6 for "play" (*tsachaq*) is a word that suggests sexual play. It is the same Hebrew word as is used in Genesis 26:8 of Isaac caressing Rebekah, his wife. In light of the fact that drinking accompanied this incident relating to the golden calf, it may very well have been a drunken orgy that Moses describes as *"out of control"* in Exodus 32:25 (*"were naked"*; KJV).

When Moses did not return as soon as the people wanted, they took matters into their own hands. This incident reveals much about dangers to true worship. First, it underscores the human tendency to worship God as we please instead of as He pleases. In 1 Corinthians 14, we see Paul correcting wrong worship, and he concludes his exhortations with the challenge, *"Let all things be done properly and in an orderly manner"* (14:40). There is always order with God, and He doesn't want man to do what seems good—He wants man to do as God instructs. The second danger revealed here occurs when leaders stop **leading** and start **following** the people. Leaders are to follow God, and the congregation is to follow the leaders who hopefully are the most spiritually mature. Worship runs awry when leaders refuse to lead and followers refuse to follow.

The worship of the golden calf (Hebrew: "young bull") was a throwback to life in Egypt where animals were worshiped. The people of God were following the world instead of God. Worldliness is always the enemy of true worship.

Read through the account of Exodus 32:1–35, and write any further observations you have. Pay attention to exactly what the sin was and how God dealt with it.

____

____

____

The people of Israel wanted a god they could control. They wanted something they could see and feel and manipulate. They were not willing to wait as God instructed but wanted to be in charge of their own worship. Their specific sin was to make an idol and worship it. God's means of dealing with the sin was death.

Moses was on the mountain to get the laws of God, while the people were down below breaking them. When Moses came down off the mountain, carrying the two stone tablets upon which God had written the Ten Commandments, he threw them to the ground in disgust. His breaking of the tablets was a physical picture of their breaking of the laws.

Think about the application to us in this example of wrong worship. True worship is not about us, it is about Him—what He desires and deserves. Israel allowed their worship to be shaped by the pagan culture they had left behind instead of by the defining of God Himself.

Did You Know?

EGYPTIAN INFLUENCES

During the process of Moses asking Pharaoh for the release of the people, a compromise was offered. Pharaoh said he would allow them to make sacrifices to their God within Egypt. Moses refused this offer, knowing that the Egyptians considered some animals such as the cow as sacred and worshiped them. To sacrifice them would no doubt have caused an uproar in Egypt. The worship at the golden calf was undoubtedly a digression back to the influences of Egypt.

NADAB AND ABIHU

Lesson Ten **DAY TWO**

God was very exact and careful as He instituted through Moses a system of worship. Yet immediately on the heels of the inauguration of the priestly service we find another example of false worship. This time the offense is not as widespread as with the golden calf but is significant nonetheless and dealt with quickly and seriously. You see, God will not allow us to treat Him casually or without reverence. If we are to worship Him, we must appreciate how important it is not to be careless or flippant in our worship. It need not always be a somber thing to come into God's presence, but it is always a serious one. God is saying something about the nature of true worship through how He deals with the false worship of Nadab and Abihu.

Read Leviticus 10:1–11. What was the sin of Nadab and Abihu, and how did God deal with it?

____

____

____

____

Word Study

STRONG DRINK

One of the admonitions that flows out of Nadab and Abihu's encounter with God is the command for the priests not to drink wine or strong drink (from the Hebrew root word, *shakar,* which means to make drunk). The command of Leviticus 10:9 not to drink suggests that part of the reason for Nadab and Abihu's foolish choice is that they may have been drunk, though this is not stated with certainty.

Nadab and Abihu apparently used coals of fire that were not taken from the bronze altar as prescribed by the Lord (Leviticus 16:12). The fact that it was not God's fire underscores that He cannot accept man's works. We must worship His way. Nadab and Abihu did not take the worship of God seriously and did not worship God His way. The consequence of this sin was calamitous—immediate death! It was a supernatural death, as fire came from the cloud of glory that rested over the mercy seat, killing them but not burning up their clothes or bodies (v. 5).

According to verse 3, what was the reason God dealt so seriously with this sin?

God's explanation to Moses was *"By those who come near to Me I will be treated as holy, and before all the people I will be honored."* True worship must respect God's holiness. This is why there are not "many roads to God" as inter-faith emphasis suggests. True worship also involves "honoring" the Lord.

APPLY What does this teach us about our own worship?

We must make certain we respect God's holiness (which requires dealing with sin), and we must be sure that our worship honors Him. There can be no flippancy or irreverence in our worship.

True Worship

RESPECTING GOD'S HOLINESS

The sin of Nadab and Abihu reflects an important principle that is also found in the sin of Ananias and Saphira (Acts 4:32—5:11). Both situations occurred at the beginning of the institution of a new manner of worshiping God. The incident of Nadab and Abihu occurred at the introduction of Tabernacle worship. In the New Testament we see a similar example at the introduction of worship through the Church. The message from this seems to be that God wanted to make sure each got started with an emphasis on respecting His holiness.

This narrative must be kept in the context of the whole Bible to be fully understood. It does not reflect a God who reacts unjustly or harshly over a simple mistake. What God did was a necessary example to the ages that because He is holy, He must be treated as such. In a scientific laboratory, sterile equipment must be handled as such or it will be stained by unsterile hands. This is a good physical picture of holiness.

📖 Read Acts 4:32—5:11. What was the sin, and how did God deal with it?

The sin of Ananias and Saphira was not simply that they kept part of the money for themselves but that they lied to the Holy Spirit (Acts 5:3). They tried to worship God without respecting who He is. The consequence was immediate and dramatic death, by which God underscored the seriousness of true worship.

What was the result of how God dealt with Ananias and Saphira?

In Acts 5:11 we are told, *"And great fear came upon the whole church, and upon all who heard of these things."* Since we are among those who have heard of these things, we too should bring from their testimonies a holy reverence for God.

God wants to walk in relationship with man, but He will not allow man to profane His holiness with worship that does not take Him seriously. These examples of wrong worship send a clear statement from the Lord that He is to be treated with reverence.

The Rebellion of Korah

Lesson Ten **DAY THREE**

We have been looking at worship from some of the negative examples of Scripture. We are trying to define true worship, in part, by looking at what is rejected. It is important in this process to recognize that worship is not merely the rituals we perform or the services we observe. Worship is all that we say and do. The next incident of false worship we want to look at is the rebellion of Korah. It is a story of rebellion against God's order and structure. It is also a rebellion against the leadership God has put in place. There is much we can learn from the negative example of Korah.

Read Numbers 16:1–50. What was Korah's argument, and what was wrong with his perspective?

Did You Know?

WHO WAS KORAH?

Korah, who conspired with Dathan and Abiram against Moses, was the son of Izhar, the brother of Amram, the father of Moses and Aaron, making him a cousin of these leaders of Israel (Exodus 6:21; Numbers 16:1–49). Perhaps part of his grievance was rooted in his close relationship to Moses but relatively minor role in leadership.

In Numbers 16:3 Korah and his following argued that Moses and Aaron were wrongly hoarding the leadership role. They rightly said, *"all the congregation are holy"* (see Exodus 19:6), but they failed to recognize that Moses and Aaron were God-appointed leaders. The Kohathites had a God-appointed role (see Numbers 4:1–20), but instead of being satisfied with it, they coveted the roles of Moses and Aaron and the priests.

How did God affirm His calling of Aaron?

God confirmed His calling and choosing of Aaron for the priesthood by the miracle of the budding rod so there would be no doubt in anyone's mind of His will and purpose. Aaron was not there of his own choice but by the choice of God Himself.

How did God deal with the rebellion?

God made an example of this sin of rebellion against His appointed leaders by judging them with immediate and dramatic death. The ground opened up swallowing Korah, Dathan, and Abiram along with their tents. The other rebels were consumed by fire that *"came forth from the Lord"* (Numbers 16:35). The incense burners of the rebels were beaten into plates to form an outer covering to the altar. This altar covering served as a warning of the just judgment of God (vv. 38–40). Such examples of God's wrath seem harsh at first glance, but it is important that we look at them from God's point of view. First, God must deal harshly in some instances in order to speak clearly of His holiness. However, this does not mean that He will always intervene in such a dramatic fashion. Second, we must appreciate that physical death is not the same as spiritual death. We must be careful of reading more into these judgments than is there. We are not told that Korah was sentenced to eternal damnation.

What does this incident of Korah teach us about potential hindrances to our worship?

Put Yourself In Their Shoes

SONS OF KORAH

At least eleven of the Psalms are attributed to the "sons of Korah." It would appear that his children repented of his rebellion and went on to useful service to the Lord. It is important to recognize that children can learn from the mistakes of their parents.

Sin is serious to God, and so is leadership. True worship must respect this. If we grumble and complain against God's appointed leaders, we will be unable to worship as we should. Even if we have trouble trusting leadership, we must trust God, who appoints leaders to accomplish His purpose.

What is the main way God defines our role in His body as New Testament believers?

In the New Testament era, God defines our role in His body by how He has gifted us spiritually and by His burdening and calling to specific tasks and roles. However He calls us, it is His choosing, not merely the accomplishment of man. True ministry that is of the Lord is received—not achieved.

How does this example of Korah affect our view of right and wrong worship? Clearly the leading of worship was appointed and designed by God.

He selected the tribe of Levi and appointed the roles they would play in worship. We cannot rebel against God's order and values and not bring judgment on ourselves. God will not take a vote of public opinion to determine whom He calls and to what task.

SAUL AT GILGAL

Lesson Ten **DAY FOUR**

Worship is important to God. He desires it—and He deserves it! Yet He cannot accept wrong worship. One of the Old Testament examples of wrong worship occurred at the beginning of the monarchy. Israel had asked for a king to lead them. The desire for a king was not wrong—the law allowed for it—but Israel was wrong in what they wanted in a king. They wanted to be like the other nations. They rejected God as their king in favor of following the world. God ended up judging them by giving them exactly what they wanted. He gave them Saul as king. Often God's greatest judgment on us is giving us what we want so that through the failure of our desires we can learn to want what He wants for us. Saul was such a failure. The incident, which led to his ultimate rejection as king, revolved around his role in wrong worship and teaches us of the seriousness of worshiping God—God's way.

Several years passed in the reign of Saul, and God allowed him to pursue his own ambitions. In 1 Samuel 15, we see God place a new test in front of him—a new opportunity for him to demonstrate a willingness to fully follow God. The Amalekites were perhaps the most savage and inhumane of all the Canaanites, and during Israel's wilderness journey they cruelly attacked God's people from the rear, killing the weak and elderly stragglers (Exodus 17:8–13). Verse 33 of 1 Samuel 15 indicates children were also among their victims. Though five hundred years had passed since they were placed under divine judgment, God had not forgotten their wickedness. Saul is commanded by God to "utterly destroy" (literally, "put under a ban") the Amalekites. This involved destroying the cities, killing all the inhabitants, and even destroying all their animals and possessions. Though quite severe, this was a just punishment, as God considered the land so stained by their sin that nothing was to be spared.

Word Study
"UNDER THE BAN"

The Hebrew word *charam* or *cherem* means "devoted" or "under the ban." Something put "under the ban" referred to something set aside totally for God's purposes. The spoils of Jericho were "devoted" or literally "under the ban"—set apart, as it were, as first fruits belonging to the Lord (Joshua 7). Leviticus 27:28 speaks of a devoted offering, and 27:29 speaks of a person under the ban ("utterly destroy"—1 Samuel 15:3, 8–9, 18, 20) whose crimes merited execution as did the Canaanites of Joshua's day.

Read 1 Samuel 15. According to verses 7–9, how much of God's command in verse 3 did Saul honor?

____

____

____

____

____

Saul killed all the people except for Agag, the king, and he destroyed everything worthless. Yet he saved the valuable things because, as the text says, *"Saul and the people . . . were not willing to destroy them utterly."* Saul probably saved Agag as a trophy of his victory, a common practice of the pagan nations. The greatest boast a conquering king could have would be to bring the vanquished king back in chains to be mocked and displayed.

To us it appears that Saul was partially obedient, but how does God view Saul's actions (v. 11)?

God says Saul has *"... turned back from* **following Me,** *and has not carried out My commands."* Notice, God does not say that Saul carried out part of His commands. What we would call partial obedience, God calls disobedience.

In verse 12, we see Saul's selfish focus reflected in the fact that he *"set up a monument for himself."* His first comment when he sees Samuel the prophet is to affirm his obedience to God. Samuel, already knowing Saul's disobedience, gives him an opportunity to repent by asking about the animal noises in the background.

Look at verses 15, 20 and 21, and identify whom Saul blames and how he excuses his disobedience.

In verse 15, trying to explain away the animals that should have been destroyed, Saul says *"they"* have brought them. He says *"the people"* spared the best, and then tries to excuse *"the people"* by indicating their intent to use the animals for sacrifices. In verses 20–21, Saul proclaims his own obedience while again throwing the blame on the people.

What is Samuel's response in verses 22–23 to how Saul explains his lack of obedience?

OBEDIENCE

"And Samuel said, 'Has the LORD as much delight in burnt offerings and sacrifices as in obeying the voice of the LORD? Behold, to obey is better than sacrifice, And to heed than the fat of rams.'" (1 Samuel 15:22)

Samuel makes it clear that saving the animals for sacrifice is not the offering the Lord desires. God would rather have Saul's obedience than his religious offerings. Animal sacrifices were simply an excuse, for as we saw in verse 9, the real problem was that Saul and the people *"were not willing"* to utterly destroy the animals. The fact that they saw value in them shows that they did not have God's perspective about sin.

But before we are too quick to cast a judging eye on Saul and Israel, how often do we offer up our sacrifices of time, money, and praise on Sunday when we have not been obedient throughout the week? It's easy to think we're doing fine because our actions fit the religious requirement when our hearts are still full of sinful, stubborn willfulness.

APPLY Are there areas in your life in which you have tried to substitute good things for obedience to the Lord?

Samuel's response makes it clear that the "sacrifice" excuse is unacceptable. The Lord prefers obedience to sacrifices (v. 22), and we should not forget that these animals were "under the ban." This means that they were so stained by sin that God would not allow Israel to keep them even though these animals were valuable. How could something under the ban possibly be an acceptable sacrifice when offerings were to be without blemish? Samuel equates Saul's rebellion with *"divination,"* or witchcraft, and his insubordination with *"idolatry."* Truly, failing to submit to God is a form of idolatry, for it places our will over His and is a practical form of worshiping self. Even the good things in our life are worthless when they are corrupted by our willfulness.

📖 Read verses 24–25 and 30. What signs do you see of Saul's repentance or lack of repentance in these verses?

____

____

____

____

We cannot look into Saul's heart, but we can observe his actions. His confession in verse 24, instead of including remorse, is couched with an excuse (again blaming the people). It is significant that Saul asks Samuel, not God, to pardon his sin. Verse 30 reveals that Saul cared more about his standing with the people than his standing with God. Notice he says *". . . that I may worship the LORD* **your** *God"* (emphasis added).

If we are wise we will learn from the mistakes of Saul.

Saul stands in stark contrast to King David, who, though he sinned greatly in adulterous and murderous acts, prayed that God might *"create"* in him a clean heart (Psalm 51:10). Saul only wanted his actions pardoned. We must not mistake remorse over the consequences of sin with true repentance over sin itself. Saul acknowledged that he *"transgressed the command of the LORD"* (v. 24), but there is no indication that he saw himself as wrong in doing so. Quite to the contrary, he defended his actions. True confession is agreeing with God that an action is wrong and then repenting of that action. Such contrition is tragically absent in Saul.

Think about this example of false worship. What Saul initiated as an act of worship God viewed as utterly worthless. Worse than that, God saw Saul's actions as rebellion akin to witchcraft and idolatry. Jesus, in His indictment of the Pharisees, quotes the prophet Isaiah who says, *"This people honors Me with their lips, but their heart is far away from Me"* (Matt. 15:8; compare to Isaiah 29:13). The words of Jesus and Isaiah capture very well the nature of Saul's "worship."

For Me to Worship God

Lesson Ten **DAY FIVE**

God desires and deserves our worship. Yet not all worship is acceptable to God. He cannot allow us to approach Him unless we approach in His way. We saw in our first lesson the contrasting worship of Cain and Abel. Each brought an offering to the Lord, but only one was accepted. In this lesson, we have seen some of the examples from Scripture of worship that God could not accept. I hope you are looking at these narratives from the Old Testament with more than merely historical interest. There is much in each of these situations that applies to you and me today. As we close this lesson, we want to look to the Lord for how we can apply to our own lives and worship the principles we have gleaned from the rejected worship of others.

We saw that on the heels of God's deliverance through the Red Sea, Israel bowed in pagan debauchery before an idol of gold. What an amazing thought! Those, who only days before were singing the praises of Jehovah, were now worshiping a worthless statue that had no power whatsoever to deliver them. They were worshiping the work of their own hands. This act of false worship shows us that in the absence of leadership and truth, it only takes a short time for us to lose vision and for our worship to digress into an orgy of self.

As you consider the worship in which you have witnessed and participated, what are some examples you have seen of worship that was not according to truth?

Idols are not limited to golden statues, nor are they relics of the past with no impact upon today. We are just as prone to idol worship as our ancestors. Look at the list below, and check some of the idols you are tempted to worship today.

___ money	___ self	___ relationships
___ your job	___ pleasure	___ travel
___ leaders	___ experiences	___ emotion
___ recreation	___ friendships	___ success
___ possessions	___ other: ______________	

Idols are not limited to golden statues, nor are they relics of the past with no impact upon today. We are just as prone to idol worship as our ancestors were.

The Old Testament solution to idol worship was to tear down the false idols. Is there something you sense the Lord is calling you to tear down because it has become an idol in your life?

In the examples of Nadab and Abihu and of Ananias and Saphira, we see the danger of approaching God in a careless and flippant manner, treating those things which are holy as profane. Leviticus 10:3 admonishes us, *"By those who come near to Me I will be treated as holy, and before all the people I will be honored."*

What are some ways you have seen the Lord dishonored or mistreated in worship?

Is there any area you sense the Lord is convicting you regarding right worship?

Perhaps as we considered the rebellion of Korah, you did not immediately see it as an issue of worship. Yet these were the men who were charged with leadership in worship. Korah was a Levite—a leader in the Tabernacle. His sin was judged, but it was not removed from the heart of man. We are just as vulnerable today to grumbling against leadership and God's place for us as Korah was. It is always far easier to criticize the leadership of others than it is to lead perfectly ourselves. As Jesus made plain, only those without sin are worthy to cast stones. Yet He who alone could condemn us is the very One who serves as our advocate.

Think of your own worship. Have you been guilty of grumbling against your pastor or worship leader?

Are there others in spiritual leadership that you have complained against in private (or even public)?

Romans 14:4 says, *"Who are you to judge the servant of another? To his own master he stands or falls; and stand he will, for the Lord is able to make him stand."* Except when there is clear violation of the Word of God, we must allow each other to follow the Lord in the dictates of conscience. We cannot set ourselves above the Lord in judging the service of others.

If there is any forgiveness you need to seek or restitution that should be made, do not neglect it. As a general rule, "so far as the offense is known, the repentance must be shown."

APPLY Finally, in Saul we see the negative example of the form of worship that was fulfilled to please men instead of God. As you consider the weaknesses of Saul, do you struggle with any of these sin-rooted attitudes staining your worship?

___ impatience with God
___ not worshiping according to truth
___ worshiping to be seen by men
___ worrying more about how your worship looks to men than to God
___ giving that which you don't want to God and saving the best for self
___ blaming others for your mistakes and wrong choices
___ failing to repent when confronted with things that are wrong in your life

"Create in me a clean heart, O God, and renew a steadfast spirit within me."
Psalm 51:10

Repentance is more than simply remorse. Saul was remorseful but unwilling to repent. He grieved over the consequences of his sin but not the sin itself. What a contrast we have in the king who followed him on the throne, David! When confronted with his sin, he was broken and contrite. He not only longed for forgiveness but for cleanness. Meditate again upon the words of David in Psalm 51:10: *"Create in me a clean heart, O God, and renew a steadfast spirit within me."* David not only wanted to be forgiven, but he also wanted to be changed. Psalm 51 was the result of David writing down his prayer to the Lord, and it ministers to us thousands of years later.

As you consider what you have learned from this week's lesson, write out a prayer of your own expressing your heart.

Take some time in your worship to thank God for the roles He has given you (and others) in the body. Thankfulness is one way to express trust in God's way to worship Him.

Notes

Notes

True Worship

Worshiping God in Spirit and in Truth

Over the past ten lessons, we have seen worship from Adam to Aaron, and we have walked the path of the priest into the Tabernacle. We have viewed each piece of furniture in the Tabernacle and have seen how each piece was a touch point in our relationship with God—a sign pointing to true worship. In the offerings, we have seen the necessity of dealing with personal sin and surrendering to the Lord. In looking at the Tabernacle, we see that ultimately worship is entering into the presence of the Lord with a heart of surrender and living there as a worshiper—experiencing the love of the Father, the mercy of the Son, and the refreshing life of the Spirit. We were created for such a life in His presence.

True worship flows from the heart of one who walks in the fear of the Lord, who withholds nothing from God.

True worship is seeing the Lord for who He is and surrendering to Him. As Abraham's worship in Genesis 22 shows us, true worship flows from the heart of one who walks in the fear of the Lord, one who withholds nothing from

Some of the True Worshipers in Scripture

NAME	SCRIPTURE	NAME	SCRIPTURE
Abel	Genesis 4:3–8; Hebrews 11:4	Zacharias and Elizabeth	Luke 1—2
Enoch	Genesis 5:21–24; Hebrews 11:5–6	Joseph and Mary	Matthew 1:18–25; Luke 1:26-56
Abraham and Sarah	Genesis 12—24; 22:5; Hebrews 11:8–19	The Magi	Matthew 2:1–12
Isaac	Genesis 22:5; 26:25; Hebrews 11:20	John the Baptist	John 1:19–36; 3:22–36
Jacob	Genesis 28:18–22; 35:7; 48—49; Hebrews 11:21	Peter, Andrew, James, John, and Nathaniel	Luke 5:11; John 1:35–51 (note Peter)
Moses and Aaron	Exodus, Leviticus, Numbers; Hebrews 11:23-29	The Disciples	Matthew 14:23; 28:17
Gideon	Judges 7:15; Hebrews 11:32-34	Thomas	John 20:24–29
David	2 Samuel 12:20; Acts 13:32; Hebrews 11:32–34	Early Church in Jerusalem	Acts 2:41–47; 4:24–31
Isaiah	Isaiah 6:1–13 John 12:41; Hebrews 11:32, 37	The Leaders in Antioch	Acts 13:1–3
Elijah	1 Kings 18:1–46	Lydia in Philippi	Acts 16:14

God, and one who obeys His word promptly and fully (see Lesson Two). In this lesson we want to see more of who God is and how He leads us in that kind of worship. In this lesson, we will see the will of the Father for our worship, the work of the Son in bringing us into true worship, and the ways of the Spirit in continually leading us in worship. As we seek the Lord and surrender to Him, may our hearts truly worship and find our deepest joy in Him.

Lesson Eleven **DAY ONE**

THE FATHER SEEKS TRUE WORSHIPERS

What is the will of the Father in our worship? In John 4:23–24 Jesus told the woman at Jacob's well that the Father is **seeking** true worshipers. Then He said, *"God is Spirit, and those who worship Him must worship in spirit and truth,"* from the heart with nothing hidden (4:24). In Days Two and Three, we will look more at what Jesus said to this woman about worship; however, our focus today will be on God the Father and His will. What does it mean that God seeks those who will worship Him in spirit and truth? Let's start with His first "seeking" in Genesis.

Word Study
WORSHIPING IN TRUTH

"In truth"—The Greek word for "truth," *aletheia*, is from the root *alethes*, which literally means "not hidden," "unconcealed," or "no secret." When we worship in truth, we hide nothing from God. We are open and honest with Him.

Look at Genesis 3:9–11. What is the Lord God seeking from Adam?

___

___

___

God asked, *"Where are you?"* But God certainly knew Adam's location. When Adam responded by saying he was afraid and hid because he was naked, God focused on the heart of the matter, *"Have you eaten from the tree of which I commanded you that you should not eat?"* God wanted Adam to admit where he stood spiritually. Why was Adam hiding in shame? Was it as a consequence of his disobedience? To admit where he was in respect to location would be to admit where he was in respect to his heart. It would be to admit **why** he was hiding. God wanted Adam to tell the truth, to be honest and open from the heart, from the inner man—the inner thoughts, desires, and choices. Likewise, God desires that we follow Him and worship Him from the heart.

"For the LORD does not see as man sees; for man looks at the outward appearance, but the LORD looks at the heart."

I Samuel 16:7b (NKJV)

Read Psalm 51. Here we find the same heartbeat for true worship. This is David's testimony of coming back to the Lord, back to true worship. What do you find in verse 6 that relates to how God dealt with Adam in Genesis 3 or that connects to worship *"in spirit and truth"*?

___

___

___

___

God revealed to David that He desires *"truth in the innermost being"* (v. 6). The Hebrew word for "innermost being" (*tuwchah*) literally means "overlaying" or "covering" and was used to describe the kidneys (organs that are concealed). The term "innermost being" is used figuratively in Psalm 51 to refer to our innermost thoughts—where God wants truth to reside. Speaking of truth, the Hebrew word for "truth" used here (*'emeth*) has the basic meaning of firmness or faithfulness. It refers to someone or something that is consistent. The word carries the idea of being without deceit. God wants us to walk before Him in truth and honesty from the heart. He wants us to be transparent before Him and always ready to agree with Him and His Word (the Truth). God wants worship to come from the innermost recesses of our souls.

"I have no greater joy than to hear that my children walk in truth."

3 John 1:4 (KJV)

The second part of Psalm 51:6 says that God will make him know wisdom *"in the hidden part."* God wants us to have His wisdom in the depths of our minds and hearts. If we are to walk in truth, we must be taught truth from God through His Word. God is the only source of true wisdom, or as James 3:17 aptly states, *"the wisdom from above."*

📖 Read James 3:13–18. Write out a description of the wisdom God wants us to have and contrast it with the wisdom that is not from above.

The "wisdom" from earth, flesh, or Satan is full of strife, disorder, and evil. It is marked by bitter jealousy, selfish ambition, arrogance, and self-seeking. It is neither true nor reliable. Rather, it is deceitful and hypocritical because it wants to get its own way any way it can. This "wisdom" is the mark of someone who has not been instructed by God or has refused God's instruction. On the other hand, the wisdom from above is pure and peaceable, coming from the pure heart of God and able to bring peace to the heart of man. It is gentle or forbearing, patient when mistreated, not lashing out trying to right wrongs in the energy of the flesh. The one who has the wisdom from above is reasonable with others. In other words, he or she is easily persuaded by what is right. This person listens to others and is willing to be compliant, willing to yield to the righteous requests of others. The one marked by the wisdom from above is especially yielded to the desires and demands of God, hence a true worshiper. He or she is also marked by mercy and by a willingness to help others. Such a person does not waver back and forth or behave two-faced like those marked by the hypocritical wisdom of the world, the flesh, or the devil. God's wisdom is consistent, whole, and wholesome and is a mark of a true worshiper.

True Worship

SINCERE WORSHIP

Worship "in spirit and truth" refers to worship from an open, honest heart. It means worshiping "from the heart with sincerity," not intellectual reasoning alone, empty ritual, or lifeless "Sunday" tradition and form. True worship is loving God with all one's heart, mind, soul, and strength.

How would the wisdom from above relate to worshiping God "in spirit and truth?"

Worldly or fleshly wisdom **never** leads to worship in spirit and truth, since it tends to be hypocritical, hiding selfish motives. It seeks its own will. It does not deal with sin, but rather intensifies sin; whereas, true worship always deals with sin. God's wisdom *"is first pure"* (James 3:17) and therefore calls one to purity and honesty before the Lord. It calls for one to deal with **any** sin. In the Tabernacle, the priest had to address sin first—at the bronze altar. The bronze altar is a picture of the cross, the altar of judgment for sin and the place where

True worship is faith in action, and true faith is worship in action (Genesis 22:1–18; Hebrews 11:1–6)

Christ's blood was poured out for sin. As the bronze altar was a place of temporary cleansing, the cross became the place for ultimate cleansing and purity for sinful man. A truly wise man admits his sin before God and seeks His forgiveness and cleansing. Confession is the starting point for walking and worshiping in spirit and truth.

📖 Read Psalm 51:10, 15–17, and note the additional insights about worship. According to verses 12–15, what results did David long for in his life?

David's focus is on a clean heart and an upright spirit (v. 10). He wanted to be right from the heart, not just externally or ceremonially correct. He knew that tabernacle worship and the offerings were not to be a religious ritual. He understood that God is concerned with the attitude of the heart. In verse 15 he prays for a worshiping heart, understanding that outward sacrifice is not the essential element in worship (51:16–17). The primary element God wants is a heart that deals with sin and surrenders fully to Him. That is the surrender of faith. Then there can be joyful service flowing out of a willing spirit, as he testifies in 51:12–14. As a result, sinners will be converted and become true worshipers. In seeking the Lord in spirit and truth, David knows that he will again joyfully sing and declare the praises of the Lord in his life.

Several lessons ago we looked at Abraham as a true worshiper of God. In Genesis 22, God tested what was in Abraham's heart. It was a test of faith as well as a test of true worship. Abraham passed the test. God tests us too, in small and large ways. As in Abraham's case, sometimes the test will be whether or not we are walking in the fear of the Lord. At other times, God will focus more on surrender that withholds nothing from Him. Sometimes the focus will be on prompt, full obedience in some area. In any case, the tests come to show us how true our worship and faith are and how we are doing as true worshipers of God.

APPLY Stop and think of some ways you may have been tested recently. Talk to the Lord about these things.

God tested Abraham's trust. Abraham trusted God's test.

The Father seeks true worshipers—those who are honest before Him, who fear Him, deal with sin, and surrender to His will. How did Jesus speak about these truths? We will see this in His encounter with the woman at the well in our studies for Days Two and Three.

Jesus Speaks the Word about True Worshipers, Part One

Lesson Eleven **DAY TWO**

In John 4, Jesus and His disciples journeyed into the land of Samaria, north of Jerusalem, and came to Jacob's well outside the village of Sychar. It was around noon, and the disciples went into the village to buy food. Jesus, weary from the journey, sat by the well, where a woman came to draw water. Much to her surprise, Jesus asked her for a drink of water. Jews and Samaritans did not talk with one another, nor was it the custom for men to say anything to women, but Jesus did. For this Samaritan woman, the conversation that followed took a surprising turn, as Jesus began speaking about "living water." What did Jesus mean by "living water," and what could this water have to do with worship? Watch carefully as Jesus leads this woman into becoming a true worshiper.

Read John 4:10–24 and answer the questions that follow.

What did Jesus tell the woman in 4:10?

____

____

____

____

____

Jesus began by speaking about *"the gift of God."* He told her that if she knew the gift of God and **Who** it was that spoke to her, her whole life would change. If she knew who Jesus was as the Giver of the gift of God, then she would ask Him, and He would give her "living water." The woman was puzzled about Jesus' statements concerning water, since Jesus had nothing with which to draw water out of Jacob's well, and there appeared to be no other place to get water. What was He talking about?

Jesus wanted the woman to know more about this offer of living water. What did He tell her in John 4:13–14? How did she respond according to John 4:15?

____

____

____

____

____

____

Jesus clearly explained that there are two kinds of water, one that quenches thirst temporarily and another that quenches thirst permanently. This second kind of water did not come from a well like Jacob's well. It was a gift from Jesus Himself. It was water that went deep into a man or woman and in that place became a well of water springing up, always available, never

Did You Know?

LIVING WATER

"Living Water" refers to pure, running water as opposed to cistern water or some other standing water which could be stagnant, even polluted. The people of Jesus' day recognized living water as water that came from the freeflowing rains, from rivers, from springs, or from wells fed by a spring. It was refreshing, life-giving, abundant, and free—a true picture of the salvation Jesus brings.

"Therefore with joy you will draw water from the wells of salvation."

Isaiah 12:3 (NKJV)

running dry. This living water was eternal, and in drinking it one began experiencing eternal life. The woman readily agreed to get this water if she could. What would it take?

Review John 4:16–18. What did Jesus ask, and what did He reveal? In light of her desire for living water, why do you think He did this?

____

____

____

____

Jesus asked the woman to call her husband to which she responded, *"I have no husband."* Then Jesus revealed the truth about her life. She had had five husbands, and the man she was then living with was not her husband. He pinpointed her sin as a step toward giving her living water. He pointed out her spiritual deadness so He could give her eternal life.

Did You Know?

MOUNT GERIZIM

Mount Gerizim is the mountain in Samaria from which the Israelites pronounced the blessing (Deuteronomy 11:29–30; 27:11–12). It stands opposite Mount Ebal, the mountain from which the curses were pronounced (Deuteronomy 11:29; 27:13; Joshua 8:30–35). Around the time of Alexander the Great, the Samaritans built a temple for the worship of God on Mount Gerizim. According to the historian Josephus, John Hyrcanus, the Maccabean destroyed that temple in 128 B.C. Just as in Jesus' time, the current inhabitants of this region still regard Mount Gerizim to be holy.

The woman stated her belief that Jesus must certainly be a prophet. In making that statement, she was admitting that He had spoken the truth about her. Anyone who could pinpoint her life and her sin in that way surely must be a prophet who knew God in a supernatural way.

Look again at John 4:19–20. What topic did the woman bring up? Why do you think she did this?

____

____

____

The woman began talking about the right **place** for worship. She wanted the focus moved off herself and her lifestyle and onto another topic. She directed the conversation to a debate between *"our fathers"* (the Samaritans) and where they worshiped and *"you people"* (the Jews) and where they worshiped. Since the issue had pointed to a matter of right and wrong, she shifted the conversation to an issue beyond her situation and asked about the **right place** for true worship. Jesus was more interested in a **right heart** for worship.

Jesus gave very clear direction about the right place for worship and the meaning of true worship. What did He tell the woman in John 4:21–24?

____

____

____

The geographical place for worship was not an issue in Jesus' mind (Jerusalem or Mount Gerizim). The issue is the place of the heart. God seeks those who worship Him *"in spirit and truth."* The focus of the heart and the condition of the heart is God's concern. How did this relate to the woman to whom He was talking? What is the relationship between what Jesus said about worshiping in spirit and truth and His earlier question about the woman's live-in boyfriend? How do worship and the woman's personal life relate to the matter of receiving "living water?" We will answer these questions in Day Three.

APPLY How is your heart? Is there some sin you are trying to hide? (Do you want to change the subject?) Deal with whatever the Holy Spirit has shown you. He will always lead you to truth and true worship.

Jesus Speaks the Word about True Worshipers, Part Two

Lesson Eleven **DAY THREE**

When we look at Jesus' words in John 4:10, 13–14, 16–18 and 21–24, we can see some very important connections. Jesus had introduced the woman to the fact that there was a "gift of God" to be given. Then He began showing her who He is as the Giver so that she could ask Him for that gift. When Jesus brought up the issue of the woman's lifestyle, He was revealing truth. He was seeking to get her to the truth about Himself and the truth about her life. He wanted the woman to experience the joy of the "living water" He offered, but He knew that her sin had to be dealt with first. She had to be honest about her sin. To get "living water" from Jesus, one must ask for it. The woman had asked for the living water, but her asking had to be in line with who Jesus is and **how** He gives *"the gift of God"* (living water). How does this living water connect to worship in spirit and truth?

Read John 4:25–30. What happened in the life of this woman at the well? What was the turning point for her?

____

____

____

____

When the woman at the well first began to talk with Jesus, she did not know He was the Messiah. She did know that the Messiah would announce the truth about all things (especially the things about God and true worship). Jesus then revealed Himself as the Messiah: *"I who speak to you am He."* In the Greek language He literally said to her, "I AM" (*ego eimi*), the designation for the Lord in the Old Testament (Exodus 3:14–15). When Jesus revealed Himself to her, the connection was made in her heart. When He turned to her as Messiah, faith was born. She turned to Him, knowing somehow that He could take care of her sin. She was willing to surrender to Him and His salvation. At that point, the woman lined up her life before Him as her Messiah and knew He could give her living water.

Now read John 4:39–42. What did the woman tell the villagers? What does her statement tell you about her?

____

____

____

____

Word Study WORSHIP

The New Testament uses three Greek words for worship: *proskuneō*, *sebomai*, and *latreuō*. The word *proskuneō* literally means "to kiss the hand toward someone," carrying the idea of honoring or showing reverence with a kiss of homage. *Proskuneō* can also mean to bow, kneel, or prostrate oneself before another, emphasizing the **attitude** and **action of submission.** The word *sebomai* means "to worship and adore," emphasizing the **attitude of reverence** with the root idea being "to fall before." *Latreuō* means to wholeheartedly serve the will of the one being worshiped, not out of compulsion but freely. The word *sebomai* emphasizes the **action of service.** John 4:24 uses *proskuneō*. Matthew 4:10; Luke 1:74; 2:37; and Romans 12:1 use *latreuō*. *Sebomai* is used in Mark 7:7 and Acts 16:14; 18:7, 13.

"AND YOU SHALL LOVE THE LORD YOUR GOD WITH ALL YOUR HEART, AND WITH ALL YOUR SOUL, AND WITH ALL YOUR MIND, AND WITH ALL YOUR STRENGTH."

Mark 12:30

She ran to tell the villagers about this Jesus who *"told* [her] *all the things that* [she had] *done."* She was honest and transparent from the heart. That statement was a public admission or agreement that said in essence, "All of you know what kind of life I have lived. He revealed the sin in my life and He is right. You must come see this man. Surely He is the Christ." They came to see for themselves.

How do the events of verses 25–30 relate to worship in spirit and truth? How does this relate to all we have seen in the study of worship at the Tabernacle?

____

____

____

____

____

The Father seeks those who will worship Him in spirit and truth. When Jesus revealed Himself as the Messiah, the woman realized the full picture that included her sin, her Savior, and her surrender to Him. When she saw Jesus for who He is, she became honest about her sin; she was going in the right direction. Jesus knew this honesty regarding her sin was essential if she would worship in spirit and truth. We have seen the focus on our sin, our need of a Savior, and the importance of surrender to the Lord throughout our study of the Tabernacle. We must deal with sin. We must deal with what is "on the inside," for that is where the real person is. God wants "real people" as His worshipers—people who surrender to Him from the heart and worship Him with all that is within them.

What did the Samaritan villagers do according to John 4:39–42?

____

____

____

When the Samaritan villagers heard the woman's testimony and saw her honesty and transparency, they knew something had changed about her. They knew this Jesus must be someone very unique. They came to see Him, and Jesus revealed Himself as the Christ to them. They, too, believed in Him as their Savior, their Messiah. They, too, became worshipers of the Father and of the Lord Jesus in spirit and truth—knowing He could take care of their sin debt and change their believing, yielded hearts. The Father still seeks such as these to be His worshipers (John 4:23).

"If we say that we have no sin, we are deceiving ourselves, and the truth is not in us."

I John 1:8

We have seen that true worship must be in spirit and truth, dealing with sin God's way and yielding to Jesus as Lord and Savior. From the beginning, God dealt with the sin of Adam. God showed David that it was the heart that mattered, and a cleansed heart mattered more than anything else. Jesus made that clear to the woman at the well. He also made it clear that the place to meet God and to worship Him now was neither the Tabernacle of centuries past nor the Temple in Jerusalem. The Father is interested in an honest heart, truth in the inner man. The Father wants to meet man spirit to Spirit based on truth—the truth about who He is as Holy God and the truth about who each person is as a sinner in need of a Savior. What does it mean to "walk in truth" as a child of God? We will study aspects of this question in Day Four.

THE HOLY SPIRIT LEADS TRUE WORSHIPERS

What role does the Holy Spirit play in true worship? Several incidents in Jesus' ministry reveal the work of the Holy Spirit in leading us in true worship. We start several months after the ministry of Jesus in the Samaritan village of Sychar. Jesus and His disciples were in Jerusalem for the Feast of Tabernacles. This feast occurred on the fifteenth through the twenty-first of the month Tishri (around our October 1–7). It is perhaps the most joyous of the seven feasts, since it celebrates the harvest of fruit and grain as well as the spiritual cleansing that takes place on the Day of Atonement, just five days earlier. The high priest had offered the sin offerings and burnt offerings on that Day, and the Lord had accepted them. A feast of great rejoicing then took place before the Lord—a time of celebration and worship that lasted a full seven days. People would come to Jerusalem from all over the land and take branches of palm, myrtle, and other trees and set up makeshift huts and lean-tos in remembrance of the time Israel lived in tents in the wilderness. This great worship celebration looked back on the forgiveness and faithfulness of God and looked forward to the fullness of His promises in the Messiah and His reign.

During this feast, Jesus spoke once again about "living water." This time it was on *"the Great Day of the Feast,"* the seventh and last day. * A little history will help us understand what happened and the significance of what Jesus said. At the Temple, every day of the feast the High Priest would rise early in the morning, take a golden pitcher, and, accompanied by several musicians, would walk down to the Pool of Siloam and draw out water. He walked back, and when he came to the Water Gate another priest blew three trumpet blasts, and the people quoted Isaiah 12:3, *"Therefore with joy you will draw water from the wells of salvation"* (NKJV). He entered the Temple at the time of the morning sacrifice and with great ceremony walked around the bronze altar in the outer court, then poured the water at the base of the altar. The pouring out of water signified the Lord pouring out His salvation from heaven through the Messiah, the son of David. Then the choir sang Psalm 118. When they came to verse 25, the worshipers shook palm branches toward the altar. They believed that whenever the Messiah came, He would bring a day when God would pour out His Spirit, bringing salvation to the nations, and there would be great joy as the people worshiped Him (Isaiah 12:3–6). This was a worship celebration.

On the seventh day of the Feast, "the Great Day," the High Priest with the golden pitcher marched around the altar seven times. At the point when the worshipers were repeating Psalm 118:25, *"Save now, I pry, O LORD; O LORD, I pray, send now prosperity"* (NKJV), he poured out the water. At that point Jesus made a remarkable declaration (John 7).

📖 Read the astonishing proclamation Jesus made on the last day of the feast, *"the Great Day."* It is found in John 7:37–38. What did Jesus say? Compare this with Isaiah 55:1, 6–7 and write your insights.

____

____

____

Did You Know?

THE LAMPS OF THE FEASTS

In Jesus' day, the **lighting of lamps** in the Temple occurred at the end of the first day of the Feast of Tabernacles. Four large lampstands over 70 feet high were lit in the Court of the Women, giving light to the whole temple area. This symbolized the *Shekinah* glory that had once filled the temple in Solomon's day and spoke of the prophesied light to come (Isaiah 9:2). (See Alfred Edersheim's *The Temple, Its Ministry and Services* [Grand Rapids, Wm. B. Eerdmans, 1983], pp. 283–285.)

*See Alfred Edersheim, *The Life and Times of Jesus the Messiah,* Part II, Book IV (Grand Rapids: Wm. B. Eerdmans, 1971), chap. vii, pp. 157–161. Also see Edersheim's *The Temple, Its Ministry and Services* (Grand Rapids: Wm. B. Eerdmans, 1983) pp. 268–287.

Jesus cried out that if anyone was thirsty, he could come to Him and drink and find "living water." This "water" would fill a man's heart and overflow in his life. His invitation sounded very similar to the invitation of Isaiah 55, where the Lord called all that were thirsty to *"come to the waters . . . without cost."* The call to *"come to the waters"* is an invitation to forsake sin and call on the Lord for salvation. Isaiah pointed to God's promise of mercy and abundant pardon (Isaiah 55:7). Recognition of God's promises indicates the beginning of a life of true worship.

Did You Know?

LIVING WATER FROM THE POOL OF SILOAM

Jesus spoke of "Living Water." The term "Living Water" suggests free-flowing water from a spring or from rain rather than from a cistern or stagnant pool. As part of the festivities on the "Great Day of the Feast" (John 7:37–39), the High Priest filled a golden pitcher with "living" water from the Pool of Siloam in the southern part of Jerusalem and carried it back to the Temple. Coming from the Gihon Spring and flowing underground through Hezekiah's Tunnel, this water appeared to come from the innermost parts of Jerusalem. It was a picture of the "Living Water" coming out of the innermost being of one alive and filled with the Holy Spirit.

What was the condition for receiving this promise of "living water" according to John 7:37–38?

___

___

___

___

Who did Jesus connect with this gift of "living water" in John 7:39?

___

___

___

___

To receive the living water of Jesus, all one had to do was recognize his thirst, come, and drink. John 7:38 speaks of the necessity of coming with a believing heart, believing in Jesus as the giver of "living water"—the salvation promised ages ago by the prophets. That gift of "living water" was the very presence and life of the Spirit of God whom believers would receive after Jesus went to the cross, resurrected Himself, and ascended. His death for sin and His triumphant resurrection provided everything necessary for man to know the joy of forgiveness and eternal life.

📖 The work of the Spirit is essential if we are to be true worshipers. What else did Jesus reveal about the Spirit and His work? Look at John 16:7–15 along with John 6:63 and compare those verses. Record your insights.

___

___

___

___

___

Jesus promised that the Spirit would give life and guide believers into all the truth, which includes true worship. The Spirit would glorify Christ and lead people to worship Him. Jesus assured His disciples that the Spirit would reveal sin so that it could be dealt with. The Spirit would also lead men away from self-righteousness to true righteousness by convincing them to put their faith in Christ and His work on the cross. The Spirit would speak Christ's words, those words that are spirit and life, full and rich and living like the "living water" that Christ had so eloquently described.

The apostle Paul also testified about the work of the Spirit in his life and how this work affected his worship. Look at Philippians 3:2–3. What two actions did Paul equate with true worship in the Spirit? What connections do you see to John 7:37–39 and John 16:7–15?

____

____

____

Did You Know?

PAUL'S WARNING

Three times in Philippians 3:2 Paul used the word "beware," pointing to certain religious people who sought to lead the Philippian believers astray from true worship and away from knowing and following Christ. Paul called these religious people "dogs," "evil workers," and "the false circumcision." These people were known for false worship based on false teaching—the teaching that Jesus was not enough for salvation. They believed there must be outward circumcision and ritual; therefore, their teachings amounted to a belief in false religion, not of the true relationship Jesus brings. True worship focuses on Christ and knowing Him in His fullness—not on what one can attain in the flesh.

Those who worship in the Spirit also boast or *"glory in Christ"* and *"put no confidence in the flesh."* Paul did not boast in any merits of his own or in any outward ceremonial laws, for they could not give life. The Lord Jesus gave him life, even as Paul testified in Philippians 1:21, *"for to me to live is Christ."* Christ was his life because he was united with Him by faith. He had come to Christ and received Him by faith. Christ came to live in Paul and to flow through him. Paul boasted about Jesus and all He had done for him. In giving Jesus all the credit, he made sure everyone knew he put absolutely no confidence in the flesh. The Greek word for "confidence" is a word that means to be persuaded. Paul refused to be persuaded to trust in the "flesh" for anything. He knew that no man is saved by any connection to flesh—by physical birth or heritage, by the works of the Law, or by any number of rituals (see Philippians 3:4–10). Only as one places confidence in Christ for salvation, and then for his daily walk, can he be the kind of worshiper that pleases God.

True worship includes not only our initial trust in Christ for salvation, but also our trust in the Holy Spirit to empower us and direct us day by day. The Spirit leads us in knowing Christ more fully, in growing in faith, and in telling others of the salvation Christ can give them. The Holy Spirit also leads us to walk away from any legalistic standard, old or new, or anything that our proud flesh can work for, get credit for, and boast about. The Spirit wants us to drink the refreshing water of life, rejoice in our walk with Jesus, and allow that "living water" to overflow to others around us. The Spirit desires to lead us in worship throughout the day, every day, that we might know the joy of surrender and the fullness of His Spirit. The Holy Spirit did that with Paul and will do that with each of us as we allow Him.

For Me to Worship God

Lesson Eleven **DAY FIVE**

What does it mean for you and me to walk in true worship today? We know it is still the Father's will that we worship in spirit and truth. He is still looking at the heart of each of us. He still wants truth to reside and reign in the inner man. Jesus the Son has spoken clearly His Word about what it means to worship and follow Him. Just as the Lord was pleased with Abraham's walk of worship, so He is pleased when we obediently walk in the fear of the Lord in surrender, withholding nothing from Him. The Holy Spirit is still leading believers in the ways of God, leading them in that walk of true worship.

The Holy Spirit is still leading believers in the ways of God, leading them in a walk of true worship.

As we think through our familiar "For Me to Worship God" portion of our lesson, we must always keep in mind the central truth that worship is surrender. It is surrender to God's view of sin and to His remedy for sin. It is surrender to Jesus as Lord and Savior of our lives. It is surrender to the indwelling Holy Spirit and the mysterious ways of the Spirit. If you have ever witnessed examples of this type of surrender in a person's life, then you have seen the picture of a true worshiper. The psalmist knew something of this walk of surrender when in Psalm 84:10 he said, *"For a day in Thy courts is better than a thousand outside. I would rather stand at the threshold of the house of my God, than dwell in the tents of wickedness."* One day in the presence of God is better than a thousand anywhere else because when we are in God's presence, we can experience walking in the fullness of God. We can know the joy of life as it was meant to be. In the New Testament each believer is God's Temple, designed to experience the fullness of God's presence on a daily basis. What are some ways we can walk in God's presence and experience this fullness? A look in the New Testament uncovers the answers to that question.

Did You Know?
PAGAN WORSHIP

Pagan worship in Paul's day often included lewd acts of drunkenness and immorality. In pagan worship, the worshiper was often unconscious of his drunken actions. God wants worship in truth, in honesty, in sincerity, and with **all** one's mind.

📖 Read Ephesians 5:18 in the context of 5:15–18. What does God command? What connections to worship do you see?

____

____

____

____

____

God commands that we never be drunk with wine (or any other substance), since drunkenness is dissipation—a waste! Excessive consumption of any substance allows that substance to control us and lead us into a squandered life, a life wasted on foolish choices and foolish actions. Instead of allowing alcohol, drugs, food, or any other earthly entity to control us, God wants each of us to be filled and controlled by His Spirit. The words *"be filled"* can be translated "be continuously filled" or "allow yourself to be filled continually." God wants us to surrender, to yield to the control of His Spirit each moment of the day.

"Let the word of Christ dwell in you richly in all wisdom; teaching and admonishing one another in psalms and hymns and spiritual songs, singing with grace in your hearts to the Lord." (Colossians 3:16 KJV)

When we think of worship as surrender, we see that yielding all to the filling or control of the Holy Spirit is worship to God. In that yielding, God desires that we experience His joyous presence as He guides and guards us in all we do. It is God's will (5:17) that we walk wisely, avoid evil, and make the most of our time (5:15–16).

Recall that in both the Tabernacle and the Temple the priests and the people worshiped the Lord through sacrifices, through various offerings, and through the fellowship of the peace offering. Worship was a daily event, a weekly event (Sabbath), a monthly event (New Moon), as well as a seasonal event (the celebration in the feasts). There were times when the glory of God filled the Tabernacle and the Temple; His presence was manifested in such a way that Moses and Aaron, and later, the priests could not minister. They were filled with awe and wonder, overwhelmed by His presence (Exodus 40:34–35; 2 Chronicles 6:11–14) At other times, the joy and celebration of the people filled the Temple and the city (Nehemiah 8).

📖 Read Ephesians 5:19–21. Four evidences are listed in these verses of one who is filled with the Spirit.

Look again at Ephesians 5:19, and describe the first two evidences of the Spirit's fullness in a believer in Christ.

The first two evidences given of a person filled with the Spirit are **speaking** and **singing** with a worshiping heart. One who is full of the Spirit is surrendered to the Lord, submitted to His will. With that heart of surrender, he praises the Lord before others through speaking and singing. Vocal praise can come through psalms, hymns, and spiritual songs. Psalms are songs that are sung or spoken and often accompanied with stringed or other musical instruments. (The Greek word *psalmos* referred to the plucking of strings.) The Greek word used here for "hymns" (*humnos*) referred to verses of poetry that proclaim a message, especially a message of praise, and the word for "songs" (*odē*; related to the English "ode") referred to songs of poetry initiated and directed by the Spirit. Actually, the term *"spiritual songs"* can refer to all three types of song.

Extra Mile

DESCRIPTIONS OF WORSHIP

Read I Chronicles 16, the description of worship at the Tabernacle in David's day. What marked that time period? What similarities to Ephesians 5:18–21 do you see? Then look at the worship recorded in Revelation 4–5. What marks that worship in heaven?

What is the third evidence of a Spirit-filled person according to Ephesians 5:20? How does this relate to what we have seen about worship in the past lessons? (You may want to look at 1 Thessalonians 5:18 as well.)

Just as the Israelites often brought an offering of thanksgiving, so the person full of the Spirit will offer thanksgiving to God. However, it will not be just an occasional offering. **Giving thanks** (the third evidence) becomes an everyday, all-day reality in our relationship with Christ. It is God's will for us to be thankful to Him, and the Spirit always leads us to do the will of God.

Extra Mile

THE SPIRIT-FILLED CHRISTIAN

Read Ephesians 5:22—6:9. How does a Spirit-filled Christian act as a wife or husband (5:22–33), as a child (6:1–3), as a father (6:4), and as a worker or employer (6:5–9)?

Describe the fourth result of being filled with the Spirit in Ephesians 5:21? (You may want to look for additional insights in Ephesians 4:11–16, especially verse 16.)

A believer who is filled with the Spirit will walk with a servant's heart—ready and willing to serve others. Each will look out for the benefit of others as he or she walks in the fear of Christ. Serving the needs of others is what the Church should strive for as the Body of Christ (as seen in Ephesians 4:11–16). All entities of the Church are to show reverence and submission to Jesus Christ, the Head. They are to be controlled by the Head and directed for the benefit of all. Each entity exists to fulfill God's will. What God wants to do, where He wants to go, and what He wants to say should be clearly revealed in each person who is filled with His Spirit. When the Temple was filled with God's presence, His will was always done, and it brought great rejoicing to the people. When individual believers are filled with the Spirit, there is joy and gladness, and others are served with love.

The **filling** of the Spirit is not a once-in-a-lifetime event but a daily reality. Jesus said that we should deny ourselves, take up our cross daily, and follow Him (Luke 9:23). Why? We must die to our "self" or our "flesh" every day. To be filled with His Spirit, we must be emptied of selfishness. He wants no competition from our vain interests. We must realize that the "flesh" never gets any better. The only right place for our flesh is the place of death on the cross. Jesus provided for that in His death. In Him, we can enter into death by faith so that we might experience His Life. Exchanging physical death for eternal life is the "Great Exchange." Jesus did not come to make us slightly better. He came to give us a new life, to fill us with His Life, to change us forever. He came to live in us and to manifest Himself through us to others. That is why He sent His Spirit to indwell us as He promised. We are His temples now, and He wants to fill us each moment of each day.

Recall that in Lesson Two we talked about being filled with the Spirit. A temple is meant to be a place filled with God's presence—to show what God is like. Let's review that truth and its application.

APPLY Let's put all we have seen into one focused application. How can your life be God's dwelling place, a place of true worship? Your life can be God's dwelling place when you walk as His Temple, where sin is dealt with, forgiveness is experienced, and the fullness of His Spirit is real and lasting. You may be asking, "How can I walk in the fullness of the Holy Spirit and become the temple God wants me to be?" Someone once shared with me three very simple truths that summarize and help us answer this question on a daily basis.

☑ **Confess** any and all sin to God. Agree with Him about your sin and don't argue about it (1 John 1:9). When we agree with Him, we are walking in the fear of the Lord.

☑ **Present** yourself to God to be filled and controlled by His Spirit (Romans 12:1–2). To surrender means to withhold nothing.

☑ **Ask** Him in faith to fill you with His Spirit. He commanded us to be filled (controlled) in Ephesians 5:18, and so we know that is His will (1 John 5:14). He is not reluctant. (Don't depend on feelings; depend on Him and His Word by faith.) Expect Him to fill you as you obey His Word.

Before we finish today's lesson, it would be good to look at the worship we will experience for all eternity. Read Revelation 21:1–6; 22–27; and 22:1–5. What do these verses say about our eternal home and our worship in that place?

____

____

____

____

____

"Search me, O God, and know my heart; try me, and know my anxious thoughts; and see if there be any hurtful [wicked] way in me, and lead me in the everlasting way."

Psalm 139:23–24

". . . Behold, the tabernacle of God is among men, and He shall dwell [tabernacle] among them, and they shall be His people, and God Himself shall be among them. . . ."

Revelation 21:3

God's ultimate destiny for His children is unbroken fellowship and pure worship of Him as their Heavenly Father—an unhindered, undistracted, unsoiled walk with Him in the light of His presence. In heaven, all will walk in the fear and reverence of the Lord. Everyone will obey all He says and will surrender to Him—withholding nothing. Heaven is a home of deepest love, purest joy, and sweetest peace. In light of our future heavenly blessings and worship of the Lord, God calls us right now to a life of worshiping Him in spirit and truth—a life that will take us into eternity, where our worship will finally be perfected.

Spend some time with the Lord in prayer right now.

Lord, You alone are worthy of pure worship, of my purest surrender. Thank You for opening the way for me to know You and become a true worshiper of You, for convicting me of sin, forgiving me, and coming into my life by Your Spirit. I praise You as the Lamb slain, yet undeserving of death, especially a death on the cross for my sins. May my surrender to You be worthy of Your sacrifice. May I present to You a heart of wisdom and worship, a heart that walks in the fear of the Lord, that surrenders (withholding nothing), and that obeys You promptly and fully. Teach me all it means to worship in the Spirit, to glory in Christ Jesus, and to put no confidence in the flesh (Philippians 3:3). In Jesus' worthy name, Amen.

"And he [the angel] said to me, '. . . worship God.'"

Revelation 22:9

Write your own prayer of worship to the Lord. Use the space below to record your prayer or to journal your thoughts and insights.

Entering into Full Fellowship with God

THE GATE: This is **The Place of Entry.** The one entrance pictures the reality that there is no other way to God than through Jesus. To worship Him we must know Him (John 10:7; 14:6). **Have you come to Jesus for salvation, or are you trying other "doors"? Do you know Jesus as your personal Lord and Savior?**

THE BRAZEN ALTAR: This is **The Place of Reconciling.** It was a place of death where sin could be dealt with. The Altar of the Old Testament is a picture of the Cross of the New Testament, where the Lamb of God was slain for the sins of the world, where each believer died in Him and dies daily to the world, the flesh, and the temptations of the evil one. It is not those in rebellion to God who can worship, but those who have been reconciled to God through the death of His Son (Romans 5:10; Colossians 1:20; Ephesians 2:16). This pictures not only salvation, but the ongoing process of dealing with sin (1 John 1:7–9). **Are you walking dead to "self" and alive to God? Is there any sin from which you are unwilling to turn?**

THE BRASS LAVER: This is **The Place of Cleansing.** It pictures the sanctification that comes from the *"washing of water with the Word"* (Ephesians 5:26). The Word of God sets us apart in our thinking and living (Romans 12:1–2; John 17:17) and is central to the worship of God, for *"God is spirit, and those who worship Him must worship in spirit and truth"* (John 4:24). **Are you allowing the Spirit of God to use the Word of God to transform your mind? Do you continually look to the Lord for the truth about life so that you are increasingly believing what He says and becoming what He wants? Do you surrender daily to Him through His Word?**

THE GOLDEN LAMPSTAND: This is **The Place of Light.** It was the only source of light in the Holy Place, and it pictures the light of God's leading in our daily walk. To worship God, we must have a lifestyle of seeking and doing the will of God as He leads. **Are you walking in the light as He is in the light (1 John 1:7)? Are you letting your light shine as Jesus taught in Matthew 5:14–16, or are you hiding that light?**

THE TABLE OF SHOWBREAD: This is **The Place of Dining.** It speaks of finding our sustenance in the Lord and being satisfied with Him and His presence. He has said He will never leave us nor forsake us (Hebrews 13:5–6). The Bread of His presence speaks of practicing His presence daily and living a life of seeking Him (John 6:26–40). If He is who we pursue, then we will always be satisfied. If something else is our priority we will always be frustrated (John 4:34). **What is your satisfaction level? Are you seeking the Lord, or are you being semi-satisfied with the "junk-food" substitutes of the world, the "flesh," and the devil? How is your appetite for the things of God, for His Word, for His will?**

THE GOLDEN ALTAR OF INCENSE: This is **The Place of Prayer.** It speaks of the role of true prayer in worship. Neither impure incense nor impure prayer is acceptable to God (Exodus 30:34–38; Revelation 5:8; 8:3–4). There is no real worship without two-way communication between the Lord and us. **Is your praying like the pure incense of the Tabernacle—made according to God's directions? Are you seeking the will of God (1 John 5:14–15)? Is your prayer life "salted" (free from the decay of flesh), "pure" (without mixed motives and selfishness—James 4:1–10), or "holy" (like the prayer of those "lifting up holy hands without wrath and dissension"—1 Timothy 2:8)?**

THE ARK OF THE COVENANT AND THE MERCY SEAT: This is **The Place of Fellowship.** The ark is the throne of God (2 Samuel 6:2) sitting in the presence of God (Exodus 25:22). Once we have faithfully followed the path of the priest, we are able to bask in the reality of God's presence (the Shekinah Glory was seen in the Holy of Holies). Here we can worship in the purest way. Here in the Holy of Holies within the Veil (Hebrews 10:19–22), we can rest in His sovereignty and life-giving ability (as seen in Aaron's Rod that budded to full life and fruitfulness), His sufficiency (as seen in the Golden Jar of Manna), and in His fulfillment of His holy standards (as seen in the Tablets of the Law)—a fulfillment through the Righteous Life of the Lord Jesus (Matthew 5:17). Now by His righteous death, His sacrificial blood, His resurrection, and His reigning life we can come boldly and confidently before His throne and commune with Him (Hebrews 4:14–16, 10:19–22). We can live in His holy, loving presence. **Are you communing with the Lord day by day? Are you practicing His presence wherever you go? Are you satisfied and joyful in the Lord? Does your life and your words speak of the reality of knowing the Lord personally? Are you telling others how they too can come to Jesus Christ, find His forgiveness and abundant life and begin living the eternal life He wants them to live?**

As you look over this "Path," consider where you are. Evaluate your walk with the Lord, your fellowship with Him, and your worship of Him. Are you worshiping Him in spirit and truth—in the light of the truths found in the Tabernacle? Take time to take this walk and begin following God like He wants you to follow Him.

Notes

Notes

Christ, Our High Priest

Leading Us into True Worship and Fellowship with God

We have looked at many facets of the Tabernacle in the Old Testament. We have seen the pieces of furniture, the path of the priest in the Tabernacle, and the various offerings and sacrifices presented there. We have looked at false and true worship and the importance of making sure we are walking in true worship.

God purposed that when we look at the Tabernacle in the Old Testament, we see the need to approach God in Spirit-filled worship and remain in His presence in fellowship. The epistle to the Hebrews tells us that the Tabernacle is a shadow of the heavenly Tabernacle where we have our High Priest, the Lord Jesus Christ, who intercedes for us daily. His blood continually speaks of our cleansing before God and of our access to the Father. We have continual access to His throne, which includes confident and continuous prayer, unbroken fellowship with Him, and reliance upon His strength and power for living a faith-filled, Spirit-powered life. We can experience this life of worship by experiencing His presence and walking in His power. He came as High Priest to bring the fullness of His Spirit into our lives. In this final lesson of our study, we will see what it means to follow and experience Christ as our High Priest.

True Worship

JESUS, OUR HIGH PRIEST

Jesus Christ is *"a merciful and faithful High Priest"* (Hebrews 2:17); *"High Priest of our confession"* (3:1); *"a great High Priest"* (4:14); *"High Priest after the order of Melchizedec"* (5:10); *"a High Priest forever after the order of Melchizedec"* (6:20); *"a High Priest, holy, innocent, undefiled, separated from sinners and exalted above the heavens"* (7:26); *"a High Priest who has taken His seat at the right hand of the throne of the Majesty in the heavens"* (8:1); *"a High Priest of the good things to come"* (9:11); *"a Great Priest over the house of God"* (10:21).

The Substance of the Shadows in the Tabernacle (Hebrews 8:5; 10:1). Jesus Christ Is . . .

The Tabernacle	Our High Priest	Our Offering And Sacrifice	The Blood	The Veil	The Holy of Holies	The Mercy Seat	The Shekinah Glory
John 1:1, 14 ("dwelt" or "tabernacled," Greek—*skénoó*); Revelation 21:3	Hebrews 2:17; 3:1; 4:14–15; 5:5–10; 6:20; 7:26–28; 8:1, 3; 9:11; 10:21	Hebrews 7:27; 9:14, 28; 10:10, 12; John 1:29, 36; 6:51; 10:15–18; 1 Peter 1:19; 1 Corinthians 5:7; Ephesians 5:2	Hebrews 9:12-14; 10:19; 13:12; 20; 1 Peter 1:19	Hebrews 10:19-20 [Note: Matthew 27:51; Mark 15:38; Luke 23:45]	John 2:19-21 [Greek—*naos*]	Hebrews 2:17; 9:5; Romans 3:25; 1 John 2:2; 4:10 [Greek—*hilastérion*]	John 1:14; 17:22, 24; 2 Corinthians 3:18; 4:4, 6; Matthew 17:2; 2 Peter 1:16–18

"Since therefore, brethren, we have confidence to enter the holy place by the blood of Jesus, by a new and living way which He inaugurated for us through the veil, that is, His flesh, and since we have a great high priest over the house of God, let us draw near with a sincere heart in full assurance of faith, having our hearts sprinkled clean from an evil conscience and our bodies washed with pure water." (Hebrews 10:19–22)

Lesson Twelve **DAY ONE**

OUR SOVEREIGN HIGH PRIEST

What do the Scriptures reveal about Jesus, who is called *"a merciful and faithful High Priest"* in Hebrews 2:17? In the book of Hebrews, we are introduced to the person and ministry of this High Priest, and we see how His ministry should apply to our everyday lives. From the beginning of Hebrews, we see a majestic portrait of Jesus, a portrait that spans time and eternity and brings us into the very presence of our sovereign Lord.

The book of Hebrews paints a remarkable picture of Jesus in the first four verses of chapter 1. Read Hebrews 1:1–4 with 4:14, and describe what you discover about **who Jesus is.**

____

____

____

____

Jesus is, first of all, the Son of God, exactly like His Father in His nature and one with the Father in all His purposes. He is the heir of all things, and all things are placed under His Lordship. This Jesus is the radiance (the outshining) of the Glory of God, the clear manifestation of God in the flesh. As a man, He is the incarnation of the *Shekinah* glory. He is God Himself in every detail and, at the same time, fully man. He has the very nature of God and knows what it is to be a man in every way. He is greater than any angel—after all, He created them—and has a name greater in honor and excellence than all of them.

In Hebrews 1:1–4, 10 and 4:14, what do you find about the work Jesus did and now does?

____

____

____

____

We also learn about Jesus' work in John 17 (sometimes called the High Priestly prayer of Jesus). Hebrews 1:1–2 speaks of God's speaking through His Son. What do you see in John 17:1–8 about the work of Jesus and about what He has spoken?

Word Study
EXACT IMPRESSION

Hebrews 1:3 speaks of Jesus as *"the **exact representation** of His nature."* The words "exact representation" are translated from the Greek word, *charaktḗr,* meaning "a stamp or impression." The word was used in the first century to refer to the character or impression made by a seal or a die cut, like an engraving that makes an exact impression of a letter or a seal. Jesus is exactly like His Father and revealed the Father when He walked on this earth. He said in John 14:9, *"He who has seen Me has seen the Father."*

Did You Know?
THE SCEPTER

The scepter was a symbol of the power and authority of a king. The ruler used it to indicate his decisions and held it out as a sign of approval or to allow one to approach his throne. Hebrews 1:8 says concerning the Son, *"the righteous scepter is the scepter of His kingdom"* Every thought Jesus has, every decision He makes, every direction He takes is righteous in every detail. His kingdom is right in every way.

Jesus is the creator of the heavens, the earth, and the ages—all that is—and is now sustaining and upholding all things. He came as the God-Man, died on a cross, and made purification for our sins so that we can know His personal forgiveness. He arose from the dead and ascended through the heavens. He finished the work the Father gave Him to do. Therefore, He now sits at the right hand of the Majesty on high. In His work as the God-Man, He has done all the Father gave Him to do and has spoken all that the Father gave Him to say. Because of what He has done and what He has said, we can know God and the eternal life He gives.

What added insights about Jesus do you see in Hebrews 1:8–9?

Jesus, the Son, is the sovereign Lord. He is God, and His throne is forever. His scepter is a righteous scepter, which means that His reign is marked by righteousness in every way—everything He does, everything He says, every decision He makes. He always loves righteousness and hates lawlessness.

What are the angels commanded to do according to Hebrews 1:6?

The angels, who are part of the "all things" the Son created and now upholds, have always known that the Son is **God** and have worshiped Him. When the Father brought Him into the world as the "firstborn," the angels were commanded to worship Him then as well. As a man, He was still God and worthy of worship, not only by the angels but by us as well.

In light of who Jesus is and what He has done, what are we called and commanded to do according to Hebrews 2:1–3?

As the sovereign Lord, Jesus is able to bring about all He has promised. We must pay close attention to all that Jesus has said and all He has done. He wants us to listen to Him and know by personal experience the salvation He bought—the salvation revealed in the Word He spoke. We have written for us in the Old and New Testament scriptures the "salvation" of which He spoke first through the prophets, then through His earthly ministry, and finally through what was spoken and written by those who heard. As we listen to our sovereign Lord and follow Him, we will not drift into neglect in our walk or into unbelief in our relationship with Him.

"And the Word became flesh, and dwelt among us, and we beheld His glory, glory as of the only begotten from the Father, full of grace and truth"

John 1:14

Did You Know?

THE FIRSTBORN

In Scripture, the term "firstborn" does not necessarily mean born first. Psalm 89:20, 27 speak of David as firstborn though he was not born first. These verses ultimately refer to the Messiah as God's firstborn, *"the highest of the kings."* It is a term that refers to preeminence, to an exalted position, and in Jesus' case refers to His position as the God-Man, God in the flesh, who is Lord.

We have a sovereign Lord who is our High Priest. He is the all-powerful Creator, worthy of worship by all His creation. Not only is He powerful, but He is also good and righteous in every way.

Lesson Twelve **DAY TWO**

OUR SYMPATHETIC HIGH PRIEST

"Jesus is Lord" was a foundational confession of the early Church. In that short confession is the truth that Jesus is the sovereign God and that our sovereign Lord is Jesus the Man, the God-Man. The epistle to the Hebrews is very clear on this truth and paints a dynamic portrait of the Lord Jesus as the God-Man who understands us and sympathizes with us. We can learn much as we look at our Lord who is also our **sympathetic** High Priest.

What do you discover about Jesus in Hebrews 2:9–10?

____

____

____

____

For a little while, Jesus was made lower than the angels and had to face the suffering of death. He tasted death for everyone in fulfilling the Father's plan to bring many sons to glory, to the place of reflecting the character and nature of God. God designed for His children to become mature sons who walk in the fullness of the life of God, that is, in the reality of His glory. Recall how we have seen in the study of the Tabernacle how He clearly showed His glory to Israel in the wilderness, especially in the Tabernacle. He wants to show His glory now with each of His children, each being a "temple" or "tabernacle" of His Spirit. It was necessary for the Lord Jesus to experience suffering in becoming the mature man His Father wanted Him to be. Although Christ suffered greatly, at no time did He ever lose His sinless perfection. He remains sinless to this very day and will forever remain sinless. The word "perfect" refers to being mature, to completing a course, to reaching the intended goal.

Word Study
PROPITIATION

Jesus made "propitiation" for our sins (Hebrews 2:17). The words *"make propitiation"* are translated from the Greek word, *Hiláskomai*. The word *Hiláskomai* comes from the root word *Hilasmós*, which describes the means by which one is satisfied or appeased. According to *The Complete Word Study Dictionary New Testament* (©1992, AMG Publishers, pp. 768–770), "Jesus Christ . . . becomes *Hilasmós*, the means which is acceptable to God to satisfy His righteousness or His justice. . . . [Therefore Jesus] provides the satisfaction demanded by God's justice whereby the removal of sins is attained. . . . *Hilasmós* refers to Christ as the One who not only propitiates but offers Himself as the propitiatory sacrifice. He is both the sacrifice and the officiating High Priest" who sacrificed Himself for us.

Read Hebrews 2:14–15, 17, and 18, and write a description of Jesus' time on earth? What did He face as a man, and what does it mean to us?

____

____

____

____

____

Jesus partook of flesh and blood as a man. He was made like us in every area. He had the feelings, the physical needs, the weariness, and the temptations of a man. Those temptations were part of His sufferings. Because He never yielded in the slightest measure to any temptation He faced, He bore the full weight of every temptation, the full pressure each could bring. Jesus knew about the sins men faced from a man's perspective and from God's perspective. Therefore, when it came time to offer Himself as the sacrificial substitute and die for those sins, He went to the cross with a full knowledge of our sin and our need for atonement. He was willing to show mercy and was faithful to His Father and to us in His death. He died as a merciful and faithful High Priest. In dying on the cross as the sinless sacrifice, Jesus fully satisfied the justice of God, removing our sin debt and thus removing our death sentence. We need no longer fear death since Christ has taken our sin judgment on Himself, delivering us from enslavement to the fear of death and judgment.

We need no longer fear death since Christ has taken our sin judgment on Himself.

What do you find about our High Priest in Hebrews 4:15?

____

____

____

Jesus can sympathize with each of us because He was *"tempted in all things,"* in all areas of life. This does not mean He faced every single temptation that we have ever faced or will face. For example, Jesus was never tempted to "run a red light" or commit any other traffic violation. However, He was tempted to go past the authority of His Father and turn stones into bread after forty days of fasting (Matthew 4). Each of the temptations Jesus faced was rooted in a legitimate desire—bread for a hungry man, protection from harm, and the opportunity to rule the world. All of these desires were things that would come His way in the Father's will and in the Father's perfect timing. The temptation was to do the right thing but in the wrong way, in the wrong timing, for the wrong reason, under the wrong authority. Jesus faced the devil's arsenal of doubt, deceitful thoughts, and presumption on the Word of God, but He never budged an inch from His Father's will. He followed His Father in every choice, and He can lead us in following Him as well.

We must understand this truth. Jesus faced **every type** of temptation we face. However, there is one big difference—we are tempted according to the desires and weaknesses of our sinful flesh. Jesus did not have a sin nature, nor any sinful flesh. He was born of a virgin with no earthly father. He was conceived *"of the Holy Spirit"* (Matthew 1:20). That meant He did not inherit the sin nature of Adam (Romans 5:12, 19; 1 Corinthians 15:22), rather Jesus fully expressed the nature of His Heavenly Father, who could do no evil (James 1:13; 1 Peter 2:22). Jesus said in John 14:30 that the prince of this world (Satan) *"has nothing in Me."* There was and is still no connection between Satan and Jesus. When Satan tempted Jesus, he could find nothing in Jesus that corresponded to any sin or to the nature of sin.

When Satan tempted Jesus, he could find nothing in Jesus that corresponded to any sin or to the nature of sin.

Think of this picture. Temptation is like moving a magnet over several metal objects. If there are pieces of iron, it is the nature of that iron to be drawn to the magnet. However, if the magnet moves over a piece of aluminum, nothing happens! It is not the nature of aluminum to be drawn to the magnet. In the same way, we are born with a sin nature that is drawn in certain ways to the magnet of temptation. We can even increase that drawing force by repeated yielding, by giving in to temptation. Jesus was born of His Father and the virgin Mary. He had the nature of His Father. He had no sin nature passed down from Adam to Him. There was nothing in Him that ever responded to any temptation. It was not His nature to desire any wrong or to sin in any way—thought, word, or deed. It was His nature to hate evil in every form.

Jesus also has a full understanding of sin because no sin ever dulled His spiritual senses. Like a healthy person who can quickly sense the smell of rotten food, Jesus knows what is sinful and what is not by the "stench" or repulsiveness of that sin. A sick person can be dulled in his or her senses. Like a leper who cannot feel any pain in his hands or feet because the nerve endings have died, so a sinner is insensitive to sin until he is "healed" and awakened to the wretchedness of sin. Jesus was always aware and awake to anything that was sinful. This heightened awareness of sin added to His suffering on the cross. His sensitivity to sin was greater than any man ever knew or will ever know. While Jesus knows what we face and sympathizes to the fullest extent, He never condones our sin or treats it lightly. He came to die for that sin, to crush evil and to deliver us out of sin.

Word Study

OUR SYMPATHETIC HIGH PRIEST

Jesus sympathizes with our weaknesses (Hebrews 4:15). The Greek word for "sympathizes" is ***sumpathéō***, meaning "to feel with," "to suffer with," "or to experience something with someone." The idea in this word is more than a sympathetic thought. It is to actually feel the experience when we face it. Jesus not only understands us, He enters into our experience. He wants us to come to Him for His grace and mercy in our time of need.

Read Hebrews 2:18 and 4:15–16. What do those verses tell you about our sympathetic High Priest? What should be our response to Him according to those verses?

____

____

____

____

____

____

Because Jesus has been tempted in the things He suffered, He understands the tests and temptations we face. Not only does He understand, but He also sympathizes. He identifies with us and is ready and able to come to our aid in those temptations. He desires to help us and knows **how** to help us; Jesus has been where we are. He calls us to come to Him, to the throne of grace (not the throne of judgment). There we will find mercy and grace, that is, the enabling power of God. His promise is that He will give well-timed help—help that comes exactly when we are facing the temptation.

Hebrews 5 talks about how the earthly priests lived and acted toward those who came to them. Read Hebrews 5:1–2. What characterized the priests? In light of what we have seen about Jesus thus far, how much more can Jesus guide us?

____

____

____

____

____

The priests at the Tabernacle and at the Temple were beset with weakness; they dealt with their frailty throughout their lives. Because of their own weaknesses they could *"deal gently with the ignorant and misguided"* and were ever ready to offer sacrifices for the people. Can Jesus do that? He suffered. He was weary. He had human weaknesses, yet He was without sin. Jesus faced every type of temptation we face, so He knows more than anyone does what we go through. He can deal perfectly and gently with us in our ignorance and in our misguided ways.

Hebrews 3:1 calls us to "consider Jesus." He is our sympathetic High Priest who fully understands us, is always aware of our needs, and wants to come to our aid. Therefore, we must believe Him and trust Him rather than doubting Him or wandering in unbelief. Not only are we to consider our **sympathetic** High Priest, but Scripture calls us to know Him as our **sacrificial** High Priest. When we know Him in this way, we will be drawn to follow Him more closely than ever. We will see that in Day Three.

Our Sacrificial High Priest

Lesson Twelve **DAY THREE**

When we begin to look at the sacrifice of our High Priest, we begin to see the greatest of contrasts. We see the contrast between the old covenant and the new covenant. We see the contrast of the Old Testament sacrifices and the sacrifice of Christ. We see the temporal results of one and the eternal results of the other. When we look at our everyday walk of following God, we see a new day—a day of ready access to the true Holy of Holies, where Christ sits enthroned. We see an open heaven and open fellowship for each of us.

📖 Read Hebrews 10 and answer the questions below that pertain to this chapter in the Bible.

What was the benefit of the Old Testament sacrifices in taking away sin, according to Hebrews 10:1–4, 11?

___

___

___

The sacrifices of the Old Testament were a shadow of what was to come. They could neither bring cleansing to the worshiper nor removal of his sins. They could only remind one of sins year after year until the perfect sacrifice would come. The blood of bulls and goats, those sacrifices offered most notably on the Day of Atonement, could not take away sins. All the sacrifices of the old covenant could never take away sins.

How did Christ view the Old Testament sacrifices according to Hebrews 10:5–9?

___

___

___

Christ knew that none of the sacrifices of the Old Testament could take away sins. He knew that His Father did not desire more and more sacrifices. There was no need for more burnt offerings and sin offerings day after day and year after year. The Father looked to that one sacrifice that could take away sins, the sacrifice of His only Son. Jesus knew His body was prepared to be that sacrifice; that was His Father's will, and He willingly went to the cross as that sacrifice.

"For this reason the Father loves Me, because I lay down My life that I may take it again. No one has taken it away from Me, but I lay it down on My own initiative, . . . This commandment I received from My Father."

John 10:17–18

What do you find about the offering of the body of Christ in Hebrews 10:10?

____

____

____

Did You Know?

THE ASHES OF A HEIFER

The ashes of a heifer are described in Numbers 19 for the outward cleansing of defilement from touching something dead. Hebrews 9:13 speaks of this sprinkling and cleansing. The ashes are the evidence that the sacrificial heifer was consumed in the fires of judgment on sin and impurity. Hebrews 9:14 parallels the blood of Christ with those ashes—Jesus' blood poured out points to the fires of judgment on sin and impurity being fully quenched. We do not have to carry a burden of guilt or a dirty conscience. The application of the blood of Christ by faith gives inward cleansing of the conscience from dead works (all we have said or done apart from His Spirit). Jesus frees us to worship and serve God clean and guilt-free in the life and power and joy of His Spirit.

The offering of the body of Jesus was the will of God. Jesus gave that offering once for all, and His body is never to be offered again. By that offering, every believer stands sanctified, set apart to salvation. This is a radical contrast with the sacrifices of the old covenant.

What was the result of the sacrifice of Christ? In other words, what did He do after He offered Himself, and what does this mean according to Hebrews 10:12?

____

____

____

Jesus offered Himself as the one sacrifice for sins for all time. Never would there be a need for another sacrifice. His sacrifice was totally sufficient; the work was finished! Therefore, Jesus sat down at the right hand of God. In the earthly Tabernacle and Temple, there was no place for the high priest to sit down because the work was never finished. How different is the picture in Heaven, where Christ sits enthroned—His work of redemption complete and His promises awaiting their proper fulfillment in history.

What was the **result** of the sacrifice of Christ as far as believers are concerned? Read each of these verses, and record your insights.

10:10

____

____

10:14

____

____

Doctrine

CHRIST "SAT DOWN"

Hebrews 1:3 introduces us to the exalted Lord Jesus, who *"sat down at the right hand of the Majesty on high"* after making purification of sins. There was no place for Aaron to sit in the Tabernacle because his work was never finished. Jesus finished the work He came to do. Christ fully dealt with our sins as we see in Hebrews 8:1 (He *"has taken His seat"*); 10:12 *("having offered one sacrifice for sins for all time, sat down")*; and 12:2 *(Jesus . . . endured the cross . . . and has sat down")*.

10:15–16

____

____

10:17–18

____

____

10:19–20

____

____

Through the offering of the body of Jesus, believers have been sanctified or made holy. This means that believers have been cleansed and set apart as a special people unto God and His purposes. The sanctification of believers is both a settled fact and an ongoing process. We **are sanctified** (set apart) and we are **being sanctified** (continually set apart and increasing in maturity). To fulfill His will in His children in daily life, God has written His law on their hearts and minds. He has given us a new spiritual genetic code, a new nature that corresponds with the nature of God and that stands in opposition to the "flesh" with which we war. The Spirit of God leads us in what is right, which includes putting to death the deeds of the flesh (see Romans 8:3–14). The Spirit directs His children, and that direction is **always** in line with the Word of God. The Spirit assures us that all our sins are forgiven and forgotten; they will never be brought up against us. The offering of Jesus paid for those sins—once and for all, openingthe way for us to live in His presence knowing we are forgiven, cleansed, and welcomed. We can know a freedom from guilt, judgment, and condemnation. We can know the exhilaration and joy of being accepted in Christ, with an openness to walk welcome in His presence.

Because of the Sacrifice of our High Priest, Hebrews 10:22–25 gives us three commands, each beginning with *"let us."* What do you find the Holy Spirit commanding us. . . .

In Hebrews 10:21–22?

How can we "draw near" to God according to these verses?

In Hebrews 10:23?

How can we hold on to our hope according to this verse?

In 10:24?

According to verse 25, how can we encourage others to *"love and good deeds"*?

True Worship

REMEMBRANCE OF CHRIST

Should we remember or dwell on past sins if they have already been forgiven? The Lord says, "THEIR SINS . . . I WILL REMEMBER NO MORE" (Hebrews 10:17). In contrast, First Corinthians 11:23–26 speaks of the remembrance of Jesus—His body broken and His blood poured out for redemption and forgiveness. This is the remembrance He wants us to have, and we observe this remembrance in the Lord's Supper.

"This hope we have as an anchor of the soul, a hope both sure and steadfast and one which enters within the veil, where Jesus has entered as a forerunner for us, having become a high priest forever according to the order of Melchizedek."

Hebrews 6:19–20

God wants us to draw near to Him with a true, sincere heart, confident in the completed work of Jesus our High Priest. As the pieces of the Tabernacle and the priests who served there were sprinkled outwardly, our faith can rest in Him, knowing that, inwardly, our hearts have been sprinkled clean. In the Tabernacle, we see open access to God for the priests. But unlike the priests who only had access to God during certain ritualistic occasions in the Tabernacle and Temple, we can now have that same access **at all times**. We can openly confess our hope and confidence in all God's promises, because Jesus is faithful in all He has ever done or said. With that confidence in Jesus, we can encourage one another to walk in faith, in love, and in good deeds, knowing He will faithfully guide and direct us. To do that we must spend time with other believers to be encouraged and to encourage them, especially in light of the approaching day when we must give an account for our faith and the behavior it produced.

Jesus opened the way for us to come into the Holy Place by His own blood. Hebrews 6:18 speaks of the *"strong encouragement"* we have because of our hope in Him. Hebrews 6:19–20 paints an ancient picture to help us apply His sacrifice to daily life and to strengthen our faith and hope in Him. In the harbors around the Mediterranean Sea, there were large stones (at least one, often more) firmly embedded at the edge of the shore. These stones, known as the *anchoria* (Latin) or *agkura* (Greek), served as the anchor rock, a mooring for ships. Sometimes a ship could not come into port using its sails, and so a "forerunner" would sail ashore in a small boat, carrying a line from the ship. The forerunner then tied the ship to the *anchoria.* That line was tied to the bow of the ship and was sometimes called an *anchoria* because of its attachment to the rock. Once tied, the ship was *"sure and steadfast"* (Hebrews 6:19), not because of an ordinary anchor dragging the sea floor somewhere, but because of the solid hold of the *anchoria* in the harbor. Those on the ship could lay hold of the line, the *anchoria*, and with it draw near within the harbor. Jesus our High Priest has gone before us as our "forerunner" and tied us into the harbor *"within the veil."* We are anchored to live in His presence, fellowshipping in the Holy Place (Hebrews 10:19–22).

Lesson Twelve **DAY FOUR**

OUR STRONG HIGH PRIEST

Our High Priest calls us to come near, to come with confidence into the Holy Place. There He wants us to fellowship with Him, to find grace and mercy for our needs, and to stand strong in faith, trusting Him in every situation we face. Hebrews 11 presents those who followed God, people who walked with God by faith. Hebrews 11:6 tells us that true faith, like that of Enoch, believes "God is," that God is **God** and that He is a rewarder to those who diligently seek Him. Those in Hebrews 11 looked to God for His strength as their God, as the rewarder, as the guide and guard of their lives. Even those who faced martyrdom continued to look to Him as their strength in life, knowing He would fulfill all His promises sooner or later. Those who trust God to **guide** and **guard** them along the paths of life seek the Lord and find Him to be faithful. They worship Him. When we look at the people mentioned in Hebrews 11, we see true faith and worship in action. Like those in Psalm 84 who dwell in God's house in Zion, they *"go from strength to strength"* (84:7). How are we to walk in that faith and His strength for our lives?

📖 Hebrews 11 gives the testimony of Abraham who *"grew strong in faith"* (Romans 4:20) as well as the testimonies of other men and women of faith. How did these people practice their faith, and what did they endure? Read Hebrews 11:8–10, 24–27, 32–40 and list the things these people endured as they were made strong in faith.

Abraham left his country not knowing fully where he would live or what turns the journey would take. He left the culture (and idolatry) of Ur to live in tents in the land of Canaan, as he looked for the fulfillment of all the promises God made to him. Moses had the opportunity to live in the affluence and power of the courts of Pharaoh, but chose instead to endure rough treatment with God's people. By faith, he saw the true riches of following God, confident there was a reward for him and all who followed by faith. His endurance came through *"seeing Him who is unseen,"* believing God's Word to him and waiting on the fulfillment of God's promises at their proper time. In addition to Moses, many others faced numerous difficulties—wars and battles, wild animals and wilderness wanderings as well as mocking, scourging, chains, imprisonment, death by the sword, stoning or even being sawn in two (the report of Isaiah's death). Yet, what those in Hebrews 11 endured cannot be compared with the wonder that will come in the Resurrection, when with all God's children they receive their reward and the fullness of God's promises.

📖 Hebrews 12:1–2 shares the testimony or witness of **how** the men and women of faith endured in running their race. With the words *"let us* **also,**" Hebrews 12:1 introduces us to three characteristics of these witnesses that we are told to emulate. What are those characteristics?

Like a runner in a race who would never wear needless gear, we must *"lay aside every encumbrance,"* anything that **slows** us in the race. This "encumbrance" may be something that on the surface appears harmless in and of itself, but it slows our pace; it causes us to lag behind. We must also jettison the sin that *"entangles us,"* that which **stops** us from making progress in the race. Sin is something that misses the mark of God's will. These entanglements or sins are wrong, unrighteous, and God wants none of them in our lives. Once we have taken care of the things that hinder, we must look to what will help us make progress. What will **strengthen** us in our race? To endure, we must look away from any thing on which we depend and focus on Jesus. As we look to Him, our faith is strengthened. In Him, we find the ability to bear up under the rigors of the race marked out for us. Jesus is our

"How blessed are those who dwell in Thy house! They are ever praising Thee. How blessed is the man whose strength is in Thee; in whose heart are the highways to Zion!"

Psalm 84:4–5

LOOKING UNTO JESUS

Christ and the writers of Scripture spoke of those who followed in faith, ***looking to Jesus*** (see Hebrews 12:2 KJV). Jesus said Moses *"wrote of Me"* (John 5:46), and Hebrews 11:27 says Moses *"endured, as seeing Him who is unseen."* Jesus stated, *"Abraham rejoiced to see My day,"* and John 8:56 tells us Isaiah *"saw His glory, and he spoke of Him"* (John 12:41).

Doctrine
AUTHOR AND PERFECTER

Jesus is the Beginner and Completer of our faith (Hebrews 12:2). He starts faith, and He brings it to its full goal or completion. As He is the Alpha and the Omega, the Beginning and the End for all of human history, so He is the Beginner and the Completer of the faith in which we walk. As we look to Him, we can grow in faith.

Extra Mile
THE CRUCIFIXION

What insights do you see about Jesus and His crucifixion in Psalm 22 and the other accounts of the crucifixion in Matthew 26:47–68; Mark 14:43–65; 15:1–39; Luke 22:47–71; 23; John 18—19; and 1 Peter 2:22–23?

strong High Priest who understands what it means to endure, and He can give us His strength to endure.

Hebrews 12:2 tells us to endure, *"fixing our eyes on Jesus."* We have seen that Christ was tempted in all things yet never sinned and that He can come to our aid. What more can we learn about how strong our High Priest is?

Read Hebrews 12:2–3 along with Matthew 27:11–51, one of the accounts of the crucifixion. What do the Scriptures show He "endured"?

____

____

____

____

Jesus faced great shame, hostility, and hatred in going to the cross. He was mocked and ridiculed in all the trials He faced (there were three Jewish trials and three Roman trials). He was scourged, given a mock scepter and a crown of thorns, a king's robe and mock praise. He was crucified naked on a Roman cross, bearing the shame of a criminal and the pain of our sin, forsaken by His own Father. He endured it all, trusting His Father and knowing there was great joy set before Him.

Moses endured, *"seeing Him who is unseen"* (11:27). We endure in the same way, *"fixing our eyes on Jesus."* Hebrews 12:3 says, *"For consider Him who has endured"* the cross and the hostility of sinners *"so that you may not grow weary and lose heart."* Those things can easily happen to someone running a race. The words *"grow weary and lose heart"* literally mean "to become weary and give up." What are you facing in the race?

Hebrews 12:4–9 shows us the child-training ("discipline" or "chastisement"—Greek, *paideía*) God uses to strengthen us to endure. What else do you observe in those verses?

____

____

____

____

Looking at Jesus and all He faced will help us focus on the Father's ways with us. We have not come close to enduring what Jesus faced; we have not waged war to the point of bloodshed in striving against sin. We can easily forget the exhortation God has given us in His Word. To be a son of God, one must experience and respect the Father's child-training by never treating Him or the training lightly. When we are reproved and corrected by the Lord, we must guard against fainting or wanting to give up. His training, reproof, and scourging are all marks of His love as our Father. As we yield to Him and His training, we will grow strong. As we face the difficulties that can come with child-training, we know that we can call on Him for help, and He will answer. He does not just send help; He **is** our help and our strength. Knowing we are loved and linked to Him and His purposes gives us a sense of purpose in all of life. God is working throughout the lives of all who trust Him, training ("disciplining") us all along the way.

It is vital to understand that God trains us in many ways. He uses many circumstances and many people to influence us throughout our lives. Sometimes His training is **corrective** or **preventive**—to stop us in sin or to keep us from sin. Sometimes His training is **instructive.** Instructive training comes in the form of principles and guidelines that show us the way. God has a variety of ways in which He applies each of these types of training. Some situations in life include all three types of training: corrective, preventive, and instructive. He sometimes brings **barriers** into life—things that keep us from going the wrong way, things that hedge our way like a hedge of thorns, protecting us. Though these barriers may occasionally hurt us temporarily, they are never meant for our harm, only for our good. Such barriers can actually be very instructive. At other times **blessings** from God may be used as an instructive form of training. Sometimes God gives us an unexpected blessing that helps us know Him better. Blessings can also confirm God's will in a particular area or encourage us to endure. Both **barriers** and **blessings** are loving **boundaries** that the Lord places around our lives to train us in His holiness. They lead us to His best for our lives. Hebrews 12:10–11 speaks about this.

Word Study

A FATHER'S INSTRUCTION

Ephesians 6:4 speaks of *"the discipline* [Greek—*paideia*] *and instruction* [Greek—*nouthesía*] *of the Lord." Paideía* is the caring, corrective, and all-encompassing child training of Hebrews 12. *Nouthesía* refers to instruction and admonition which can take one of two forms: words of encouragement that guide and direct as well as words of reproof that stop, correct, and redirect. Our Father encourages while He corrects us.

What is the result toward which the Lord aims according to Hebrews 12:10–11?

___

___

___

The Lord wants us to receive His training so we know and experience His holiness in all of life, experiencing what it means to be set apart to Him and His ways. We must cooperate with Him to be fully trained. As we see God's sovereignty explained from chapters 1 and 12 of the epistle to the Hebrews, we see how God can work things in our lives to train us that we may come to experience His holiness. God's holiness refers to His being set apart from His creation in a special way. It includes His total satisfaction with Himself, with His ways, with His wisdom, with who He is. God is always right, and all the actions and words that come from Him are right. He wants us to share that satisfaction of holiness with Him as we surrender by faith to Him and His ways. Surrender opens the way for knowing God's satisfaction and partaking of the *"peaceful fruit of righteousness."* That includes the peace of right relationships—the peace and harmony that exists when we are right with God and with others.

How do we experience this to the fullest? How are we to walk in life experiencing our sovereign and sympathetic High Priest? How are we to know the full meaning of His sacrifice and live in His strength? We will see these things in Day Five.

FOR ME TO WORSHIP GOD

Lesson Twelve **DAY FIVE**

We have looked at Jesus our High Priest and have seen what He has done for us. The Lord wants us to understand His priestly role in a very practical, daily way. He wants us to walk in the assurance of His sovereignty and strength, to know the joy of His presence

Remember that Christ is taking us to His glory—to the fullness of His presence, the completion of His purpose, and the total satisfaction of His heart.

and the reality of His victory over sin. Remember, He is taking us to glory—to the fullness of His presence, the completion of His purpose, and the total satisfaction of His heart (Hebrews 2:10; 2 Corinthians 3:18). Even now we are moving from one level of glory to another; we are learning what it means to experience His presence as in the Holy of Holies (10:19–22). How can we experience this more fully?

First of all, we must recall what God has revealed about Himself. He is the God who is **able** to accomplish His will in our lives as we follow and worship Him. Look at each of the verses listed below that deal with God's ability, then record what each verse is saying and how that verse can make a difference in how you worship and follow Him.

Hebrews 2:18—He is able______________________________

____

____

Hebrews 4:12–13—The Word of God is able ____________________

____

____

Hebrews 7:25—He is able ______________________________

____

____

Jude 1:24—He is able ________________________________

____

____

Ephesians 3:20—He is able _____________________________

____

____

____

It is evident that the Lord is able to come to our aid in any temptation or trial we face. As we walk with Him and pay attention to His Word, He shows us our hearts and motives, and then we receive a true evaluation of our thoughts and deeds. When we draw near to God, we discover that *"He is able to save* [us] *forever"* (Hebrews 7:25), or as some translate, "able to save us completely" in every way. That is His ability, and we can rest in Him to finish the salvation He has begun. We **are** saved from the penalty of sin; we are **being** saved from the power of sin; we **will be** saved from the presence of sin. We will one day know the fullness of His salvation as we rejoice in our resurrection bodies (see Philippians 1:6; 2:13; 3:20–21; 4:13). This is guaranteed because He has the power to keep us from stumbling and to make us stand before Him—*"in the presence of His glory blameless with great joy"* (Jude 1:24). Until that day, we continue to worship and follow Him, listening to Him through His Word and calling on Him in prayer. We are assured that His power will continue to work within us, showing us His sovereign hand and His sympathetic heart, applying the full power of His sacrifice as He trains us to trust and rely on Him. He is making us the children He wants us to be.

Jesus Christ, Our High Priest

Sovereign High Priest	**Sympathetic High Priest**	**Sacrificial High Priest**	**Strong High Priest**
Hebrews 1	Hebrews 2—5	Hebrews 6—10	Hebrews 11—13
We can rest assured of His sovereign power and care.	We can walk in His sympathetic care in every of life.	We can know His forgiveness, His presence within, and enter into joyful fellowship with Him	We can know His strength for every day, for every circumstance, in every place we go.

True faith and worship start with this clear revelation that "God is able." How then can this revelation become real in daily life? How is Jesus to be real as **my** High Priest? How do I access this ability of God in my life? How do I fulfill what Hebrews 12:12–13 commands? Those verses state, *"Therefore, strengthen* [literally, "make straight"] *the hands that are weak and the knees that are feeble, and make straight paths for your feet, so that the limb which is lame may not be put out of joint, but rather be healed."* Many of the people addressed in Hebrews were weary, tired of the race, facing rejection, dealing with doubts about Christ, and in danger of stumbling badly. The Lord wanted them to run a strong race, and He wants the us to do the same. How are we to do that?

True faith and worship start with this clear revelation that "God is able!"

Proverbs 3:5–6 speaks about the Lord making our paths **straight**. If we are to walk (or run) on straight paths (Hebrews 12:12–13), we must know what those paths are. That means we must follow God in what He says, for example in Hebrews 12:1–11, especially the command in verse 2 to fix our eyes on Jesus.

APPLY Proverbs 3 gives us some very practical guidance as to what it means to walk with God. Look at each of the commands from Proverbs 3:5–6? Read each phrase and the questions that follow below and consider how these phrases from Scripture apply to your life.

"Trust in the Lord with all your heart" [a command]—Are things getting in the way of your trust? What helps you trust or walk in faith? What helps your heart ("all your heart") focus on the Lord and the things of God?

"Do not lean on your own understanding"—"Lean" means "to depend upon" for support. Are you relying on God's wisdom? Are you guarding against depending only on your own understanding and opinions? [Note: This command does not say, "do not **use** your own understanding." It says *"do not* **lean** *on"* it.] Are you spending time in God's Word (His understanding)?

Are there any situations you are facing which you are tempted to handle on your own?

____

____

____

____

"In all your ways acknowledge* [know] *Him" [a command]—Are you knowing or experiencing God in all your ways? What are some of the "ways" of your life in which you have seen God at work? What are some of your "ways" that need His touch? Are you spending time in prayer giving Him those "ways"?

____

____

____

____

____

____

The Lord promises that if one follows His commands in Proverbs 3:5–6, He will make the paths straight; He will remove the things that cause one to stumble. But how can we consistently walk on straight paths? Hebrews 12 tells us the Lord will "child-train" each of His children, but we must understand **how** He does that. We must understand His ways, especially His "training" ways.

Each of us should interact with the Lord in the circumstances of life, instead of reacting to the circumstances

We all know that no one is effectively trained in anything unless he or she cooperates with the trainer, listening with a learner's heart and applying the training to life. In order to follow God, we must learn to interact with our Trainer, the Lord. One of the ways to interact with the Lord is to ask the questions, "What are You saying in this situation, Lord? How should I respond in this situation? What is Your way in this? What are You teaching me in this?" Each of us should **interact** with the Lord in the circumstances of life **instead of reacting** to circumstances. Often, full of fear or doubt, we react to the circumstance, to the people involved, or even to the Lord, instead of interacting with Him in trust and worship.

This **interaction** is the essence of Proverbs 3:5–6. When verse 6 says to *"acknowledge Him,"* it uses the Hebrew word *yada,* which means to know by experience. The word is used in the Old Testament in the contexts of sailing a vessel, hunting wild game, playing a musical instrument, and of the close, intimate relationship of a husband and wife. The author of the proverb wants us to know or acknowledge the Lord, to experience Him in all our ways, and to trust Him to make our paths straight. God promises to give us a stable walk, an "unstumbling" walk. The paths in which He leads us and trains us require that we trust Him and lean not on our own limited understanding. God knows what will cause us to trip or stumble, so He leads us to watch each step. But to receive guidance from the Lord, we must continually interact with Him. We must live a life of drawing near, of trusting Him as our High Priest.

When Jesus walked on this earth, He was the perfect High Priest in every way. When He was interrupted, He continually looked for what the Father was doing. What looked like an interruption was often one of the Father's appointments to fulfill His will. Jesus never "reacted" to the circumstances around Him without seeking His Father's will. Jesus always interacted with His Father and with the people who appeared on the surface to be an interruption (that is the way His disciples often saw them). For example, in Mark 5:21–43, Jesus was on the way to Jairus' house because Jairus' daughter was sick. As Jesus walked, a woman with an issue of blood came up, touched Him, and was immediately healed. Jesus knew this was no ordinary encounter. The people around Him failed to recognize what was taking place. Jesus stopped and talked with her, confirmed her faith, and rejoiced in her healing. Then some came saying that Jairus' daughter had died and that there was no need for Jesus to come. To Jairus, the interruption caused by the woman with the issue of blood must have seemed to be a delay of denial that resulted in his daughter's death. How could his daughter possibly be healed now? However, this was a delay of destiny for the woman and for Jairus' daughter. Jesus went on to Jairus' house and raised his daughter from the dead. Jairus' daughter and the sick woman are two examples of how Jesus revealed Himself as the sovereign and almighty Lord; as a man sympathetic to the needs around Him; as the one able to deliver from disease and death; and the one able to strengthen—regardless of the challenge.

Make sure you keep your feet in the paths that Christ has laid out for you—the straight paths of His holiness.

Hebrews 10–13 shows us this interactive design of God throughout the history of His people as well as in our own day. We have been brought into the presence of God through the blood of Jesus our High Priest and Mediator. Whether pictured from the Holy of Holies (10:19) or from Mount Zion (12:22), Jesus our Mediator, our *Shekinah Glory*, speaks clearly to us. Do not lose heart or think of quitting in the race of faith. God has a guaranteed future when all that faith holds now will be unveiled, when His presence will be fully revealed and His promises fulfilled. Make sure you keep your feet in the paths He has laid out for you, the straight paths of His holiness. Keep looking to Him, listening to Him, being trained by Him. Keep on loving others, and encourage them to trust God. God will always be present with you to guide you by His Word and to strengthen you by His grace. Know the Way that is eternal, the Way of true worship. Worship Jesus Christ as King of kings and Lord of your life.

APPLY As you think back over all we have seen in the Tabernacle and in the life and ministry of Jesus, think of these final words about our merciful and faithful High Priest. Hebrews 13:20–21 encourages us with these words . . .

> *"Now the God of peace who brought up from the dead the great* [the **Sovereign**] *Shepherd of the sheep* [our **Sympathetic** High Priest, the One who sympathizes as a shepherd with His sheep] *through the blood of the eternal covenant, even Jesus our Lord* [our **Sacrificial** High Priest], *equip you in every good thing to do His will, working in us that which is pleasing in His sight, through Jesus Christ* [our **Strong** High Priest is doing the equipping and the strengthening to do His will], *to whom be the glory forever and ever. Amen."*

He wants His sovereignty, His sympathy, His sacrifice, and His strength made real to us. This is His will for us—nothing more, nothing less, nothing else. Won't you accept His will for your life today?

Spend some time with the Lord in prayer.

Lord, I worship You as my High Priest and yield to You as my Sovereign Lord. Thank You for loving and caring for me, for showing me mercy time and time again as my sympathetic High Priest. Thank You for Your grace, Your power that enables me to face and overcome temptation. I know my salvation is only made possible through Your sacrifice on the Cross. You bought me with Your blood and brought me to Yourself, setting me apart for Your purposes. Thank You! Thank You! Thank You, dear Lord! You delivered me out of my self-destructive path and set me on the path to real holiness and purity, real satisfaction and joy, real love and real family with You as my Father. Your strength is real for daily life, and I am so grateful. I praise You for the equipping You are doing in my life so that I might do Your will to the fullest, that I might worship You in spirit and truth, and that I might walk in a manner pleasing to You. In Jesus' name, Amen.

Write your own prayer of worship to the Lord or make a journal entry that reflects your worship of Him.

Notes

Notes

How to Follow God

Starting the Journey

Did you know that you have been on God's heart and mind for a long, long time? Even before time existed you were on His mind. He has always wanted you to know Him in a personal, purposeful relationship. He has a purpose for your life and it is founded upon His great love for you. You can be assured it is a good purpose and it lasts forever. Our time on this earth is only the beginning. God has a grand design that goes back into eternity past and reaches into eternity future. What is that design?

The Scriptures are clear about God's design for man—God created man to live and walk in oneness with Himself. Oneness with God means being in a relationship that is totally unselfish, totally satisfying, totally secure, righteous and pure in every way. That's what we were created for. If we walked in that kind of relationship with God we would glorify Him and bring pleasure to Him. Life would be right! Man was meant to live that way—pleasing to God and glorifying Him (giving a true estimate of who God is). Adam sinned and shattered his oneness with God. Ever since, man has come short of the glory of God: man does not and cannot please God or give a true estimate of God. Life is not right until a person is right with God. That is very clear as we look at the many people who walked across the pages of Scripture, both Old and New Testaments.

Jesus Christ came as the solution for this dilemma. Jesus Christ is the glory of God—the true estimate of who God is in every way. He pleased His Father in everything He did and said, and He came to restore oneness with God. He came to give man His power and grace to walk in oneness with God, to follow Him day by day enjoying the relationship for which he was created. In the process, man could begin to present a true picture of Who God is and experience knowing Him personally. You may be asking, "How do these facts impact my life today? How does this become real to me now? How can I begin the journey of following God in this way?" To come to know God personally means you must choose to receive Jesus Christ as your personal Savior and Lord.

- First of all, you must admit that you have sinned, that you are not walking in oneness with God, not pleasing Him or glorifying Him in your life (Romans 3:23; 6:23; 8:5-8).
- It means repenting of that sin—changing your mind, turning to God and turning away from sin—and by faith receiving His forgiveness based on His death on the Cross for you (Romans 3:21-26; 1 Peter 3:18).
- It means opening your life to receive Him as your living, resurrected Lord and Savior (John 1:12). He has promised to come and indwell you by His Spirit and live in you as the Savior and Master of your life (John 14:16-21; Romans 14:7-9).
- He wants to live His life through you—conforming you to His image, bearing His fruit through you and giving you power to reign in life (John 15:1,4-8; Romans 5:17; 7:4; 8:29, 37).

You can come to Him now. In your own words, simply tell Him you want to know Him personally and you willingly repent of your sin and receive His forgiveness and His life. Tell Him you want to follow Him forever (Romans 10:9-10, 13). Welcome to the Family of God and to the greatest journey of all!!!

Walking on the Journey

How do we follow Him day by day? Remember, Christ has given those who believe in Him everything pertaining to life and godliness, so that we no longer have to be slaves to our "flesh" and its corruption (2 Peter 1:3-4). Day by day He wants to empower us to live a life of love and joy, pleasing to Him and rewarding to us. That's why Ephesians 5:18 tells us to *"be filled with the Spirit"*—keep on being controlled by the Spirit who lives in you. He knows exactly what we need each day and we can trust Him to lead us (Proverbs 3:5-6). So how can we cooperate with Him in this journey together?

To walk with Him *day by day* means ...

- reading and listening to His Word day by day (Luke 10:39, 42; Colossians 3:16; Psalm 19:7-14; 119:9).
- spending time talking to Him in prayer (Philippians 4:6-7).
- realizing that God is God and you are not, and the role that means He has in your life.

This allows Him to work through your life as you fellowship, worship, pray and learn with other believers (Acts 2:42), and serve in the good works He has prepared for us to do—telling others who Jesus is and what His Word says, teaching and encouraging others, giving to help meet needs, helping others, etc. (Ephesians 2:10).

God's goal for each of us is that we be conformed to the image of His Son, Jesus Christ (Romans 8:29). But none of us will reach that goal of perfection until we are with Him in Heaven, for then "we shall be like Him, because we shall see Him just as He is" (1 John 3:2). For now, He wants us to follow

Him faithfully, learning more each day. Every turn in the road, every trial and every blessing, is designed to bring us to a new depth of surrender to the Lord and His ways. He not only wants us to do His will, He desires that we surrender to His will His way. That takes trust—trust in His character, His plan and His goals (Proverbs 3:5-6).

As you continue this journey, and perhaps you've been following Him for a while, you must continue to listen carefully and follow closely. We never graduate from that. That sensitivity to God takes moment-by-moment surrender, dying to the impulses of our flesh to go our own way, saying no to the temptations of Satan to doubt God and His Word, and refusing the lures of the world to be unfaithful to the Lord who gave His life for us.

God desires that each of us come to maturity as sons and daughters: to that point where we are fully satisfied in Him and His ways, fully secure in His sovereign love, and walking in the full measure of His purity and holiness. If we are to clearly present the image of Christ for all to see, it will take daily surrender and daily seeking to follow Him wherever He leads, however He gets there (Luke 9:23-25). It's a faithful walk of trust through time into eternity. And it is worth everything. Trust Him. Listen carefully. Follow closely.

Following God

THE LEADER'S GUIDEBOOK

LIFE PRINCIPLES FOR WORSHIP FROM THE TABERNACLE

Preface

A Leader's Guide is for leaders. What does it mean to be a leader? The apostle Paul stands as one of the most noteworthy leaders in all of human history. In 1 Corinthians 3:10, Paul states, *"According to the grace of God which was given to me, as a wise master builder I laid a foundation, and another is building upon it. But let each man be careful how he builds upon it."* Upon close examination, that verse speaks volumes about leadership. As a small group leader you are building on a foundation laid by someone before you. What is the counsel of the Holy Spirit to us through the apostle Paul? What was he saying to the Corinthians that applies to us today?

First, Paul speaks of being a wise master builder. The Greek word he uses for master builder, *architekton*, is where we get our word, "architect." But *architekton* pictures more than simply the act of designing a building. It comes from two root words: *arche,* meaning "beginning," "origin," or "the person that begins something" and *tekton,* which means "bringing forth," "begetting," or "giving birth." *Architekton* carries the idea of one who leads forth, who goes first, who is the first to bring something to light. As a small group leader, you have the opportunity to guide people in the discovery of what it means to follow God. As you discuss each of the lessons and the people and concepts you will meet in those lessons, you and your group will learn some eternal truths about what it means to follow Jesus day by day.

Paul speaks of another aspect of being a Spirit-filled leader, and it is the essential work of *"the grace of God."* All Paul did, all he taught, every spiritual truth he helped others to see, was by the grace of God. It should be the same for you. You must depend on the Lord to be the Teacher for these lessons. By His Spirit, He will guide you in understanding His Word and His ways with His children. He will open the pages of Scripture. He alone knows the heart of each group member, and He alone has the wisdom you and your group need to walk through these lessons and to make the applications to daily life.

In 1 Corinthians 3:10, the Greek word for "*building*" refers to continuous, ongoing building, and pictures placing brick upon brick, stone upon stone. We are building day by day as we spend time with the Lord in His Word and obey what He is teaching us. As you walk through each lesson week after week, another stone can be added to the life of each group member, another truth can be built into each life, and another set of truths can be added to what God is doing in you as a group. Each group will be unique. Each week will be unique. The creativity and work of the Spirit of God will ebb and flow in different ways in each heart and in the group as a whole. You as a leader have the opportunity to encourage your group to be watching for the building work of the Spirit of God. Some insights will come when each is alone with the Lord. Other insights will not be seen until you come together as a group. The Spirit of God uses both means. It is a continuous adventure of discovering more about Him, His ways, and what it means to follow Him.

With this Leader's Guide, we want to come alongside and help you lead your small group in **following God** more closely and more consistently. Be a focused, attentive leader/builder. Paul said *"let* **each** *man be careful how he builds."* That means each of us. No one is exempt. As a small group facilitator, you will have the opportunity to lead others and experience one of the greatest times of building lives. Let us lead as "*careful*" builders, depending on the grace and the wisdom of God.

Following His leadership,

Wayne A. Barber | Eddie Rasnake | Richard L. Shepherd

Table of Contents

Causes of a Poor Study Group

The best way to become a better discussion leader is to regularly evaluate your group discussion sessions. The most effective leaders are those who consistently look for ways to improve.

But before you start preparing for your first group session, you need to know the problem areas that will most likely weaken the effectiveness of your study group. Commit now to have the best Bible study group that you can possibly have. Ask the Lord to motivate you as a group leader and to steer you away from bad habits.

How to Guarantee a Poor Discussion Group:

1. Prepare inadequately.
2. Show improper attitude toward people in the group (lack of acceptance).
3. Fail to create an atmosphere of freedom and ease.
4. Allow the discussion to wander aimlessly.
5. Dominate the discussion yourself.
6. Let a small minority dominate the discussion.
7. Leave the discussion "in the air," so to speak, without presenting any concluding statements or some type of closure.
8. Ask too many "telling" or "trying" questions. (Don't ask individuals in your group pointed or threatening questions that might bring embarrassment to them or make them feel uncomfortable.)
9. End the discussion without adequate application points.
10. Do the same thing every time.
11. Become resentful and angry when people disagree with you. After all, you did prepare. You are the leader!
12. End the discussion with an argument.
13. Never spend any time with the members of your group other than the designated discussion meeting time.

Helpful Hints

One of the best ways to learn to be an effective Bible discussion leader is to sit under a good model. If you have had the chance to be in a group with an effective facilitator, think about the things that made him or her effective. Though you can learn much and shape many convictions from those good models, you can also glean some valuable lessons on what not to do from those who didn't do such a good job. Bill Donahue has done a good job of categorizing the leader's role in facilitating dynamic discussion into four key actions. They are easy to remember as he links them to the acrostic ACTS:

*A leader ACTS to facilitate discussions by:

Acknowledging everyone who speaks during a discussion.
Clarifying what is being said and felt.
Taking it to the group as a means of generating discussion.
Summarizing what has been said.

*Taken from *Leading Life-Changing Small Groups* ©1996 by the Willow Creek Association. Used by permission of Zondervan Publishing House.

Make a point to give each group member ample opportunity to speak. Pay close attention to any nonverbal communication (i.e. facial expressions, body language, etc.) that group members may use, showing their desire to speak. The four actions in Bill Donahue's acrostic will guarantee to increase your effectiveness, which will translate into your group getting more out of the Bible study. After all, isn't that your biggest goal?

Dealing with Talkative Timothy

Throughout your experiences of leading small Bible study groups, you will learn that there will be several stereotypes who will follow you wherever you go. One of them is **"Talkative Timothy."** He will show up in virtually every small group you will ever lead. (Sometimes this stereotype group member shows up as "Talkative Tammy.") "Talkative Timothy" talks too much, dominates the discussion time, and gives less opportunity for others to share. What do you do with a group member who talks too much? Below you will find some helpful ideas on managing the "Talkative Timothy's" in your group.

The best defense is a good offense. To deal with "Talkative Timothy" before he becomes a problem, one thing you can do is establish as a ground rule that no one can talk twice until everyone who wants to talk has spoken at least once. Another important ground rule is "no interrupting." Still another solution is to go systematically around the group, directing questions to people by name. When all else fails, you can resort to a very practical approach of sitting beside "Talkative Timothy." When you make it harder for him (or her) to make eye contact with you, you will create less chances for him to talk.

After taking one or more of these combative measures, you may find that "Timothy" is still a problem. You may need to meet with him (or her) privately. Assure him that you value his input, but remind him that you want to hear the comments of others as well. One way to diplomatically approach "Timothy" is to privately ask him to help you draw the less talkative members into the discussion. Approaching "Timothy" in this fashion may turn your dilemma into an asset. Most importantly, remember to love "Talkative Timothy."

Silent Sally

Another person who inevitably shows up is **"Silent Sally."** She doesn't readily speak up. Sometimes her silence is because she doesn't yet feel comfortable enough with the group to share her thoughts. Sometimes it is simply because she fears being rejected. Often her silence is because she is too polite to interrupt and thus is headed off at the pass each time she wants to speak by more aggressive (and less sensitive) members of the group. It is not uncommon in a mixed group to find that "Silent Sally" is married to "Talkative Timothy." (Seriously!) Don't mistakenly interpret her silence as meaning that she has nothing to contribute. Often those who are slowest to speak will offer the most meaningful contributions to the group. You can help "Silent Sally" make those significant contributions. Below are some ideas.

Make sure, first of all, that you are creating an environment that makes people comfortable. In a tactful way, direct specific questions to the less talkative in the group. Be careful though, not to put them on the spot with the more difficult or controversial questions. Become their biggest fan—make sure you cheer them on when they do share. Give them a healthy dose of affirmation. Compliment them afterward for any insightful contributions they make. You may want to sit across from them in the group so that it is easier to notice any nonverbal cues they give you when they want to speak. You should also come to their defense if another group member responds to them in a negative, stifling way. As you pray for each group member, ask that the Lord would help the quiet ones in your group to feel more at ease during the discussion time. Most of all, love "Silent Sally," and accept her as she is—even when she is silent!

Tangent Tom

We have already looked at "Talkative Timothy" and "Silent Sally." Now let's look at another of those stereotypes who always show up. Let's call this person, **"Tangent Tom."** He is the kind of guy who loves to talk even when he has nothing to say. "Tangent Tom" loves to chase rabbits regardless of where they go. When he gets the floor, you never know where the discussion will lead. You need to understand that not all tangents are bad, for sometimes much can be gained from discussion that is a little "off the beaten path." But diversions must be balanced against the purpose of the group. What is fruitful for one member may be fruitless for everyone else. Below are some ideas to help you deal with "Tangent Tom."

Evaluating Tangents

Ask yourself, "How will this tangent affect my group's chances of finishing the lesson?" Another way to measure the value of a tangent is by asking, "Is this something that will benefit all or most of the group?" You also need to determine whether there is a practical, spiritual benefit to this tangent. Paul advised Timothy to refuse foolish and ignorant speculations, knowing that they produce quarrels. (See 2 Timothy 2:23.)

Addressing Tangents:

1) Keep pace of your time, and use the time factor as your ally when addressing "Tangent Tom." Tactfully respond, "That is an interesting subject, but since our lesson is on ________________, we'd better get back to our lesson if we are going to finish."
2) If the tangent is beneficial to one but fruitless to the rest of the group, offer to address that subject after class.
3) If the tangent is something that will benefit the group, you may want to say, "I'd like to talk about that more. Let's come back to that topic at the end of today's discussion, if we have time."
4) Be sure you understand what "Tangent Tom" is trying to say. It may be that he has a good and valid point, but has trouble expressing it or needs help in being more direct. Be careful not to quench someone whose heart is right, even if his methods aren't perfect. (See Proverbs 18:23.)

5) One suggestion for diffusing a strife-producing tangent is to point an imaginary shotgun at a spot outside the group and act like you are firing a shot. Then say, "That rabbit is dead. Now, where were we?"

6) If it is a continual problem, you may need to address it with this person privately.

7) Most of all, be patient with "Tangent Tom." God will use him in the group in ways that will surprise you!

Know–It-All Ned

The Scriptures are full of characters who struggled with the problem of pride. Unfortunately, pride isn't a problem reserved for the history books. It shows up today just as it did in the days the Scriptures were written. Pride is sometimes the root-problem of a know-it-all group member. **"Know-It-All Ned"** may have shown up in your group by this point. He may be an intellectual giant, or only a legend in his own mind. He can be very prideful and argumentative. "Ned" often wants his point chosen as the choice point, and he may be intolerant of any opposing views—sometimes to the point of making his displeasure known in very inappropriate ways. A discussion point tainted with the stench of pride is uninviting—no matter how well spoken! No one else in the group will want anything to do with this kind of attitude. How do you manage the "Know-It-All Ned's" who show up from time to time?

Evaluation

To deal with "Know-It-All Ned," you need to understand him. Sometimes the same type of action can be rooted in very different causes. You must ask yourself, "Why does 'Ned' come across as a know-it-all?" It may be that "Ned" has a vast reservoir of knowledge but hasn't matured in how he communicates it. Or perhaps "Ned" really doesn't know it all, but he tries to come across that way to hide his insecurities and feelings of inadequacy. Quite possibly, "Ned" is prideful and arrogant, and knows little of the Lord's ways in spite of the information and facts he has accumulated. Still another possibility is that Ned is a good man with a good heart who has a blind spot in the area of pride.

Application

"Know-It-All Ned" may be the most difficult person to deal with in your group, but God will use him in ways that will surprise you. Often it is the "Ned's" of the church that teach each of us what it means to love the unlovely in Gods strength, not our own. In 1 Thessalonians 5:14, the apostle Paul states, *"And we urge you, brethren, admonish the unruly, encourage the fainthearted, help the weak, be patient with all men."* In dealing with the "Ned's" you come across, start by assuming they are weak and need help until they give you reason to believe otherwise. Don't embarrass them by confronting them in public. Go to them in private if need be. Speak the truth in love. You may need to remind them of 1 Corinthians 13, that if we have all knowledge, but have not love, we are just making noise. First Corinthians is also where we are told, *"knowledge makes arrogant, but love edifies"* (8:1). Obviously there were some "Ned's" in the church at Corinth. If you sense that "Ned" is not weak or faint-hearted, but in fact is unruly, you will need to admonish him. Make sure you do so in private, but make sure you do it all the same. Proverbs 27:56 tells us, *"Better is open rebuke than love that is concealed. Faithful are the wounds of a friend, but deceitful are the kisses of an enemy."* Remember the last statement in 1 Thessalonians 5:14, *"be patient with all men."*

Agenda Alice

The last person we would like to introduce to you who will probably show up sooner or later is one we like to call **"Agenda Alice."** All of us from time to time can be sidetracked by our own agenda. Often the very thing we are most passionate about can be the thing that distracts us from our highest passion: Christ. Agendas often are not unbiblical, but imbalanced. At their root is usually tunnel-vision mixed with a desire for control. The small group, since it allows everyone to contribute to the discussion, affords "Agenda Alice" a platform to promote what she thinks is most important. This doesn't mean that she is wrong to avoid driving at night because opossums are being killed, but she is wrong to expect everyone to have the exact same conviction and calling that she does in the gray areas of Scripture. If not managed properly, she will either sidetrack the group from its main study objective or create a hostile environment in the group if she fails to bring people to her way of thinking. "Agenda Alice" can often be recognized by introductory catch phrases such as "Yes, but . . ." and "Well, I think. . . ." She is often critical of the group process and may become vocally critical of you. Here are some ideas on dealing with this type of person:

1) **Reaffirm** the group covenant.
   At the formation of your group you should have taken time to define some ground rules for the group. Once is not enough to discuss these matters of group etiquette. Periodically remind everyone of their mutual commitment to one another.

2) **Remember** that the best defense is a good offense.
   Don't wait until it is a problem to address a mutual vision for how the group will function.

3) **Refocus** on the task at hand.
   The clearer you explain the objective of each session, the easier it is to stick to that objective and the harder you make it for people to redirect attention toward their own agenda. Enlist the whole group in bringing the discussion back to the topic at hand. Ask questions like, "What do the rest of you think about this passage?"

4) **Remind** the group, "Remember, this week's lesson is about ______________."

5) **Reprove** those who are disruptive.
   Confront the person in private to see if you can reach an understanding. Suggest another arena for the issue to be addressed such as an optional meeting for those in the group who would like to discuss the issue.

Remember the words of St. Augustine: "In essentials unity, in non-essentials liberty, in all things charity."

Adding Spice and Creativity

One of the issues you will eventually have to combat in any group Bible study is the enemy of boredom. This enemy raises its ugly head from time to time, but it shouldn't. It is wrong to bore people with the Word of God! Often boredom results when leaders allow their processes to become too predictable. As small group leaders, we tend to do the same thing in the same way every single time. Yet God the Creator, who spoke everything into existence is infinitely creative! Think about it. He is the one who not only created animals in different shapes and sizes, but different colors as well. When He created food, He didn't make it all taste or feel the same. This God of creativity lives in us. We can trust Him to give us creative ideas that will keep our group times from becoming tired and mundane. Here are some ideas:

When you think of what you can change in your Bible study, think of the five senses: (sight, sound, smell, taste, and feel).

SIGHT:
One idea would be to have a theme night with decorations. Perhaps you know someone with dramatic instincts who could dress up in costume and deliver a message from the person you are studying that week. Draw some cartoons on a marker board or handout.

SOUND:
Play some background music before your group begins. Sing a hymn together that relates to the lesson. If you know of a song that really hits the main point of the lesson, play it at the beginning or end.

SMELL:
This may be the hardest sense to involve in your Bible study, but if you think of a creative way to incorporate this sense into the lesson, you can rest assured it will be memorable for your group.

TASTE:
Some lessons will have issues that can be related to taste (e.g. unleavened bread for the Passover, etc.). What about making things less formal by having snacks while you study? Have refreshments around a theme such as "Chili Night" or "Favorite Fruits."

FEEL:
Any way you can incorporate the sense of feel into a lesson will certainly make the content more invigorating. If weather permits, add variety by moving your group outside. Whatever you do, be sure that you don't allow your Bible study to become boring!

Handling an Obviously Wrong Comment

From time to time, each of us can say stupid things. Some of us, however, are better at it than others. The apostle Peter had his share of embarrassing moments. One minute, he was on the pinnacle of success, saying, *"Thou art the Christ, the Son of the Living God"* (Matthew 16:16), and the next minute, he was putting his foot in his mouth, trying to talk Jesus out of going to the cross. Proverbs 10:19 states, *"When there are many words, transgression is unavoidable. . . ."* What do you do when someone in the group says something that is obviously wrong? First of all, remember that how you deal with a situation like this not only affects the present, but the future. Here are some ideas:

1) Let the whole group tackle it and play referee/peacemaker. Say something like, "That is an interesting thought, what do the rest of you think?"
2) Empathize. ("I've thought that before too, but the Bible says. . . .")
3) Clarify to see if what they said is what they meant. ("What I think you are saying is. . . .")
4) Ask the question again, focusing on what the Bible passage actually says.
5) Give credit for the part of the answer that is right and affirm that before dealing with what is wrong.
6) If it is a non-essential, disagree agreeably. ("I respect your opinion, but I see it differently.") Let it go —some things aren't important enough to make a big deal about them.
7) Love and affirm the person, even if you reject the answer.

Transitioning to the Next Study

For those of you who have completed leading a **Following God** Group Bible Study, congratulations! You have successfully navigated the waters of small group discussion. You have utilized one of the most effective tools of ministry—one that was so much a priority with Jesus, He spent most of His time there with His small group of twelve. Hopefully yours has been a very positive and rewarding experience. At this stage you may be looking forward to a break. It is not too early however, to be thinking and planning for what you will do next. Hopefully you have seen God use this study and this process for growth in the lives of those who have participated with you. As God has worked in the group, members should be motivated to ask the question, "What next?" As they do, you need to be prepared to give an answer. Realize that you have built a certain amount of momentum with your present study that will make it easier to do another. You want to take advantage of that momentum. The following suggestions may be helpful as you transition your people toward further study of God's Word.

- ❑ Challenge your group members to share with others what they have learned, and to encourage them to participate next time.
- ❑ If what to study is a group choice rather than a church-wide or ministry-wide decision made by others, you will want to allow some time for input from the group members in deciding what to do next. The more they have ownership of the study, the more they will commit to it.
- ❑ It is important to have some kind of a break so that everyone doesn't become study weary. At our church, we always look for natural times to start and end a study. We take the summer off as well as Christmas, and we have found that having a break brings people back with renewed vigor. Even if you don't take a break from meeting, you might take a breather from homework—or even get together just for fellowship.
- ❑ If you are able to end this study knowing what you will study next, some of your group members may want to get a head start on the next study. Be prepared to put books in their hands early.
- ❑ Make sure you end your study with a vision for more. Take some time to remind your group of the importance of the Word of God. As D. L. Moody used to say, "The only way to keep a broken vessel full is to keep the faucet running."

Evaluation

Becoming a Better Discussion Leader

The questions listed below are tools to assist you in assessing your discussion group. From time to time in the Leader's Guide, you will be advised to read through this list of evaluation questions in order to help you decide what areas need improvement in your role as group leader. Each time you read through this list, something different may catch your attention, giving you tips on how to become the best group leader that you can possibly be.

Read through these questions with an open mind, asking the Lord to prick your heart with anything specific He would want you to apply.

1. Are the group discussion sessions beginning and ending on time?
2. Am I allowing the freedom of the Holy Spirit as I lead the group in the discussion?
3. Do I hold the group accountable for doing their homework?
4. Do we always begin our sessions with prayer?
5. Is the room arranged properly (seating in a circle or semicircle, proper ventilation, adequate teaching aids)?
6. Is each individual allowed equal opportunity in the discussion?
7. Do I successfully bridle the talkative ones?
8. Am I successfully encouraging the hesitant ones to participate in the discussion?
9. Do I redirect comments and questions to involve more people in the interaction, or do I always dominate the discussion?
10. Are the discussions flowing naturally, or do they take too many "side roads" (diversions)?
11. Do I show acceptance to those who convey ideas with which I do not agree?
12. Are my questions specific, brief and clear?
13. Do my questions provoke thought, or do they only require pat answers?
14. Does each group member feel free to contribute or question, or is there a threatening or unnecessarily tense atmosphere?
15. Am I allowing time for silence and thought without making everyone feel uneasy?
16. Am I allowing the group to correct any obviously wrong conclusions that are made by others, or by myself (either intentionally to capture the group's attention or unintentionally)?
17. Do I stifle thought and discussion by assigning a question to someone before the subject of that question has even been discussed? (It will often be productive to assign a question to a specific person, but if you call on one person before you throw out a question, everyone else takes a mental vacation!)
18. Do I summarize when brevity is of the essence?
19. Can I refrain from expressing an opinion or comment that someone else in the group could just as adequately express?

20. Do I occasionally vary in my methods of conducting the discussion?

21. Am I keeping the group properly motivated?

22. Am I occasionally rotating the leadership to help others develop leadership?

23. Am I leading the group to specifically apply the truths that are learned?

24. Do I follow through by asking the group how they have applied the truths that they have learned from previous lessons?

25. Am I praying for each group member?

26. Is there a growing openness and honesty among my group members?

27. Are the group study sessions enriching the lives of my group members?

28. Have I been adequately prepared?

29. How may I be better prepared for the next lesson's group discussion?

30. Do I reach the objective set for each discussion? If not, why not? What can I do to improve?

31. Am I allowing the discussion to bog down on one point at the expense of the rest of the lesson?

32. Are the members of the group individually reaching the conclusions that I want them to reach without my having to give them the conclusions?

33. Do I encourage the group members to share what they have learned?

34. Do I encourage them to share the applications they have discovered?

35. Do I whet their appetites for next week's lesson discussion?

Getting Started

The First Meeting of Your Bible Study Group

Main Objectives of the first meeting: The first meeting is devoted to establishing your group and setting the course that you will follow through the study. Your primary goals for this session should be to . . .

- ❑ Establish a sense of group identity by starting to get to know one another.
- ❑ Define some ground rules to help make the group time as effective as possible.
- ❑ Get the study materials into the hands of your group members.
- ❑ Create a sense of excitement and motivation for the study.
- ❑ Give assignments for next week.

Before the Session

You will be most comfortable in leading this introductory session if you are prepared as much as possible for what to expect. This means becoming familiar with the place you will meet, and the content you will cover, as well as understanding any time constraints you will have.

Location—Be sure that you not only know how to find the place where you will be meeting, but also have time to examine the setup and make any adjustments to the physical arrangements. You never get a second chance to make a first impression.

Curriculum—You will want to get a copy of the study in advance of the introductory session, and it will be helpful if you do the homework for Lesson One ahead of time. This will make it easier for you to be able to explain the layout of the homework. It will also give you a contagious enthusiasm for what your group will be studying in the coming week. You will want to have enough books on hand for the number of people you expect so that they can get started right away with the study. You may be able to make arrangements with your church or simply order books online. We would encourage you not to buy books for your members. Years of small group experience have taught that people take a study far more seriously when they make an investment in it.

Time—The type of group you are leading will determine the time format for your study. If you are doing this study for a Sunday morning time or other regular meeting time, the time constraints may already be prescribed for you. In any case, ideally you will want to allow forty-five minutes to an hour for discussion.

What to Expect

When you embark on the journey of leading a small group Bible study, you are stepping into the stream of the work of God. You are joining in the process of helping others move toward spiritual maturity. As a small group leader, you are positioned to be a real catalyst in the lives of your group members, helping them to grow in their relationships with God. But you must remember, first and foremost, that whenever you step up to leadership in the kingdom of God, you are stepping down to serve. Jesus made it clear that leadership in the kingdom is not like leadership in the world. In Matthew 20:25, Jesus said, *"You know that the rulers of the Gentiles lord it over them, and their great men exercise authority over them."* That is the world's way to lead. But in Matthew 20:26–27, He continues, *"It is not so among you, but whoever wishes to become great among you shall be your servant, and whoever wishes to be first among you shall be your slave."* Your job as a small group leader is not to teach the group everything you have learned, but rather, to help them learn for themselves and from each other. It is a servant's role.

If you truly are to minister to the members of your group, you must start with understanding where they are, and join that with a vision of where you want to take them. In this introductory session, your group members will be experiencing several different emotions. They will be wondering, "Who is in my group?" and deciding "Do I like my group?" They will have a sense of excitement and anticipation, but also a sense of awkwardness as they try to find their place in this group. You will want to make sure that from the very beginning your group is founded with a sense of caring and acceptance. This is crucial if your group members are to open up and share what they are learning.

During the Session

OPENING: 5–10 MINUTES GETTING TO KNOW ONE ANOTHER

Opening Prayer—Remember that if it took the inspiration of God for people to write Scripture, it will also take His illumination for us to understand it. Have one of your group members open your time together in prayer.

Introductions—Take time to allow the group members to introduce themselves. Along with having the group members share their names, one way to add some interest is to have them add some descriptive information such as where they live or work. Just for fun, you could have them name their favorite breakfast cereal, most (or least) favorite vegetable, favorite cartoon character, their favorite city or country other than their own, etc.

Icebreaker—Take five or ten minutes to get the people comfortable in talking with each other. Since in many cases your small group will just now be getting to know one another, it will be helpful if you take some time to break the ice with some fun, nonthreatening discussion. Below you will find a list of ideas for good icebreaker questions to get people talking.

____ What is the biggest risk you have ever taken?

____ If money were no object, where would you most like to take a vacation and why?

____ What is your favorite way to waste time?

____ If you weren't in the career you now have, what would have been your second choice for a career?

____ If you could have lived in any other time, in what era or century would you have chosen to live (besides the expected spiritual answer of the time of Jesus)?

____ If you became blind right now, what would you miss seeing the most?

____ Who is the most famous person you've known or met?

____ What do you miss most about being a kid?

____ What teacher had the biggest impact on you in school (good or bad)?

____ Of the things money can buy, what would you most like to have?

____ What is your biggest fear?

____ If you could give one miracle to someone else, what would it be (and to whom)?

____ Tell about your first job.

____ Who is the best or worst boss you ever had?

____ Who was your hero growing up and why?

DEFINING THE GROUP: 5–10 MINUTES SETTING SOME GROUND RULES

There are several ways you can lay the tracks on which your group can run. One is simply to hand out a list of suggested commitments the members should make to the group. Another would be to hand out 3x5 cards and have the members themselves write down two or three commitments they would like to see everyone live out. You could then compile these into the five top ones to share at the following meeting. A third option is to list three (or more) commitments you are making to the group and then ask that they make three commitments back to you in return.

Here are some ideas for the types of ground rules that make for a good small group:

Leader:

____ To always arrive prepared

____ To keep the group on track so you make the most of the group's time

____ To not dominate the discussion by simply teaching the lesson

____ To pray for the group members

____ To not belittle or embarrass anyone's answers

____ To bring each session to closure and end on time

Member:

____ To do my homework

____ To arrive on time

____ To participate in the discussion

____ To not cut others off as they share

____ To respect the different views of other members

____ To not dominate the discussion

It is possible that your group may not need to formalize a group covenant, but you should not be afraid to expect a commitment from your group members. They will all benefit from defining the group up front.

INTRODUCTION TO THE STUDY: 15–20 MINUTES

As you introduce the study to the group members, your goal is to begin to create a sense of excitement about the Bible characters and applications that will be discussed. The most important question for you to answer in this session is "Why should I study ________?" You need to be prepared to guide them to finding that answer. Take time to give a brief overview of each leson.

CLOSING: 5–10 MINUTES

- ☐ Give homework for next week. In addition to simply reminding the group members to do their homework, if time allows, you might give them 5–10 minutes to get started on their homework for the first lesson.
- ☐ Key components for closing out your time are **a)** to review anything of which you feel they should be reminded, and **b)** to close in prayer. If time allows, you may want to encourage several to pray.

Worship from Adam to Aaron

PRINCIPLES FROM THE FALL TO THE PRIESTHOOD

MEMORY **Romans 12:1–2** VERSE

"I urge you therefore, brethren, by the mercies of God, to present your bodies a living and holy sacrifice, . . . And do not be conformed to this world, but be transformed by the renewing of your mind, that you may prove what the will of God is, that which is good and acceptable and perfect."

Before the Session

- ❑ Study the lesson diligently for yourself. The more impact the Word makes in your own heart, the more enthusiasm you will communicate.
- ❑ Spread your homework out rather than trying to cram everything into one afternoon or night. You may want to use this as your daily quiet time.
- ❑ As you study, write down any good discussion questions you think of as they come to mind.
- ❑ Be transparent before the Lord and before your group. We are all learners—that's the meaning of the word "disciple."

What to Expect

Mankind was created for fellowship with God. Before sin, everything Adam did was an act of worship. The scriptural record after the fall reveals man's attempts to come back to a place of worship with God. This particular lesson is an overview to display the big picture of worship from Adam in the Garden to Aaron and the establishment of the Tabernacle. This overview lays an important foundation and sets the context for our future study of the Tabernacle. It is quite possible that many in your group will experience new insights or rich applications from their study this week. Some will realize how far they have strayed from the Word of God. Others will be affirmed in the steps of obedience they have taken. Expect the Lord to do a fresh work in you as well as in the members of the group. He waits to show Himself strong toward *"those whose heart is fully His"* (see 1 Chronicles 16:9a). Some may have questions about this study or about the Bible. You can help them see the Scriptures as God's Word written in love. They can discover that this Book is eternal wisdom and is ever able to teach, reprove, correct, and train in righteousness (2 Timothy 3:16–17).

THE MAIN POINT

The main point of this lesson is to overview worship from creation to the priesthood and to identify common principles God reveals during this time.

During the Session

OPENING: 5–10 MINUTES

Opening Prayer—You or one of your group members should open your time together in prayer.

Opening Illustration—Worship that is accepted by God (see 1 Peter 2:5) is a privilege unique to the Christian. It is not a right. I am permitted to offer acceptable worship only by the grace of God.

Consider briefly the significance of worship:

It is obedience to a divine command.

It is a means of nourishing the spirit.

It assists in achieving spiritual growth.

It encourages others in their spiritual development.

It shows the world where my priorities are.

It is one way of expressing my love for God.

It is an avenue God has provided by which I can praise His name.

It is the offering of spiritual sacrifices.

It is a way of showing my thanksgiving to God for all He has done for me.

It is a period of communion with God with the world shut out entirely.

It is an experience that should make the heart of every Christian glad!

As we meet together in this course and work through this Bible study on worship, we must make it our aim not just to study worship, but actually put principles of worship into practice. Otherwise, our time spent together will have been wasted.

DISCUSSION: 30–40 MINUTES

Main Objective in Day One: The objective for today's reading is to study Adam and Eve's fall and how God reestablished worship after sin. Below are some possible discussion questions for the Day One discussion. Check which questions you will use.

___ Why do you think Adam and Eve hid after they sinned?

___ How did their efforts to cover their sin and hide from God succeed?

___ What did God do to reestablish a relationship of worship with Adam and Eve?

___ Why do you think God killed animals to clothe Adam and Eve?

Main Objective in Day Two: Day Two focuses on the fact that there is a right and a wrong way to worship God. Check which discussion questions you will use for Day Two.

___ Why do you think God accepted Abel's offering but didn't accept Cain's?

___ Do you think there is any significance to the fact that Abel's offering was an animal and Cain's was not?

___ What do you think it means that Abel's offering was made in faith?

___ What did you learn from Hebrews 12:24 about the "blood of Abel"?

Main Objective in Day Three: The main focus in Day Three is the role of obedience in worship. Check any discussion questions for Day Three that you might use.

___ What reasons did you find for Noah finding favor in the eyes of God?

___ What do you see in Noah's obedience?

___ What did you observe in Noah's worship?

___ What stood out to you from Abraham's use of the word "worship"?

Main Objective in Day Four: Day Four takes a look at all the main references to worship in Genesis and Exodus and identifies the common principle of the response of a grateful heart. In addition to any discussion questions that may have come to your mind in your studying, the following suggested questions may prove beneficial to your group session:

___ What did you see in the passages in Genesis?

___ What did you see in the passages in Exodus?

___ Why do you think worship is an act of response?

___ What else stood out to you from Day Four?

Day Five—Key Points in Application: Day Five seeks to move us into application from our study of the first four days. Check which discussion questions you will use for Day Five.

___ Can you think of any examples from others who worshiped God in their own way instead of His?

___ What are some ways it has "cost" you to worship God?

___ For what do you need to be grateful?

___ You might want to close in a time of group prayer, giving thanks to the Lord for whatever He brings to mind.

CLOSING: 5–10 MINUTES

- ❑ **Summarize**—Restate the key points highlighted in the class.
- ❑ **Preview**—Take just a few moments to preview next week's lesson.
- ❑ **Encourage** the group to be sure to do their homework.
- ❑ **Pray**—Close in prayer.

Tools for Good Discussion

Some who are reading this have led small group Bible studies many times. Here is an important word of warning: experience alone does not make you a more effective discussion leader. In fact, experience can make you **less effective**. You see, the more experience you have the more comfortable you will be at the task. Unfortunately, for some that means becoming increasingly comfortable in doing a bad job. Taking satisfaction with mediocrity translates into taking the task less seriously. It is easy to wrongly assert that just because one is experienced, that he or she can successfully "shoot from the hip" so to speak. If you really want your members to get the most out of this study, you need to be dissatisfied with simply doing an adequate job and make it your aim to do an excellent job. A key to excellence is to regularly evaluate yourself to see that you are still doing all that you want to be doing. We have prepared a list of over thirty evaluation questions for you to review from time to time. This list of questions can be found on pages 203-204 in this Leader's Guide. The examination questions will help to jog your memory and, hopefully, will become an effective aid in improving the quality of your group discussion. Review the evaluation questions list, and jot down two or three action points below for you to begin implementing next week.

ACTION POINTS:

1. ______________________________
____

2. ______________________________
____

3. ______________________________
____

Where We Meet God

WALKING WHERE GOD IS TRULY WORSHIPED

MEMORY **I Corinthians 6:19–20** VERSE

"Or do you not know that your body is a temple of the Holy Spirit who is in you, whom you have from God, and that you are not your own? For you have been bought with a price: therefore glorify God in your body."

BEFORE THE SESSION

- ❑ Remember that your goal is not to teach the lesson, but to facilitate discussion.
- ❑ Additional study: You will benefit from loking at all the references to worship in Scripture, in both the Old and New Testaments. You may want to look in a concordance to see all the times the word "worship" is used. You can conduct this overview quickly, or you can take an extended time to look at these references and the context in which the accounts of worship are found.
- ❑ Make sure your own heart is a place of worship. Your surrender to the Lord will be an example and an encouragement to others in your group. Be willing to be transparent with the group about your own walk and what God is showing you about your worship and walk with Him. This will make it easier for them to open up.
- ❑ Don't be afraid of chasing tangents for a while if the diversions capture the interest of the group as a whole, but don't sacrifice the rest of the group to belabor the questions of one member. Trust God to lead you.
- ❑ You may want to keep a highlight pen handy as you study to mark key statements that stand out to you.

WHAT TO EXPECT

In this lesson there are many places at which to look, many people with which to deal; but each place and each person have some common characteristics. Each place and the heart of each person who has truly worshiped is a place of surrender to God. Wherever we see surrender, that is a place of worship. That surrender grows and deepens as we walk with the Lord. It is important for your group to understand this truth. Some may see one person's surrender as insignificant and another's as profound. Such logic is a trap of presumption. Surrender means giving all I know of myself to all I know of God—that knowledge grows as we follow God. As you look at each place of worship in this lesson, look at how God deals with each person. Look for those application points—those touch points to where each of us lives. Your small group time can become a time of worship, and the place you meet can become a place of worship.

THE MAIN POINT

Worship is about surrender from the heart, not about a particular place. It is not about a tent of animal skins or a temple of stones. God is interested in the temple of the heart.

During the Session

OPENING: 5–10 MINUTES

Opening Prayer—Ask someone in your group to open the session in prayer.

Opening Illustration—Why Places Are Well-Known. If a person mentions Gettysburg, people think of the Civil War battle fought there or Lincoln's famous Gettysburg address. If a person mentions the Alamo, people think of the battle fought there. If a person mentions Bethel, people think of the place where God met Jacob in a dream; Bethlehem—the birthplace of Jesus; Nazareth—the boyhood home of Jesus, Armageddon—the prophesied final battle-ground in human history; Patmos—the island where the apostle John received the Revelation; Galatia, Ephesus, Thessalonica or Philippi—the cities or areas associated with letters from Paul. When we think of a place and what happened there it becomes noteworthy in some way. When we think of our own journey with the Lord and look back at the places we have been, what places can we remember where the Lord met us in a special way, when our faith and worship moved to a new level? What about the place where we bowed and asked Him to come into our lives as Lord and Savior? Or places along the way where He met us and dealt with us about an area of surrender that needed to take place in our lives? Any place where He pinpointed something in our lives—that place is a touch point with God, a place that we look back on as a meeting place with God. He wants every place to be a place of meeting Him, of true worship and real faith. As you walk through this lesson, think of these places in your life and about your surrender. Even the place you are in now could become a place of fresh surrender and pure worship.

DISCUSSION: 30–40 MINUTES

Once your group gets talking, you will find that all you need to do is keep the group directed and flowing with a question or two or a pointed observation. You are the gatekeeper of discussion. Don't be afraid to ask someone to elaborate further or to ask a quiet member of the group what they think of someone else's comments. Time will not allow you to discuss every single question in the lesson one at a time. Instead, make it your goal to cover the main ideas of each day, and help the group to personally share what they learned. You don't have to use all the discussion questions. They are there for your discretion.

Main Objective in Day One: In Day One, the central objective of the study is to paint a picture of what a place of worship looks like and how sacrifice and surrender enter into that picture. We want to see how the men and women of old responded to God in those places. Below, check any discussion questions that you might consider using in your group session.

___ Describe your thoughts about worship in the Garden of Eden before and after sin entered?

___ God revealed Himself to Abram. How does God use His Word in your life to reveal Himself and call you to worship?

___ How does God point out areas of fresh surrender? Can you name something that God has spoken to you about recently?

___ How does God test our faith today? How have you faced tests about your own walk? How is your group doing at walking in the fear of the Lord, or in withholding nothing from the Lord, or in obeying what He has said?

Main Objective in Day Two: In Day Two, we see how God met Moses and revealed how He wanted to dwell with His people and how they were to follow Him in true worship. Below, check which discussion questions you will use for Day Two.

___ What makes a place "holy ground"? How does God want our lives to be "holy ground"?

___ How important is the Word of God in knowing how to worship the Lord? What did God's Law do for Moses and the children of Israel?

___ Why do you think God gave so much detail in the construction of the Tabernacle? Why didn't He simply let the people build whatever they thought best?

___ What did the presence of God mean to Moses, Aaron, and the people? How would you describe what happened in Exodus 40 when the Lord appeared?

___ Are there any other areas of Day Two that you would like to discuss?

Main Objective in Day Three: Day Three takes us further into the history of Israel and opens up more of the plan of God for His people. Here we see the place of the Temple and the essential place of the life and ministry of Jesus. Look over the discussion-starter questions below to see if any are applicable to your group session.

___ What similarities do you see in the building of the Tabernacle and the building of the Temple in Jerusalem? How did God respond when the Temple was completed?

___ Thinking of the Temple as a place of prayer, what applications do you see for your walk of worship and for your prayer life?

___ Jesus revealed Himself (and God the Father and God the Spirit) so that He could be known personally. How does this match what we see in the Tabernacle and in the Temple?

___ What does the word "Immanuel" and the phrase "the Word made flesh" mean to you now?

___ Did today's lesson raise any questions for you?

Main Objective in Day Four: Day Four shows us the Temple God dwells in today—the heart and life of one who places his or her faith in Jesus Christ as Lord and Savior. Review the discussion question list below, and choose any that you feel are good questions for your session.

___ What similarities do you see between the Tabernacle, the Temple, and the life of a believer in Jesus?

___ What does it mean to you that you can be a temple of the Holy Spirit?

___ Why does God always deal with sin and forgiveness before He deals with His presence in a place or in a person's life?

___ Do you have any questions about how to deal with sin?

___ Do you have any questions about how God wants to be seen in your life?

Day Five—Key Points in Application: In looking at "Where We Meet God," we must see what that means for everyday life. God wants His presence to be very real for each of His children—He is a Father who wants His children to walk with Him in all of life, all of the time, in every place. Some good application questions for Day Five include . . .

___ What kind of place does your heart need to be for God to want to meet there?

___ What can clutter a meeting place? What can be distracting when you are trying to meet with or talk to someone?

___ What will the fullness of the Spirit look like in a person's life? (Galatians 5:22–26 give added insight to what a person looks like when he or she is walking in the fullness of the Spirit.)

CLOSING: 5–10 MINUTES

- ❑ **Summarize**—Restate the key points that were highlighted in the class.
- ❑ **Remind** the group that the victorious Christian life is not attained when we try hard to be like Jesus, but only when we surrender our lives to God and let Him work through us.
- ❑ **Preview**—Take time to preview next week's lesson on **"Enter His Gates: Principles from the Fence, the Gate, and the Outer Court."** Encourage your group members to complete their homework.
- ❑ **Pray**—Close in prayer.

Tools for Good Discussion

Bill Donahue, in his book, *Leading Life-Changing Small Groups* (Grand Rapids: Zondervan Publishing House, 1996), lists four facilitator actions that will produce dynamic discussion. These four actions are easy to remember because they are linked through the acrostic method to the word, **"ACTS."** You will profit from taking time to review this information in the "Helpful Hints" section of **How to Lead a Small Group Bible Study,** which is on page 197of this Leader's Guide book.

Enter His Gates

Principles from the Fence, the Gate, and the Outer Court

Memory Psalm 100:4 Verse

"Enter His gates with thanksgiving and His courts with praise."

Before the Session

- ❑ Pray each day for the members of your group—that they spend time in the Word, grasp the message God wants to bring to their lives, and that they surrender to what God is saying.
- ❑ Do thorough preparations—don't procrastinate!
- ❑ As you go through the study, jot down any ideas or questions you want to discuss. Those, along with the questions listed throughout this Leader's Guide can personalize the discussion to fit your group. Think of the needs of your group, and be looking for applicable questions and discussion starters.
- ❑ Remain ever teachable. Look first for what God is saying to you.
- ❑ Be prepared to be transparent and open about what God is teaching you. Nothing is quite as contagious as the joy of discovering new treasures in the Word.

What to Expect

There will be varying degrees of familiarity with the Old Testament Tabernacle and its components. As we begin this week to look specifically at the parts of the structure, for some it will be review, while for others it will be entirely new. For all, it will be a new experience to look at the Tabernacle as more than a relic of ancient history. Keep drawing the focus away from the historical details and back to "What is God trying to say through the Tabernacle?" This approach will keep things practical and application-oriented.

THE MAIN POINT

In this lesson we will see what life principles can be derived from the fence, the gate, and the outer court of the Tabernacle.

During the Session

OPENING: 5–10 MINUTES

Opening Prayer—Remember that the Lord is the Teacher and wants us to depend on Him as we open the Scriptures. Ask Him to teach you as you meet together.

Opening Illustration—Etched in stone over the entrance of the First Baptist Church in Warsaw, Indiana, are the words of Psalm 100:4 which state, *"Enter His gates with thanksgiving and His courts with praise."* What a good reminder to all who enter the church that we are to enter with thanksgiving and praise! But Psalm 100:4 is preceded with the final words of the previous verse, *"We are His people and the sheep of His pasture."* Question: Why would a sheep enter the gates of the Tabernacle? To give its life totally as a sacrifice. This illustration is a good reminder to all who draw near to God. This week's lesson will begin a look at what the Tabernacle teaches us about how man is to approach God.

DISCUSSION: 30–40 MINUTES

Keep the group directed along the main highway of life principles. You may have a pointed observation that helps sharpen the focus of the group. Encourage some to elaborate further on a key point or ask a quiet member of the group what they think of someone's comments. Watch the time, knowing you can't cover every single question in the lesson. Seek to cover the main ideas of each day and help the group to personally share what they have learned.

<u>Main Objective in Day One:</u> In Day One, the main objective is for you and your study group to see the important principle that everything in the Tabernacle is "according to pattern." Each component has a meaning and a message. Check which discussion questions you will use from Day One.

___ What is the point God is making in Exodus 25:8–9?

___ How does the epistle to Hebrews explain the meaning of the "pattern" idea in Exodus?

___ Did you learn anything else from the other verses we looked at in Hebrews?

___ What did you learn about Christ being pictured in the Old Testament?

<u>Main Objective in Day Two:</u> Day Two focuses on the principles being communicated about our relationship with God by the fence of the Tabernacle. The following questions may serve as excellent discussion starters for your group session:

___ Why do you think it was important to God for there to be a fence around the Tabernacle?

___ How do you think Isaiah 59:2 relates to the fence?

___ What can we gather from the verses from Revelation about the spiritual meaning of the fine white linen?

___ What else stood out to you in Day Two?

<u>Main Objective in Day Three:</u> Day Three introduces us to the principles being communicated about our relationship with God by the Gate of the Tabernacle. Check which discussion questions you will use from Day Three.

___ What is your initial impression of the gate of the Tabernacle?

___ What stood out to you from the New Testament Scriptures we looked at about the width of the gate?

___ It what ways is Jesus our Gate of entry to the Lord in worship?

<u>Main Objective in Day Four:</u> In Day Four, we look at some of the principles being communicated about our relationship with God by the bronze altar and the bronze laver. Check which discussion questions you will use from Day Four.

___ What stands out to you as you read about the bronze altar?

___ Why do you think a sacrifice is necessary to approach God?

___ What meaning do you see in the bronze laver?

___ Did you see significance in the water of the laver?

___ What else did you learn from Day Four?

<u>Day Five—Key Points in Application:</u> The most important component of each lesson is to move into application. Below, select a question or two for your Day Five discussion.

___ What can we do to respect God's holiness more as we approach Him?

___ Obviously we "enter the gate" initially at salvation, but what applications do you see in the gate?

___ Did you see any personal applications to the bronze altar?

___ How can we apply the bronze laver practically in our walk?

CLOSING: 5–10 MINUTES

- ❑ **Summarize**—Restate the key points the group shared. Review the objectives for each of the days found in these leader's notes.

- ☐ **Ask** your group to share their thoughts on the key applications from Day Five.
- ☐ **Remind**—Using the memory verse (Psalm 100:4), remind the group of the importance of how we enter God's presence.
- ☐ **Preview**—Take a few moments to preview next week's lesson, **"The Holy Place: Principles from the Lampstand, the Table, and the Altar of Incense."** Encourage your group to do their homework and to space it out over the week.
- ☐ **Pray**—Close in prayer.

Tools for Good Discussion

One of the people who shows up in every group is a person we call **"Talkative Timothy."** Talkative Timothy tends to talk too much and dominates the discussion time by giving less opportunity for others to share. What do you do with a group member who talks too much? In the "Helpful Hints" section of **How to Lead a Small Group Bible Study** (p.197), you'll find some practical ideas on managing the "Talkative Timothys" in your group.

The Holy Place

PRINCIPLES FROM THE LAMPSTAND, THE TABLE, AND THE ALTAR OF INCENSE

MEMORY **Revelation 21:3** VERSE

"The tabernacle of God is among men, and He shall dwell among them, and they shall be His people, and God Himself shall be among them."

Before the Session

- ❑ Be sure to do your own study far enough in advance so as not to be rushed. You want to allow God time to speak to you personally.
- ❑ Don't feel that you have to use all of the discussion questions listed for this lesson. You may have come up with others on your own, or you may find that time will not allow you to use them all. These questions are to serve you, not for you to serve.
- ❑ You are the gatekeeper of the discussion. Do not be afraid to "reel the group back in" if they get too far away from the lesson.
- ❑ Pray each day for the members of your group—that they spend time in the Word, grasp the message God wants to bring to their lives, and that they surrender to what God is saying.

What to Expect

Last week's lesson should have whetted the group's appetite to go further in their study of the Tabernacle. Hopefully, your group members have begun to see how practical this study can be to their daily walk with the Lord. Remember that for nearly five hundred years, the Tabernacle served as a tool to instruct people on how God desires to be worshiped. Make sure you keep drawing the focus away from mere information and into application.

THE MAIN POINT

Regarding the Holy Place, we need to see what life principles can be derived from the lampstand, the table, and the altar of incense.

During the Session

OPENING: 5–10 MINUTES

Opening Prayer—Remember that if it took the inspiration of God for people to write Scripture, it will also take His illumination for us to understand it. Have one of the members of your group open your time together in prayer.

Opening Illustration—In his book, *What Is Worship?* J. Vernon McGee tells of the time one of his church leaders invited him to hear a symphony orchestra perform. He said he knew nothing about music, but went anyway "to be nice."

What he first heard was a horrid cacophony of individual squeals and squawks, as each musician tuned his instrument. But then, he related, when the conductor entered the scene, what a difference there was! At his cue, all those different instruments blended their voices to create truly beautiful music.

Today, McGee explains, "every man is playing his own little tune. (But) one of these days, out from the wings will step the Conductor, the Lord Jesus Christ. And when He lifts His baton, from the ends of God's universe those galactic systems will burst forth into song. Every bird, every angel, and then man will join the heavenly chorus. In the meantime, you and I can bow before Him and bring our own little souls into the harmony of heaven."

DISCUSSION: 30–40 MINUTES

Once your group gets talking, you will find that all you need to do is keep the group directed and flowing with a question or two or a pointed observation. You are the gatekeeper of discussion. Don't be afraid to ask someone to elaborate further ("Explain what you mean, Barbara?") or to ask a quiet member of the group what they think of someone else's comments ("What do you think, Dave?"). Time will not allow you to discuss every single question in the lesson one at a time. Instead, make it your goal to cover the main ideas of each day and help the group to share what they learned personally. You don't have to use all the discussion questions below. They are there for your choosing and discretion.

Main Objective in Day One: Day One focuses on the actual structure of the tent itself and the meaning behind each piece. Below, check which discussion questions you will use from Day One.

____ Do you think the purpose of the colors of the curtains was for symbolism or beauty or both?

____ What do you think is God's message from the animal skins?

____ Did anything stand out to you from the door?

Main Objective in Day Two: Day Two studies the golden lampstand and the meaning to be found in it. Check which discussion questions you will use from Day Two.

____ What stood out to you from the looks of the lampstand?

____ In what ways do you see Jesus pictured in the lampstand?

____ What are some ways you see believers pictured in the lampstand and the priest's role with it?

____ What else stood out to you from Day Two?

Main Objective in Day Three: In Day Three, we focus on the table of showbread and the meaning behind it. In addition to any discussion-starter questions that you may have in mind, the following questions may also prove useful to your group time.

____ Did anything stand out to you from the construction of the table?

____ What did you see suggested by a table set with food in the context of worship?

____ What did you learn from the New Testament passages we looked at?

Main Objective in Day Four: In Day Four, we examine the altar of incense and the meaning behind it. Below, place a checkmark next to the questions that you feel are worthy of mention in your session. Or you may want to place ranking numbers next to each question to note your order of preference.

____ What did you see in the construction of the altar of incense?

____ What do you see in its operation?

____ What message do you see in the burning of incense?

____ What stood out to you from Psalm 66:18?

____ Why do you think God dealt so harshly with Nadab and Abihu?

Day Five—Key Points in Application: Application is the most important part of each lesson. Apart from it, any study of the Tabernacle will lack in overall impact. Examine the question list below, and decide if there are any that fit your group discussion for the Day Five application time.

____ Is there anything you need to be doing differently to make sure you are walking in the light of God's Word?

____ What application do you see to fellowship with other Christians?

____ How does this lesson affect how you view your prayer life?

____ What is the main application you saw this week?

CLOSING: 5–10 MINUTES

- ❑ **Summarize**—Restate the key points that were highlighted in the class. You may want to briefly review the objectives for each of the days found at the beginning of these leader notes.
- ❑ **Focus**—Using this lesson's memory verse (Revelation 21:3), focus on the idea of the Tabernacle and God's heart toward His people.
- ❑ **Ask** group members to reveal their thoughts about the key applications from Day Five.
- ❑ **Preview**—Take a few moments to preview next week's lesson.
- ❑ **Pray**—Close in prayer.

TOOLS FOR GOOD DISCUSSION

As mentioned earlier, there are certain people who show up in every discussion group. Last week we looked at "Talkative Timothy." Another person who is likely to show up is **"Silent Sally."** She does not readily speak up. Sometimes, her silence is because she doesn't yet feel comfortable enough with the group to share her thoughts. Other times, it is simply because she fears being rejected. Often, her silence is because she is too polite to interrupt and thus is headed off at the pass each time she wants to speak by more aggressive (and less sensitive) members of the group. In the "Helpful Hints" section of **How to Lead a Small Group Bible Study** (p. 198), you'll find some practical ideas on managing the "Silent Sally's" in your group.

Enter His Presence

Principles from the Veil, the Ark, and the Mercy Seat

Memory **Hebrews 10:19–22** Verse

"Since therefore, brethren, we have confidence to enter the holy place by the blood of Jesus, by a new and living way which He inaugurated for us through the veil, that is, His flesh ... let us draw near with a sincere heart in full assurance of faith..."

Before the Session

- ❑ Resist the temptation to do all your homework in one sitting or to put it off until the last minute. You will not be as prepared if you study this way.
- ❑ Make sure to mark down any discussion questions that come to mind as you study. Don't feel that you have to use all of the suggested discussion questions included in this leader's guide. Feel free to pick and choose based on your group and the time frame with which you are working.
- ❑ Remember your need to trust God with your study. The Holy Spirit is always the best teacher, so stay sensitive to Him!

What to Expect

In this lesson, expect that all your group members will need a better understanding of the most holy place in the Tabernacle. Anticipate that a few of your group members may not be familiar with the Old Testament at all, and *Yom Kippur* will be a new and exciting idea. Some will be surprised to discover how practical and application-filled this lesson will be. Make every effort to steer the study away from being just another lesson by reminding your group members to look to their own lives and circumstances for how these principles can apply to them.

THE MAIN POINT

The objective of studying "The Holy of Holies" is to see what life principles can be derived from the Veil, the Ark, and the Mercy Seat

During the Session

OPENING: 5–10 MINUTES

Opening Prayer—Remember to have one of your group members open your time together in prayer.

Opening Illustration—A man was carried in a dream to a church. In his vision he saw the organist vigorously playing the organ, but no sound was heard. The choir and congregation began to sing, but their voices were not heard. Then the minister began, energetically, to pray, but no tones came from his lips.

The man turned in wonder to his angel guide. "You hear nothing," said the angel, "because there is nothing to hear. These people are not engaged in worship, but only in the form of worship. Their hearts are not touched, and this silence is the silence that is yet unbroken in the presence of God. But listen now."

And, listening, the man heard a child's voice, clear and distinct in all that silence, while the minister seemed to pray, and the people seemed to join. Only the child's voice was heard, because only the child's heart was touched. "That," said the guide, "is the only true worship in all this great church today: all the others are concerned with only the appearance of worship."

DISCUSSION: 30–40 MINUTES

Remember that your job is not to teach this lesson, but to facilitate discussion. Do your best to guide the group to the right answers, but don't be guilty of making a point someone else in the group could just as easily make.

Main Objective in Day One: The objective here is to gain a feel for life principles to be seen in the veil. Choose some discussion questions from the list below.

____ What do you think the veil must have looked like to those who saw it for the first time?

____ Do you think we should read meaning into the colors of the veil?

____ Why do you think God wanted Cherubim on the veil?

____ What stood out to you from Hebrews 10?

Main Objective in Day Two: In Day Two, we begin looking at the meaning in the ark of the covenant. Below, check any discussion questions you might use from Day Two.

____ What stands out to you most about the ark?

____ Why do you think God dealt so harshly with the man who touched the ark?

____ What do you think the Philistines were trying to do when they stole the ark?

____ Did today's study raise any questions for you?

Main Objective in Day Three: Day Three takes a look at the items that were placed inside the ark and their significance. Review the questions below, and see if any are suitable to your group discussion on Day Three.

____ Why did God want the "testimony" placed in the ark?

____ What stands out to you from the manna being placed inside?

____ What message do you think God is sending by putting Aaron's rod in the ark?

____ Did anything else grab your attention in your studies in Day Three?

Main Objective in Day Four: In Day Four, we see the key component of the mercy seat and its message to us. Check which discussion questions you will use from Day Four.

____ What did you find out in 1 John 2?

____ Did you see a message in the Cherubim over the mercy seat?

____ What else stood out to you from Day Four?

Day Five—Key Points in Application: The important thing to see out of Day Five is that we need to apply these principles to our own lives. Decide on some discussion-starter topics for the application section of Day Five. The following questions are suggested questions that you may want to use for your discussion:

____ Has your view of the Tabernacle changed through looking at the components?

____ How has your view of sin changed through this study?

____ Were there any areas in particular where this lesson touched your heart?

CLOSING: 5–10 MINUTES

- ❑ **Summarize**—Go over the key points of your study of the Holy of Holies.
- ❑ **Remind** group members that living a victorious Christian life is not attained when we try hard to be like Jesus, but only when we surrender our lives to God and let Him work through us.
- ❑ **Ask** them what they thought were the key applications from Day Five.
- ❑ **Preview**—Take a few moments to preview next week's lesson. Encourage group members to complete their homework.
- ❑ **Pray**—Close in prayer.

Tools for Good Discussion

Hopefully your group is functioning smoothly at this point, but perhaps you recognize the need for improvement. In either case, you will benefit from taking the time to evaluate yourself and your group. Without evaluation, you will judge your group on subjective emotions. You may think everything is fine and miss some opportunities to improve your effectiveness. You may be discouraged by problems you are confronting when you ought to be encouraged that you are doing the right things and making progress. A healthy Bible-study group is not one without problems, but is one that recognizes its problems and deals with them the right way. At this point in the course, as you and your group are nearly halfway-completed with the study of the Tabernacle as it relates to worship, it is important to examine yourself and see if there are any mid-course corrections that you feel are necessary to implement. Review the evaluation questions list found on pages 203-204 of this Leader's Guide, and jot down two or three action points for you to begin implementing next week. Perhaps you have made steady improvements since the first time you answered the evaluation questions at the beginning of the course. If so, your improvements should challenge you to be an even better group leader for the final seven lessons in the study.

ACTION POINTS:

1. ______________________________

____

2. ______________________________

____

3. ______________________________

____

Ministers to the Lord

PRINCIPLES FROM THE PRIESTHOOD

MEMORY **I Peter 2:9** VERSE

"But you are a chosen race, a royal priesthood, a holy nation, a people for God's own possession, that you may proclaim the excellencies of Him who has called you out of darkness into His marvelous light"

BEFORE THE SESSION

- ❑ Remember the Boy Scout motto: **BE PREPARED!** The main reason a Bible study flounders is because the leader comes in unprepared and tries to "shoot from the hip."
- ❑ Walk through the discussion questions below, looking at your lesson and selecting which questions you will use.
- ❑ Make sure to jot down any discussion questions that come to mind as you study.
- ❑ Don't forget to pray for the members of your group and for your time studying together. You don't want to be satisfied with what you can do—you want to see God do what only He can do!

WHAT TO EXPECT

In studying this lesson, you should realize that all of us are called to be priests to our God and to serve Him in some way. Be prepared for your group to need to overcome a mentality of applying this only to clergy and missionaries. As we look at the priesthood we should see ourselves. Be sensitive to any discussion questions that may surface in this lesson, and guard your group from applying the principles only to others rather than to themselves.

THE MAIN POINT

There are life principles to be learned for our own walk with God from studying the Old Testament priests.

DURING THE SESSION

OPENING: 5–10 MINUTES

Opening Prayer—Remember to have one of your group members open your time together in prayer.

Opening Illustration—Bill Smith. There may be no name more common in the English language. In a seminary class, one professor related an event that happened his first day in college.

His teacher professed an uncanny command of the English language. It seemed that he always pulled out the most appropriate word for the occasion. On this, the first day of school, he was calling the roll. After recognizing each student he made some pertinent comment about his name—its history, meaning, or some historically-related story. Finally, he came to Bill Smith. He said with a pause and in a reflective tone, "Bill Smith . . . that is a common name." Stirred from within, Bill arose from his seat and said in a loving but firm tone, "Sir, Bill Smith may be frequent but not common."

Who among us has not lived under the teacher's philosophy? Thinking there is nothing special about ourselves, we have concluded that we are common, everyday, ordinary. Let us continually remind ourselves that each one of us is a chosen person, a royal priest, a member of a holy nation, a person that belongs to God (1 Peter 2:9).

DISCUSSION: 30–40 MINUTES

Remember to pace your discussion so that you will be able to bring closure to the lesson at the designated time. You are the one who must balance lively discussion with timely redirection to ensure that you don't end up finishing only part of the lesson.

Main Objective in Day One: In Day One, the main objective is to see that God is behind the appointment of the priests. No one is self-appointed. Check which discussion questions you will use from Day One.

- ____ What do you think it means that Aaron and his sons were to minister as priests to the Lord?
- ____ How did God involve others in His affirmation of Aaron?
- ____ What stood out to you from the passage in Hebrews about the role of priests?
- ____ What else stood out to you from your study in Day One?

Main Objective in Day Two: In Day Two, we learn some of the significance of the priestly apparel. Choose a discussion question or two from the Day Two list below.

- ____ What stood out to you from your reading in Exodus 28?
- ____ Why do you think God was so concerned with how the priests looked?
- ____ Did anything particular grab you from the various parts of the priest's apparel?
- ____ Did your study of Day Two raise any questions for you?

Main Objective in Day Three: Day Three introduces us to a brief overview of the priestly activity. This will be discussed in more detail later. Decide on some discussion-starter questions for your session on priestly activity. Below, are some possible discussion questions for you to consider.

- ____ Why do you think God instituted sacrifices to become a part of man's worship?
- ____ What stood out to you from Hebrews 5:2 about the priestly oversight?
- ____ What did you learn from Nehemiah 8:1–3?

Main Objective in Day Four: In Day Four, we see the most significant activity of the priest—*Yom Kippur,* the Day of Atonement. This will be looked at again before we finish, but there are many practical applications here for us. Check which discussion questions you will use from Day Four.

- ____ What did God desire the attitude of the people to be on Yom Kippur?
- ____ What message do you see in the fact that it was observed year after year?
- ____ How do you think the principle of Yom Kippur applies to us today?
- ____ Did you learn anything new in comparing the Old and New covenants?

Day Five—Key Points in Application: Although there are many different applications to the priesthood, some of these will be pursued in another lesson. This time we chose to camp on the idea of seeking God's will, which was a priestly activity using the *Urim* and *Thummim.* Below, check any discussion questions that are best suited to your group for application.

- ____ The priests often sought God's will for themselves and the people. Have you ever thought of God's will as a privilege to all through the priesthood of believers?
- ____ What do you think about the formula, "Desire + Opportunity + No Red Flags"?
- ____ What other applications did you see in this week's lesson?

CLOSING: 5–10 MINUTES

- ❑ **Summarize**—Restate the key points.
- ❑ **Remind** those in your group that living a victorious Christian life is not attained when we try hard to be like Jesus, but only when we sur-

render our lives to God and let Him work through us.

- ❑ **Preview**—Take a few moments to preview next week's lesson. Encourage your group to do their homework and to space it out over the week.
- ❑ **Pray**—Close in prayer.

Tools for Good Discussion

As discussed earlier, there are certain people who show up in every discussion group that you will ever lead. We have already looked at "Talkative Timothy" and "Silent Sally." This week, let's talk about another person who also tends to show up. Let's call this person **"Tangent Tom."** He is the kind of guy who loves to talk even when he has nothing to say. Tangent Tom loves to "chase rabbits" regardless of where they go. When he gets the floor, you never know where the discussion will lead. You need to understand that not all tangents are bad. Sometimes, much can be gained from discussion "a little off the beaten path." But these diversions must be balanced against the purpose of the group. In the "Helpful Hints" section of **How to Lead a Small Group** (pp. 198-199), you will find some practical ideas on managing the "Tangent Toms" in your group. You will also get some helpful information on evaluating tangents as they arise.

The Debt of Sin

DEALING WITH SIN GOD'S WAY

MEMORY **I Peter 2:24** VERSE

"And He Himself bore our sins in His body on the cross, that we might die to sin and live to righteousness;. . ."

BEFORE THE SESSION

- ❑ Try to get your lesson plans and homework done early this week. This gives time for you to reflect on what you have learned and process it mentally. Don't succumb to the temptation to procrastinate.
- ❑ Make sure you keep a highlight pen handy to highlight any things you intend to discuss; including questions that you think your group may have trouble comprehending. Jot down any good discussion questions that come to your mind as you study.
- ❑ Don't think of your ministry to the members of your group as something that only takes place during your group time. Pray for your group members by name during the week that they would receive spiritual enrichment from doing their daily homework. Encourage them as you have opportunity.

WHAT TO EXPECT

In this lesson we look at two essential offerings, the sin offering and the guilt offering. These may be foreign ideas or seem like ancient (even unimportant) rituals to some in your group. The important thing to remember in walking through your discussion time is the heart of the matter—we must deal with sin if we are to know God and walk with Him. There are many pictures and principles God reveals through these offerings. Expect that everyone in your group will have areas of their life to which these principles will apply in some way. Be prepared to share your own journey as well as guide them toward personal evaluation of their lives and personal application to the different areas of their lives. Remember, when dealing with sin, the circle of confession is as big as the circle of offense. You and the members of your group can be an encouragement to one another to walk in the forgiveness and cleansing God wants for each of us.

THE MAIN POINT

God requires us to deal with sin, and He has made full provision for us to do so—not just to admit sin, but to find His full forgiveness.

DURING THE SESSION

OPENING: 5–10 MINUTES

Opening Prayer—It would be a good idea to have a different group member each week open your time together in prayer.

Opening Illustration—Many have heard of the hymn "It is Well with My Soul" and the tragedy that birthed it. Horatio Spafford, a lawyer and teacher, scheduled a trip to France for his family and himself, but he had to delay going because of business. He sent his wife and four daughters on to France aboard the *Ville du Havre,* planning to join them soon after. The ship collided with another vessel in the mid-Atlantic and sunk within an hour. The four daughters drowned, and their mother sent a cablegram, with the brief message, "saved alone." The four daughters had been converted in a meeting led by Dwight L. Moody in Chicago, and Mr. and Mrs. Spafford experienced great peace and strength, knowing that their daughters were in heaven. Horatio Spafford penned the words to "It Is Well with My Soul" after that tragedy. Many quote the words to the first verse, "When peace, like a river, attendeth my way, When sorrows like sea-billows roll; Whatever my lot, Thou hast taught me to say, 'It is well, it is well with my soul.' " The third verse speaks to a peace that goes beyond the temporal tragedy they faced. It is the peace of sin forgiven. Think of these words, "My sin—oh, the bliss of this glorious thought, My sin—not in part, but the whole, Is nailed to the cross and I bear it no more, Praise the Lord, praise the Lord, O my soul!" Horatio Spafford's burden of sin and guilt was an even greater burden to him than the children he had lost at sea. Yet, Mr. Spafford and his wife could know the peace of God for the grief of his soul over his children and for the burden of sin that had been taken care of by the Lord. His heart was calmed by the work of Christ on the Cross. Horatio knew the peace that only God could bring. That is the message of the sin offering and the guilt offering. These offerings were established so that the peace of forgiveness could be established between God and His people.

DISCUSSION: 30–40 MINUTES

A key objective in how you manage your discussion time is to keep the big picture in view. Your job is not like a schoolteacher's job, grading papers and tests and the like, but more like a tutor's job, making sure your group understands the subject. Keep the main point of the lesson in view, and make sure they take that main point home with them.

Main Objective in Day One: In Day One, the main objective is to see the importance of dealing with sin God's way so that man can walk with God in the right way. Start thinking now about what discussion starters you will use in your session devoted to dealing with sin. Review the question list below. Perhaps there is a question or two below that might be essential to your group time.

- ____ What insights do you see in the fact that God initiated the various offerings and how they were to be offered?
- ____ Why do your think it was important to have these offerings given on a regular basis?
- ____ What new insights did you see in the procedures associated with the sin offering?
- ____ How important is it to God that we deal with sin? How important should it be to each one of us?
- ____ What else stood out to you from Day One?

Main Objective in Day Two: In Day Two, we see the importance of making any offense right with God first, then making right any offense against another person. Check which discussion questions you will use from Day Two.

- ____ How big does an offense have to be to be an offense? What insights did you see in the ten offenses given in Leviticus 5 and 6?
- ____ How important is restitution to God? Do you want things made right or restitution given when you have been offended, wronged, or robbed in some way?
- ____ How did you respond the last time that you faced an offense? What about the last time you offended someone? [You may want to use this as a thought-provoking question, since some would not want to tell of an offense within the group meeting.]
- ____ Why is it important to deal with offenses quickly? How valuable is a "conscience void of offense"?

Be sensitive to the Spirit of God in walking through this lesson. There may be someone in your group that is wrestling with this issue of dealing with sin, especially dealing with restitution. Ask the Lord to lead you as you talk through these truths.

Main Objective in Day Three: Day Three looks at the importance of the sin offerings on the Day of

Atonement. Of even greater importance is how the Lord Jesus Christ fulfilled the will of God as our sin offering, thus taking away our sins. Take a look at the discussion question list below to see if any are applicable to your group session.

____ What does it mean to treat the Lord as holy? How can we do that or fail to do that today?

____ The Lord had to sensitize His people to the seriousness of sin and the importance of walking clean before Him. The Day of Atonement was one of the most important times for picturing clean living to the people. What in that Day shows you the seriousness of sin and dealing with it?

____ What does God use today to show us the seriousness of sin? How can we help one another deal with sin more consistently?

____ What insights about the Lord Jesus as our sin offering were especially meaningful to you?

____ Were there any questions raised by your study in Day Three?

Main Objective in Day Four: Day Four examines Isaiah 52 and 53 and looks at how the Lord Jesus fulfills the guilt offering pictured there. He is our substitute for sin, a truth we must hold dearly and a reality in which we must walk. Choose some discussion starters for your group session.

____ What do you see in Isaiah that reminds you of the things Jesus faced during His time on earth?

____ What insights about judgment on sin do you see in Isaiah 53?

____ What insights about the love of the Servant for you and me do you see in Isaiah 53?

____ What do you think it was like as Philip and the Ethiopian traveled and discussed the Scriptures about this Suffering Servant? Discuss some of the things Phillip may have told him.

Day Five—Key Points in Application: The most important application point out of Day Five is the opportunity to experience not only the forgiveness of the Lord, but also His joyful presence. After all, He made us for His enjoyment. Below, check any discussion questions that you might consider using for your application time.

____ What, for you, is the most inviting aspect of the presence of the Lord?

____ What is the most damaging aspect of sin as far as your daily life goes?

____ What keeps us from dealing with sin quickly and thoroughly? What can we do to encourage one another to deal fully with any and every sin, any and every time it comes up?

____ What is the strongest application point you observed this week?

CLOSING: 5–10 MINUTES

- ❑ **Summarize**—You may want to read "The Main Point" statement at the beginning of the leader's notes on "The Debt of Sin.
- ❑ **Preview**—If time allows, preview next week's lesson on "The Devotion of Surrender: Walking in the Joy of Surrender to Jesus Christ." Encourage your group to complete their homework.
- ❑ **Pray**—Close in prayer.

TOOLS FOR GOOD DISCUSSION

One of the issues you will eventually have to combat in any group Bible study is the enemy of **boredom.** This enemy raises its ugly head from time to time, but it shouldn't. It is wrong to bore people with the Word of God! Often boredom results when leaders allow their processes to become too predictable. As small group leaders, we tend to do the same thing in the same way every single time. Yet God the Creator, who spoke everything into existence, is infinitely creative! Think about it. He is the one who not only created animals in different shapes and sizes, but different colors as well. When He created food, He didn't make it all taste or feel the same. This God of creativity lives in us. We can trust Him to give us creative ideas that will keep our group times from becoming tired and mundane. In the "Helpful Hints" section of **How to Lead a Small Group** (pp. 200-201), you'll find some practical ideas on adding spice and creativity to your study time.

The Devotion of Surrender

WALKING IN THE JOY OF SURRENDER TO JESUS CHRIST

MEMORY **Ephesians 5:1–2** VERSE

"Therefore be imitators of God, as beloved children; and walk in love, just as Christ also loved you, and gave Himself up for us, an offering and a sacrifice to God as a fragrant aroma."

Before the Session

- ❑ Your own preparation is key not only to your effectiveness in leading the group session, but also in your confidence in leading. It is hard to be confident if you know you are unprepared. These discussion questions and leader's notes are meant to be a helpful addition to your own study but should never become a substitute.
- ❑ As an aid in your study of the offerings or for further study, you may benefit from looking over the chart "General Overview of the Offerings in the Tabernacle and the Temple" at the end of Lesson 7 in the workbook (p. 105).
- ❑ As you do your homework, study with a view to your own relationship with God. Resist the temptation to bypass this self-evaluation on your way to preparing to lead the group. Nothing will minister to your group more than the testimony of your own walk with God.
- ❑ Don't think of your ministry to the members of your group as something that only takes place during your group time. Pray for your group members by name during the week that they would receive spiritual enrichment from doing their daily homework. Encourage them as you have opportunity.

What to Expect

As with the sin offering and the guilt offering of Lesson 7, the offerings covered in this lesson may be foreign to many of the members of your group. The burnt, grain, drink, and peace offerings may seem like ancient (even unimportant) rituals, but as in the sin or guilt offerings the important thing to remember is the heart of the matter—God delights in hearts surrendered to Him and His will. He delights to work through surrendered lives. These offerings give us vivid pictures and life-changing principles for our walk with God and what it means to follow Him with a whole heart. Expect that each person in your group will have areas of their life to which these principles apply in some way. Be prepared to share your own journey as well as guide them toward personal evaluation. Remember, God is continually moving us to new depths of surrender and to a greater capacity to know Him in His fullness. Your time in "The Devotion of Surrender" can be an opportunity for each one to better evaluate where he or she is. This can also be a time of encouragement to grow in surrender. Be open to challenge the members of your group to become that daily "burnt offering"—a living sacrifice, yielded, broken, and poured out.

THE MAIN POINT

We must discover what it means to walk in surrender to the Lord and experience the delight of true worship.

During the Session

OPENING: 5–10 MINUTES

Opening Prayer—A good prayer with which to open your time is the prayer of David in Psalm 119:18, *"Open my eyes, that I may behold wonderful things from Thy law."* Remember that if it took the inspiration of God for men to write Scripture, it will take His illumination for us to understand it.

Opening Illustration—When one country surrenders to another after a war there is often what is called an "unconditional surrender." There is a deep peace in existence as long the unconditional surrender lasts. The same thing is true in our surrender to the Lord. In the Tabernacle, twice each day the burnt offering was offered up, a twice–daily reminder of surrender. Every day we must see the importance of surrender—a moment-by-moment, hour-by-hour, day-by-day, yielding up of our hearts and lives to the Lord to follow Him whatever our circumstance. The word "circumstance" pictures the "circle" (circum) in which you "stand." Regardless of the condition of the day or the circumstances we face, there can be a heart attitude and a life action of surrender. That can be followed by the experience of peace with God as well as the peace of God, from God. We can walk in that peace, know that peace, and enjoy that peace.

As you walk through the burnt offering and the grain and drink offerings that accompanied it, the devotion of surrender as well as the picture of the peace of surrender will become clearer. That is what God wants for us each day, all day.

DISCUSSION: 30–40 MINUTES

Remember to pace your discussion so that you don't run out of time to get to the application questions in Day Five. This time for application is perhaps the most important part of your Bible study. It will be helpful if you are familiar enough with the lesson to be able to prioritize the days for which you want to place more emphasis, so that you are prepared to reflect this added emphasis in the time you devote to that particular day's reading.

Main Objective in Day One: In Day One, the main objective is to understand the significance of the burnt offering and how it pictures daily surrender to the Lord as well as to His ways and His will. Choose a discussion question or two from the Day One list below.

____ What aspects of the burnt offering grabbed your attention?

____ What does the fact of a twice-daily burnt offering say to you about your daily walk with the Lord?

____ Anyone could offer a burnt offering, poor or rich. The poor were unable to offer a rich person's offering, but were instructed to offer what they could. The rich were to offer what they could afford as well. What does this say to you about how God views surrender?

____ Are there any other thoughts from Day One that you would like to discuss?

Main Objective in Day Two: We learn in Day Two the meaning of the grain and drink offerings and how they picture surrender to the Lord. Check which discussion questions you will use from Day Two.

____ What stands out to you about the grain or the drink offerings?

____ What are some of the elements of "yeast" or "honey" that can get mixed in with our walk of surrender?

____ How important is it to keep our focus on the Lord in offering ourselves to Him, especially when that involves our service for others—as a drink offering? What could get in the way of our service?

Main Objective in Day Three: Day Three introduces us to the "peace offering" showing us the peace we can walk in as a result of dealing with sin and walking in surrender to the Lord. In addition to any discussion questions you may have in mind for your group session, the following questions below may also be useful:

____ What stands out to you about the peace or fellowship offering?

____ What does the peace offering say to you about how the Lord wants to fellowship with us and wants us to fellowship with Him?

____ Proverbs 17:1 says, *"Better is a dry morsel and quietness with it than a house full of feasting with strife."* What common elements to the experience of the peace offering do you see?

____ What difference does Jesus make in how we experience the peace of God or peace with one another?

____ Were there any other questions raised by your study in Day Three?

<u>Main Objective in Day Four:</u> In Day Four, we see how the Lord Jesus perfectly fulfilled all the "sweet aroma" offerings—the burnt offering, the grain offering, the drink offering, and the peace offering. Place a checkmark next to the discussion question you would like to use for your group session. Or you may want to place a ranking number in each blank to note your order of preference.

____ What stands out to you about Jesus as our "sweet aroma" offering?

____ What was the most important thing about the offerings according to Jesus?

____ How can we get caught up in the outward forms of religion and miss the heart of what God is saying or wanting?

____ What does it mean to you that Jesus offered all of Himself for you? What do you see in His actions that showed surrender to the Father's will and love for us?

____ Are there other insights gained or questions raised from Day Four?

<u>Day Five—Key Points in Application:</u> The most important application point from Day Five is how Jesus' offering of Himself paved the way for us to truly worship God and walk with Him in joyous fellowship. Make sure your members understand all Jesus has done and how it applies to each of us. Check which discussion questions you will use from Day Five.

____ How does seeing the mercies of God (Romans 1–11) help us walk as a living sacrifice (Romans 12:1–2)?

____ How does Jesus' daily walk of surrender to His Father encourage you in your walk of surrender?

____ What are some of the ways we can present offerings to the Lord today?

____ What other applications did you see from this week?

CLOSING: 5–10 MINUTES

❑ **Summarize**—Restate the key points. You may want to reread "The Main Point" statement for "The Devotion of Surrender."

❑ **Preview**—Take time to preview next week's lesson on **"Positioning for Worship: God's Order for Transporting and Positioning of the Tabernacle."** Encourage your group members to do their homework.

❑ **Pray**—Close in prayer.

Tools for Good Discussion

From time to time, each of us can say stupid things. Some of us, however, are better at it than others. The apostle Peter certainly had his share of embarrassing moments. One minute, he was on the pinnacle of success, saying, *"Thou art the Christ, the Son of the Living God"* (Matthew 16:16), and the next minute, he was putting his foot in his mouth, trying to talk Jesus out of going to the cross. Proverbs 10:19 states, *"When there are many words, transgression is unavoidable. . . ."* What do you do when someone in the group says something that is obviously wrong? First of all, remember that how you deal with a situation like this not only affects the present, but also the future. In the "Helpful Hints" section of **How to Lead a Small Group** (p. 201), you'll find some practical ideas on managing the obviously wrong comments that show up in your group.

Positioning for Worship

God's Order for Transporting and Positioning the Tabernacle

Memory **Exodus 25:9** Verse

"According to all that I am going to show you, as the pattern of the tabernacle and the pattern of all its furniture, just so you shall construct it."

Before the Session

- ❑ Pray each day for the members of your group—that they spend time in the Word, grasp the message God wants to bring to their lives, and that they surrender to what God is saying.
- ❑ Be sure you have searched the Scriptures carefully for each day's lesson.
- ❑ While preparing for this lesson, read through the discussion questions on the following pages and select which questions you will use.
- ❑ Remain ever teachable. Look first for what God is saying to you. This will help you in understanding and relating to some of the struggles that your group members may be facing as they are seeking to make an impact on those around them.

What to Expect

Studying the issue of the positioning of the Tabernacle can at first appear to be one of the less interesting lessons in this study, but when you realize that there is meaning and purpose in every detail, finding that meaning and purpose will be a joy. Expect the members of your group to be surprised at how many practical applications there are to be found in this component of the Tabernacle. Make sure to be sensitive to those group members who did not find those applications on their own. Make sure everyone leaves with a sense of what God is saying.

THE MAIN POINT

Since God is so specific on different issues of positioning, we will find that He has a purpose and a message for us.

During the Session

OPENING: 5–10 MINUTES

Opening Prayer—Remember to ask the Lord for **His** wisdom. He promised to guide us into the truth.

Opening Illustration—Dr. Philip Brooks often told the story of a missionary who, while home on furlough, wanted to find something to take back to his mission post—something that would be accepted by all the natives. He finally decided upon securing a rather large bronze sundial. When he returned, he called the natives together, and they helped him set the dial in proper position. Then the missionary explained its function. The natives were all very pleased and very much interested. A few days later, the missionary was astonished to find that the natives had built a shelter over the sundial to protect it. Their lack of understanding rendered the sundial useless. You see, it is the positioning of the sundial that enables it to tell us what it is designed to tell us. In the same way, the positioning of the Tabernacle was essential for it to communicate what God intended.

DISCUSSION: 30–40 MINUTES

Select one or two specific questions to get the group started. By this point in the course (Week Nine), you know the talkative ones and the ones who are quiet. Continue to encourage each member in the importance of his or her input. Some of the greatest applications ever to be learned from this study course may come from someone who has said very little up to this point.

Main Objective in Day One: In Day One, the main objective is to set forward the significance of the Tabernacle as the centerpiece of the camp. Review the question list below, and decide upon some discussion starters for your group session.

____ Why do you think God was so specific about the placement of the Tabernacle?

____ What message do you see in it being always in the center of the camp?

____ What did you think about the "cross" idea in the placement of the tents?

____ What does this lesson speak to you about your own worship of God?

Main Objective in Day Two: Day Two focuses on the significance of the Tabernacle always being positioned facing East and what God is saying through that. Check which discussion questions you will use from Day Two.

____ Did anything in particular stand out to you from Exodus 26:18–22?

____ What did you see in Isaiah 64:8?

____ What pattern did you see from the Scriptures we reviewed for Day Two?

____ Why is it important that the path toward the Tabernacle was always due west?

____ Did anything else stand out to you from today's homework?

Main Objective in Day Three: Day Three is a review of the High Priest's path as he made his progression from the gate of the Tabernacle to the Holy of Holies. Each item that the High Priest passed contains a message concerning our approach to God. Some good discussion questions for Day Three include . . .

____ What stands out to you from the High Priest's path and the items found in the outer court of the Tabernacle?

____ What meaning do you see in the three items in the Holy Place?

____ What is the point of the Holy of Holies being the innermost room?

____ Did anything else grab you from today's study?

Main Objective in Day Four: Day Four examines the final component of the Tabernacle's positioning—how it was carried—and looks for applications to our worship. Check which discussion questions you will use from Day Four.

____ Why do you think God had the Israelites follow a pillar?

____ Why do you think Judah was first in line behind the pillar?

____ What significance do you see in the placement of the ark?

____ Did today's lesson raise any pertinent questions for you?

Day Five—Key Points in Application: The most important application point in this lesson is to begin looking at the path of the priest as a model for our approach to God. Below, are some suggestions for discussion questions. Feel free to come up with your own questions as well.

____ As you consider the challenges of walking with God today, which of the areas listed in your books make it difficult for you personally to keep the Lord at the center of your life?

____ Do you see any changes you need to make as a result of this lesson?

____ As you looked at the steps in the process of the priest moving toward God, which did you find most meaningful?

CLOSING: 5–10 MINUTES

- ❑ **Summarize**—Restate the key points the group shared. Review the objectives for each of the days found in the leader's notes for Lesson Nine.
- ❑ **Focus**—Make sure the group sees the importance of each reference in regards to positioning of the Tabernacle.
- ❑ **Ask** them to express their thoughts about the key applications from Day Five.
- ❑ **Encourage**—We have finished nine lessons. This is no time to slack off. Encourage your group to keep up the pace. We have three more lessons full of life-changing truths. Take a few moments to preview next week's lesson. Encourage your group members to do their homework in proper fashion by spacing it out over the week.
- ❑ **Pray**—Close in prayer.

TOOLS FOR GOOD DISCUSSION

The Scriptures are replete with examples of people who struggled with the problem of pride. Unfortunately, pride isn't a problem reserved for the history books. It shows up just as often today as it did in the days the Scriptures were written. In your group discussions, you may see traces of pride manifested in a "know-it-all" group member. **"Know-It-All Ned"** may have shown up in your group by this point. He may be an intellectual giant, or he may be a legend only in his own mind. He can be very prideful and argumentative. If you want some helpful hints on how to deal with "Know-It-All Ned," look in the "Helpful Hints" section of **How to Lead a Small Group Bible Study** (p. 199).

False Worship

Disobedience to God's Order for Worship and its Consequences

Memory **Leviticus 10:3b** Verse

"By those who come near to Me I will be treated as holy, and before all the people I will be honored."

Before the Session

- ❑ Never underestimate the importance of prayer for yourself and for the members of your group. Ask the Lord to give your group members understanding in their time in the Word and to bring them to a new level of knowing Him.
- ❑ Spread your study time over the week.
- ❑ Remember to mark those ideas and questions you want to discuss or ask as you go through the study.
- ❑ Be sensitive to the needs of your group. Be prepared to stop and pray for a member who may be facing a difficult struggle or challenge.

What to Expect

Expect that your group not only needs to understand truths in this area of false worship, but also needs to be challenged to evaluate their own worship in that light. Hopefully by this time, the pieces are beginning to fit together and they have begun looking at everything as it applies to them. Encourage them not to miss this important step of application. Next week, we will look at positive examples of worship, but there is much to be gained from a study of negative examples as well.

THE MAIN POINT

There is a wrong way to worship, and there are consequences to not following God's revealed will.

During the Session

OPENING: 5–10 MINUTES

Opening Prayer—Have one of the group members open the time with prayer.

Opening Illustration—On April 25, 1994, the news section of *Christianity Today,* reported that some fans of Elvis Presley were actually revering the king of rock and roll as a god. Pockets of semi-organized Elvis worship had taken hold in New York, Colorado, and Indiana. Worshipers raised their hands, spelled and then chanted Presley's name, worked themselves into a fervor, and prayed to the deceased star. Followers believe Elvis watches over them. If someone reports seeing Presley, the high priests at the Church of the Risen Elvis in Denver hold Elvis worship services. They enshrined a look-alike doll of Elvis in an altar surrounded by candles and flowers. This illustration is proof positive that just because something is called worship does not mean it is acceptable to God. Many times man worships the wrong thing or in the wrong way.

DISCUSSION: 30–40 MINUTES

Select one or two specific questions to get the group started in discussion. Continue to encourage each member in the importance of his or her insights and input.

Main Objective in Day One: Day One looks at the incident of false worship during the early days of the Tabernacle—worship of the golden calf—and looks for applications to us. Good discussion starters for Day One include . . .

____ What were the leaders supposed to do while Moses was on the mountain, meeting with God?

____ What did they do and what resulted?

____ Do you see dangers that relate to our worship?

____ What stood out to you from the sin and how God dealt with it?

Main Objective in Day Two: In Day Two, the main objective is to see God's dealings with Nadab and Abihu in light of the point God is making about worship. Below are some suggested questions for your discussion on Day Two. Which questions will you use for your group session?

____ What was the sin of Nadab and Abihu, and how did God deal with it?

____ Why do you think God dealt with their sin so severely?

____ What stood out to you from the story of Ananias and Saphira?

____ What do these examples say of our worship?

Main Objective in Day Three: In Day Three, the objective is to identify principles of worship from Korah's rebellion. What discussion starters do you plan to use for Day Three? Here are some suggestions:

____ What was Korah's complaint?

____ What is wrong with his perspective?

____ What does this incident of Korah teach us about potential hindrances to our worship?

____ What else stood out to you from Day Three?

Main Objective in Day Four: Day Four looks at the mistakes in worship by King Saul at Gilgal and how they apply to us. Check which questions you will use for your discussion on Day Four.

____ What stands out to you from Saul's actions here?

____ Why do you think God doesn't credit him for at least being partially obedient?

____ What do you see in Saul's responses to Samuel that reflect a lack of true repentance?

____ What else stood out to you from Day Four?

Day Five—Key Points in Application: The most important aspect of each lesson is taking time to seek to apply the truths to our own lives. Make sure you save time for this important part. Select a discussion question or two from the list below.

____ What are some examples you have seen of worship that was not according to truth?

____ What idols stood out to you from the list that are a temptation today?

____ What are some ways you have seen the Lord not honored or treated in holy in worship?

____ What are some ways we are tempted to grumble against leaders?

CLOSING: 5–10 MINUTES

- ❑ **Summarize**—Review the key points the group shared. You may want to review "The Main Point" statement for this lesson. Also, ask your group to express their thoughts about the key applications from Day Five.
- ❑ **Focus**—Using the memory verse (Leviticus 10:3), focus the group on the heart of true worship and the importance of guarding against false worship.
- ❑ **Preview**—Take a few moments to preview next week's lesson on True Worship.
- ❑ **Pray**—Close in prayer.

TOOLS FOR GOOD DISCUSSION

So, group leaders, how have the first nine weeks of this study been for you? Have you dealt with anyone in your group called **"Agenda Alice?"** She is the type that is focused on a Christian "hot-button" issue instead of the Bible study. If not managed properly, she (or he) will either sidetrack the group from its main study objective, or create a hostile environment in the group if she fails to bring people to her way of thinking. For help with "Agenda Alice," see the "Helpful Hints" section of **How to Lead a Small Group Bible Study** (pp. 199-200).

True Worship

WORSHIPING GOD IN SPIRIT AND IN TRUTH

MEMORY **Philippians 3:3** VERSE

"For we are the true circumcision, who worship in the Spirit of God and glory in Christ Jesus and put no confidence in the flesh."

BEFORE THE SESSION

- ❑ Pray for your group as they study through this week's lesson.
- ❑ Spread your study time over the week. This is like a large meal. You need time to chew each truth and digest it fully.
- ❑ As you walk through this lesson on true worship, continually keep in mind the contrast with false worship, even as the golden calf incident stands in sharp contrast to the events surrounding Moses and the Tabernacle in Exodus 25—40. This will help in guiding the discussion on true worship with your group.
- ❑ As you study, remember to jot down those ideas and questions you want to discuss or ask as you go through this lesson with your small group.

WHAT TO EXPECT

Knowing facts and figures about the Tabernacle or the Temple is useless if we do not apply these truths to our hearts, especially to our personal worship of the true God. God still seeks those who will worship Him in spirit and truth. This lesson looks at the big picture all the way from Genesis to Revelation. It will be important to help your group see the big picture without getting lost in the details. At the same time, it is essential to help focus the group on personal application of all we have seen in these eleven lessons.

Help your group see the importance of finishing what God has called them to do—even finishing this study in *Following God*. (We have only one more lesson to go after this lesson.) Encourage them to share insights that God has shown them.

THE MAIN POINT

We are to worship God in spirit and in truth, never depending on the flesh or straying into deceptive traps of idolatry and false worship.

DURING THE SESSION

OPENING: 5–10 MINUTES

Opening Prayer—Have one of the group members open the time with prayer.

Opening Illustration—Acts 17:16–34 give us one of the clearest illustrations of the importance of true worship in all of Scripture. There we see Paul declaring the matter of true worship versus false worship as a matter of life and death, even eternal life versus eternal death. He knew it was a matter for which there is ultimate accountability to Jesus Christ, the resurrected Lord. When Paul talked to the Athenians, he spoke of their altar to the "Unknown God," an altar that appeared to be "god-insurance"—they wanted to make sure there was no god that they were potentially offending by not having an altar devoted to him. In their thinking, an unrecognized god could bring a plague or famine or catastrophe, so they covered their bases by devoting an altar to any gods they failed to acknowledge. The idea of worship to them was a sobering, fearful matter; yet they understood nothing about the true God and true worship. They knew worship was important in life, but they did not have the full picture. Paul brought that full picture to them showing them they must walk in true worship. That meant walking with God, honoring Jesus Christ as resurrected Lord and Savior. The people responded in three different ways: some sneered; some wanted to hear more later; and some joined themselves to Paul and to the Lord, or literally, they glued themselves to Paul in belief and trust of this true God. Telling others about true worship versus false worship will have the same results in our day. It is a matter of life or death . . . forever. You and your group can know the reality of true worship as you follow the Lord God of heaven and His Son Jesus. You can lead others to do the same.

DISCUSSION: 30–40 MINUTES

Study diligently in your preparation time. This will help you guide the discussion as well as answer many of the questions that arise in your group. Knowing the ways of God in guiding us in true worship can help your group in many areas of their Christian walk. True worship is the foundation upon which everything else rests. It is where we start and never leave. As you trek through the lesson, seek to keep the main point the main point and be sure to leave time for the application points in Day Five. There is nothing more important than emphasizing personal application in worship.

Main Objective in Day One: In Day One, the main objective is to see that in seeking those who will worship Him in spirit and truth the Father focuses on the true condition of each heart. In addition to any discussion questions you may have in mind, the list of questions below may also contain useful discussion-starter ideas.

____ How do we try to hide sin, either in what we have done or what is in our hearts? Why do we think we can hide from God?

____ What effect can truth have on one's heart and life? How can being truthful or honest with God affect our attitude, our countenance, or our ability to make wise choices?

____ How important is wisdom in our walk with God or in our worship of Him?

____ How does our worship affect others? How does true worship (with true wisdom) affect our relationships with others?

Main Objective in Day Two: In Day Two, the main objective is to see how the Lord Jesus began to guide the woman of Samaria into the truth and to true worship. Check which discussion questions you will use from Day Two.

____ How does knowing Jesus as the Giver affect how we ask things of Him?

____ Jesus began with the woman at the well by focusing on a need (water) and how He could more than meet that need. Why would He focus on this need first?

____ Why did Jesus bring up the woman's sin? How does He do that with us? How does personal sin relate to the issue of true worship?

____ How do we try to change the subject with the Lord? Can you think of ways we substitute religion for true worship? How can we guard against substitutes for true worship?

Main Objective in Day Three: In Day Three, our main objective is to see how Jesus reveals Himself so that we can worship Him in spirit and truth. Below, are some suggested discussion starters for you to consider.

____ True worship magnifies who the Lord is in our eyes. How was Jesus magnified in the woman's eyes?

____ How do we see sin when we see the Lord for Who He is?

____ What effect does seeing the Lord for Who He is have on our lives? What effect does seeing the Lord for Who He is have in relationships with others?

____ Think of how the Lord desires truth in relationships—first with Him and then with others. How important is truth to you in the relationships you have (at home, at school, at work, in business dealings, at church)?

Main Objective in Day Four: Day Four's main objective is for you and your group to see how the Holy Spirit leads true worshipers in a walk of true worship. Check any questions that are applicable for your Day Four-discussion time.

____ What does the picture of the Spirit being like living water say to you? How does this encourage you?

____ What does it take to receive living water?

____ How is the Spirit like refreshing water?

____ What options are left open to those who refuse Jesus' offer of living water? What kind of life can they expect to live? What kind of eternity will they have?

Day Five—Key Points in Application: The most important application point in "True Worship" is found in fulfilling the purpose for which God created us—to know Him and the fullness of His Life. When we know this we can experience the joy of His presence and point others to Him so they too can know Him and His fullness of Life. Check which discussion questions you will use to help focus the applications from Day Five.

____ How are true worship and the fullness of the Holy Spirit connected?

____ What part does the Holy Spirit play in guiding us in true worship? What are some ways He leads us in worship?

____ What are some of the things that keep us from true worship or from being controlled by the Holy Spirit?

____ True worship can be "a little heaven on earth." Describe what that could look like.

CLOSING: 5–10 MINUTES

❑ **Summarize**—Restate the key points the group shared.

❑ **Focus**—Using the memory verse (Philippians 3:3), focus the group again on what it means to worship God in truth. Remind the members of your group that life is meant to be lived by His Spirit's fullness, by His power, wisdom, and grace.

❑ **Ask** them to share their thoughts about the key applications from Day Five.

❑ **Preview**—Take a few moments to preview next week's lesson on **"Jesus Christ, Our High Priest: Leading Us into True Worship and Fellowship with God."** Encourage your group members to do their homework in proper fashion by spacing it out over the week.

❑ **Pray**—Close in prayer.

Tools for Good Discussion

Well, it is evaluation time again! You may be saying to yourself, "Why bother evaluating at the end? If I did a bad job, it is too late to do anything about it now!" Well, it may be too late to change how you did on this course, but it is never too late to learn from this course what will help you on the next. Howard Hendricks, that peerless communicator from Dallas Theological Seminary, puts it this way: "The good teacher's greatest threat is satisfaction—the failure to keep asking, 'How can I improve?' The greatest threat to your ministry is **your ministry."** Any self-examination should be an accounting of your own strengths and weaknesses. As you consider your strengths and weaknesses, take some time to read through the evaluation questions list found in **How to Lead a Small Group Bible Study** on pages 203-204 of this leader's guide. Make it your aim to continue growing as a discussion leader. Jot down below two or three action points for you to implement in future classes.

ACTION POINTS:

1. ______________________________

____

2. ______________________________

____

3. ______________________________

Christ, Our High Priest

Leading Us into True Worship and Fellowship with God

Memory **Hebrews 10:19–22** Verse

"Since . . . we have confidence to enter the holy place by the blood of Jesus, by a new and living way which He inaugurated for us through the veil, that is, His flesh, and since we have a great priest over the house of God, let us draw near. . . , having our hearts sprinkled clean from an evil conscience and our bodies washed with pure water."

Before the Session

- ❑ You will certainly need to pray for your group as they walk through this final lesson in the study, *Life Principles for Worship from the Tabernacle.* Ask the Lord to give clear insight into who Christ is as our High Priest. Never underestimate the importance of prayer for yourself and for the members of your group. Pray for each of them by name.
- ❑ Spread your study time over the week.
- ❑ Remember to mark those ideas and questions you want to discuss or ask as you go through the study. Add to those some of the suggested questions listed on the following pages.
- ❑ To better see the Person of Christ you may want to look at the lessons that refer to Christ in other Following God studies: "Adam: Following God's Design" (Lesson 1) in *Following God: Life Principles from the Old Testament,* "Christ the Prophet: Worshiping in Spirit and Truth" (Lesson 12) in *Following God: Life Principles from the Prophets of the Old Testament,* "The True King in Israel: Following the King of Kings" (Lesson 12) in *Following God: Life Principles from the Kings of the Old Testament,* "The Bride of Christ: Walking in the Beauty of Holiness" (Lesson 12) in *Following God: Life Principles from the Women of the Bible Book One,* and "The Son of Man: Following His Father" (Lesson 12) in *Following God: Life Principles from the New Testament Men of Faith.*
- ❑ Be sensitive to the working of the Spirit in your group meeting, ever watching for ways to help one another truly follow and worship God.

What to Expect

We know that Jesus is Savior and Lord, but many times we forget about or fail to see the significance and importance of Jesus' role as High Priest. Many in your group will have little or no understanding of the priesthood, especially the place and role of the High Priest. Many will think of some modern form of priesthood or a priesthood from history which is foreign to the Old and New Testament ideas. When coupled with an understanding of the Tabernacle, the priesthood, and the offerings, the place of the High Priest can have great personal meaning for the members of your group. You may need to review some of the truths learned in Lessons 1–11 on the Tabernacle, priesthood, and offerings. This will help you to better explain or clarify these truths or answer questions that arise during your discussion time.

The Scriptures have much to say about Jesus as our

High Priest and perfect sacrifice. Many in your group will gain new insights into Christ's work of salvation and how it applies to each of them. Hopefully, they will see many new application points for walking with Him as **their** High Priest. Encourage them to share their insights as you guide the discussion.

THE MAIN POINT

Jesus Christ, through the fullness of both His Person and His work, brings us to Himself in salvation and to true worship and fellowship.

During the Session

OPENING: 5–10 MINUTES

Opening Prayer—Psalm 119:18 says, *"Open my eyes, that I may behold wonderful things from Thy law."* Ask the Lord to open your eyes as you meet together. Have one of the group members open the time with prayer.

Opening Illustration—Following to the Finish. I was driving on an Interstate highway one morning and got stuck in traffic. It was a time for enduring not enjoying. In the midst of that the Lord showed me a very important truth. Right in front of me was a car with the words "I Love Running" surrounding the car tag. Obviously an avid jogger owned this. On the left side of the back bumper was a half-sized bumper sticker with these words in bold print: "I FINISHED—RiverRun 15 K." This person had run the required fifteen kilometers of the RiverRun 15K and finished—no word about who won the race, or how long it took to complete their run, just that this person **finished**. What a powerful truth! That is what the book of Hebrews urges its readers. You and I are running a race. Sometimes we want to quit, to back out, but the Lord is saying keep running, keep trusting, keep looking to Jesus, the author and finisher of faith (Hebrews 12:2). For the joy set before Him, He endured the cross and has sat down at the right hand of the throne of God. You endure. It will be worth all the effort, all the struggle, all you have to face, because the rewards are far greater than any received for finishing a 15K run, for they are eternal! During your Christian "run," you can know the joy of fellowship with God and experience true worship.

As your group has looked at **Jesus Christ, Our High Priest**, each one has seen how He is our sovereign Lord, one who sympathizes with each of us, one who sacrificed Himself for us, and one who is ever strong and able to give us His strength to run the race. This lesson can be a strong encouragement to look to the Lord for strength, to focus on Him, and in so doing, to follow Him in fellowship all the way to the finish. He calls us to come into the Holy of Holies and live in His presence. Help the members of your group determine to follow to the finish.

DISCUSSION: 30–40 MINUTES

Select one or two specific questions to get the group started. This lesson on Christ, our High Priest offers many application points about how each of us is following and worshiping the Lord. He is continually guiding us in worshiping Him, and we need to encourage one another in true worship. Remember to look for those "Velcro" points where members can see something that applies to their own lives. Encourage them to share the insights the Lord has shown them during the week.

Main Objective in Day One: In Day One, the main objective is to see our High Priest as the sovereign Lord who is worthy of worship and to whom we must pay close attention. Place a checkmark next to the suggested discussion questions that you would like to use in your group session. Or you may want to use ranking numbers and rank the questions in preferential order.

____ What are some of the characteristics of the Son of God? Which ones are most meaningful to you?

____ What do you think it would be like to follow one who ruled with a righteous scepter, who followed God's will in every detail?

____ What are some ways we can pay close attention to the Lord and what He has spoken?

____ What are some things that can get in the way of listening to God and His Word? How can we neglect hearing Him and drift in our walk?

Main Objective in Day Two: In Day Two, the main objective is to see how our High Priest sympathizes with us in our sorrows, temptations, and struggles. Check which discussion questions you will use from Day Two.

____ What stands out to you about the Lord Jesus, particularly His walk on earth, facing the many sufferings He faced?

____ What does it mean to you that Jesus is "merciful and faithful"?

____ What does it mean to you that Jesus faced the full force of every kind of temptation? What does that mean when you face temptation?

____ How does the invitation to come to the throne of grace motivate you in following Jesus?

Main Objective in Day Three: Day Three focuses on our sacrificial High Priest and the work He accomplished through the cross. Some good discussion questions for Day Three include these.

____ Someone has compared the sacrifices of the Old Testament to a credit card—using the credit card covers the payment for a time, but does not pay for the item or service. The debt still has to be paid when the bill comes. What does it mean to you that Jesus paid your sin debt—no bill will ever come?

____ What difference should it make in your daily walk knowing that God wants you to come into His presence with confidence or boldness through the blood of Jesus? How should this affect your prayer time? Your decision-making process?

____ What does it mean to you that you have been set apart in a special class by the sacrifice of Jesus?

____ What other insights have you gleaned from Day Three?

Main Objective in Day Four: In Day Four, the main objective is to see our strong High Priest and how He wants to be our strength for daily life. Select a discussion question or two from the list of questions below.

____ The key element in faith is **the object of our faith** not the amount of faith. As someone has pointed out, "thin faith" in "thick ice" is more important than "thick faith" in "thin ice" if you want to walk across an ice-covered lake. What insights have you gleaned about how Abraham grew and how we grow strong in faith?

____ Even in the face of His trials, Jesus knew He was both Lord and High Priest, and that His Kingdom and His sacrificial work would stand. What insights and/or personal applications do you see about Jesus' strength in the events surrounding His trials, crucifixion, and resurrection, especially as they apply to your need for strength day by day?

____ How is the Christian life like a race? What insights have you gleaned about how to run your race?

____ What does it really mean to be satisfied? Where is true satisfaction found according to the Scriptures?

Day Five—Key Points in Application: The most important application point seen in "Jesus Christ Our High Priest" is how His work of salvation is being carried out in each of His children. He wants us to walk with a strong faith in Him, confident in His ability to fulfill the work He has begun in us. In light of that, we can look to Him as our strength for the race set before us, and we can experience the joy of true worship and fellowship. Check which discussion questions you will use to help focus the applications from Day Five.

____ What is God able to do? What fresh insights has God shown you about His ability, especially as it relates to you and your circumstances?

____ What are some ways we "interact" with the Lord? Why is it vitally important to know His Word as we interact with Him in the various circumstances of life?

____ We can get discouraged in running the race—weary, thirsty, ready to give up. How can we encourage one another in the race each of us is running?

____ What is the most significant insight the Lord has shown you concerning Jesus as High Priest (for the present and/or for the future)?

CLOSING: 5–10 MINUTES

- ❑ **Summarize**—Restate the key points the group shared. Review the main objectives for each of the days found in these leader notes.
- ❑ **Focus**—Using the memory verses (Hebrews 10:19–22), direct the group's focus to the open door into full fellowship and worship we have through the Lord Jesus, our High Priest. Note the practical applications to everyday life that His High Priesthood has for each one.
- ❑ **Ask** the group to express their thoughts about the key applications from Day Five.
- ❑ **Pray**—Close your time in prayer, thanking the Lord for the journey He has led you on over the past twelve weeks.

Tools for Good Discussion

Congratulations! You have successfully navigated the waters of small group discussion. You have finished all twelve lessons in *Following God: Life Principles for Worship from the Tabernacle*, but there is so much more to learn, so many more paths to take on our journey with the Lord, so much more to discover about what it means to follow Him. Now what? It would be wise for you and your group to not stop with this study. In the front portion of this leader's guide (in the "Helpful Hints" section of **How to Lead a Small Group Bible Study,** pp. 201-202), there is information on how you can transition to the next study and share those insights with your group. Encourage your group to continue in some sort of consistent Bible study. Time in the Word is much like time at the dinner table. If we are to stay healthy, we will never get far from physical food, and if we are to stay nourished on "sound" or "healthy" doctrine, then we must stay close to the Lord's "dinner table" found in His Word. Job said it well, *"I have not departed from the command of His lips; I have treasured the words of His mouth more than my necessary food"* (Job 23:12).

WALKING HAND IN HAND AS CHRIST'S LOVE
transforms lives